COMMERCE AND MORALITY

COMMERCE
AND
MORALITY

EDITED BY
TIBOR R.MACHAN

ROWMAN & LITTLEFIELD
PUBLISHERS

To Jamie, Kate, Thomas, and Erin

ROMAN & LITTLEFIELD

Published in the United States of America in 1988
by Rowman & Littlefield, Publishers
(a division of Littlefield, Adams & Company)
81 Adams Drive, Totowa, New Jersey 07512

Copyright © 1988 by Rowman & Littlefield

Library of Congress Cataloging-in-Publication Data

Commerce and morality.

  Bibliography: p. 233
  Includes index.
  1. Business ethics. 2. Industry and state.
I. Machan, Tibor R.
HF5387.C65 1988 174'.4 87-16635
ISBN 0-8476-7586-6
ISBN 0-8476-7587-4 (pbk.)

90 89 88 / 5 4 3 2 1

Printed in the United States of America

Contents

Preface

Business ethics is a subfield of ethics wherein the very broad questions "How should I conduct myself?" or "With what standards of conduct should I guide myself in life?" arise. The study of ethics arises in response to these basic questions since we assume that the questions are meaningful and applicable to human life.

Other fields can be similarly questioned, for example: "What is the composition of physical reality?" (physics); "What is life?" (biology); "What is the nature of voluntary exchange of goods and services?" (economics); "What is consciousness?" (psychology). Ethics, like other disciplines can also be subdivided—we may speak of the ethics of the various distinct tasks human beings can have in life—the ethics of parenting, friendship, athletics, citizenship, professions. Business ethics is a subdivision of professional ethics, just as medical, legal, or educational ethics are derived from their particular fields.

Not everyone thinks along these lines, especially those who disagree that ethics is even a bona fide field of investigation or concern for human beings. If people had no choice about what they did or if there could be no standard of right conduct for people, then ethics, as it has been largely understood throughout history, would be a bogus field.

Business ethics may best be understood as the division of ethics that addresses the question, "How should I, a person professionally engaged in commerce, conduct myself in the course of my work?" This way of understanding the field immediately suggests that commerce itself is one of the numerous, legitimate, morally justified areas of human conduct. Just as physicians focus on how to attain health, attorneys on how to cope with the law, educators on how to communicate knowledge, so professionals in business address a special human concern, namely, how to secure prosperity or the economic well-being of people by working as brokers, executives, or consultants. Special ethical questions arise for such persons and the field of business ethics addresses them.

There is another dimension that is customarily included under the heading "business ethics," namely, public policy regarding the economic affairs of a community. Much beside the strictly personal ethical questions that concern people embarking on business is included in courses and books on business ethics. Indeed, as the field now looks, those studying it are considerably more concerned with public policy and law than with personal ethics.

This book is different from others partly because it is mainly concerned with business ethics proper, as a branch of ethics in general. There are discussions of public policy issues as well, but they should be construed as secondary and derivative—following the main subject of the field, which is the study of how people in business ought to conduct themselves and why.

When philosophers or ethicists who study business ethics render judgment about various ways of conduct in the business professions, they tend to invoke utilitarian or intuitionist ethics. The former theory judges and guides human conduct by reference to whether or not it contributes to the greatest happiness, good, or well-being of the society as a whole—the general welfare. The latter passes judgment on the basis of whether what people do accords with moral intuitions or the basic moral ideals we all tend to share.

In this book, some contributors may invoke these views. The majority tend toward another perspective, namely, classical self-actualization ethics. This is a revised version of Aristotelian ethics that considers the moral life to be one that seeks the perfection or excellence of the individual as a human being. The difference between the ethics widely invoked in this work and Aristotle's is that Aristotle did not pay enough attention to human individuality, whereas contributors to this volume take the individual person's life to be of great significance for ethical purposes.

In this work, commerce itself is seen as quite proper. It is perhaps best understood as the social outcome of the widespread personal concern with the virtue of prudence or foresight, i.e., advancing one's own long-range, essential well-being. In contrast, many other discussions of business ethics see business as inherently morally suspect. This may be explained by reference to the fact that people have for many centuries been oriented toward self-fulfillment in another—supernatural—life. Profiting in this world had been decried as evil. Business has never been treated as one of the noble professions and, even in our time, most drama depicts greed as the major evil and people in business as the most vicious in our culture. This assumption does not underlie the present book.

This volume begins with a brief discussion of ethics and moral theories and then launches into discussions of several areas of business ethics as well as public policy. It ends with a brief summary of the influence of ethics on the three political-economic theories that are live options in our age—capitalism, Socialism, and welfare-statism.

This book is therefore the starting point of inquiry. We realize there is much left to be considered. Only minimal mention is made, for example, of Marxist communism (the main challenge to the business society) or capitalism. This challenge has to be taken up elsewhere.

I wish to thank the Earhart and Reason Foundations for their help with the preparation of this book. I want also to thank Arthur Hamparian of Rowman and Littlefield for his support, and Professors M. Bruce Johnson and Llad Phillips for their encouragement with my studies in business ethics.

T.R.M.

She had many things to learn about management: to be a good delegator, to make people see how to do things by asking them questions that sparked their own ideas, to fill the more boring jobs with less-qualified people, who would not be bored, and then to make them stretch.

—Kay Nolte Smith, *Mindspell*

Why didn't the government do more . . . order a warning label? Issue a regulation? Did it bow to industry pressure?

—John Dance, NBC Reports,
"Assault on Big Brother . . . Regulating the Regulators."
April 20, 1984

Introduction:

ETHICS AND ITS USES

TIBOR R. MACHAN

I thought Calder would have been interested, but bankers' ethics as
usual kept me quiet.   — Dick Francis, *Banker*

Introduction

Ethics is the discipline concerned with what standards are to guide our
choices in life. This field of concern arises in response to the question that
apparently all persons must ask, namely, "How should I conduct myself?"
And business ethics is concerned with the implications of the best answer to
that question for one distinct area of human social life, commerce.

The basic assumptions of ethics are implicit in the slogan "Ought implies
can." This means (a) if Bob ought to or should do something, he is *free to
choose* to do or not to do it, and (b) some *standard* of conduct is identifiable
with regard to Bob and other persons and their ability to make the right
choice. So the two basic assumptions underlying ethics are that we all
possess free will and that some ethical theory or system can be found that
will provide us with standards for making the best choices in our lives.

Ethics or morality has, of course, been conceived differently. Some
believe that it concerns values or the nature of goodness, but such a
characterization is too broad. We could accept the existence of values or
some idea of goodness without having to admit that ethics has any
legitimate place in our lives. This is because when we concern ourselves with
ethical or moral values, it is only those values or that kind of goodness that
we can be responsible for achieving or neglecting that are at issue. (Even the
subjects of botanists or zoologists can involve values. Whether a living thing
is growing well or badly involves a [nonmoral] evaluation of it.)

Both of the assumptions of ethics are controversial. Free will is often
denied or at least disputed, especially by those who hold science in high

1

esteem. And many also express doubt about the possibility of finding standards of conduct that can guide us all.

For example, some say that the principle of universal causality precludes free will—it would be unfounded to claim we have it when all of nature is governed by immutable laws. Others respond that, when it comes to human nature, reality shows itself to be very complicated and admits of free will, which is itself a complicated kind of causation in the world. And they say that the diversity and complexity of human life can only be explained by admitting free will. Some say that free will is an arbitrary, prescientific idea that amounts to a superstition, not a sound theory. Others reply that we couldn't even make sense of thinking about the world and trying to get to understand it without free will because inquiry must be free, unprejudiced, started without preconceptions.

Skeptics also doubt the possibility that standards for right conduct could be found. They point to the widespread disagreements in ethics. They note that ethical claims cannot be shown to be true by observation, as other claims often can be. And they tell us that certainly ethical claims cannot be proven from nonethical ones, since the proof would be an invalid or faulty one. Those who defend ethics could, in turn, make much of the widespread agreement we find across the globe and the ages. But others claim that standards can and indeed may have been found already. This is supported by our widespread convictions about ethical or moral issues, as well as by our clear need for them. The disagreement could be explained by the fact that people are free to agree or disagree and might wish to disagree when they feel threatened by the truth about ethics. Moreover, we have to prove many of our beliefs by means other than mere observation—even in science, much that is said is demonstrated with the aid of complicated theories that have much more than merely observations to back them up. And there is, finally, no good reason to deny that some of what we know about the world, for instance, life, should be inherently concerned with values. As a philosopher of science, Karl Popper said:

I think that values enter the world with life; and if there is life without consciousness (as I think there may well be, even in animals and man, for there appears to be such a thing as dreamless sleep) then, I suggest, there will also be objective values, even without consciousness.[1]

In any case, ethics is controversial. But really, this is no great cause for worry—so are most other areas of human interest. This is especially evident when we turn to the complicated dimensions of any field of study. In physics, chemistry, mathematics, economics, sociology, or political science, arguments are legion.

We will not try to deal with most controversies here, except to discuss how ethics relates to the science of economics. This is important because economics also studies business. It aims to find the basic principles of commercial or business life. But it tries to do this in a very different way from ethics.

Economics and Ethics

Both economics and business ethics concern the same field of human activity, namely, commerce. Economics is a social science, grounded upon certain assumptions about human nature and reality. Business ethics, too, rests on certain assumptions. Are the assumptions of these two fields compatible? If the answer is that they are not, then one or the other field cannot be correct about its assumptions.[2] There are some reasons to assume that these two fields are capable of being reconciled, so we must take a brief look at these reasons.

There are two features of economics that concern us here: (a) the economic view of human nature and (b) the economist's view of science.

The former is important because economics — as most economists understand it — rests on a specific view of human nature. Its analysis is based on the acceptance of the *homo economicus* view of human nature. This view sees every individual as a utility maximizer — meaning a desire-satisfier or preference-pursuer. According to the economist's understanding, human beings are — either always or mostly in the marketplace — trying to satisfy their desires and wants. The following three statements from economists should illustrate this point. First, Gary Backer states: "The combined assumptions of maximizing behavior, market equilibrium, and stable preferences, used relentlessly and unflinchingly, form the heart of the economic approach as I see it."[3]

George Stigler puts it slightly differently: "Man is eternally a utility-maximizer — in his home, in his office (be it public or private), in his church, in his scientific work — in short, everywhere."[4]

And finally, Milton Friedman states: "[E]very individual serves his own private interest. . . . The great Saints of history have served their 'private interest' just as the most money-grubbing miser has served his private interest. The *private interest* is whatever it is that drives an individual."[5]

As Friedman's and Stigler's remarks show, the assumption is not often applied simply to market behavior (commerce or exchange of goods and services).

Not all economists believe this, of course, but enough of them do so that one can claim there is a kind of imperialism going on whereby economists wish to extend the views they hold about human economic life to all human life. As scientists, they tend to insist that what they have concluded about human nature is universally applicable.[6]

This brings up the second feature of the economist's perspective.

Scientific economics must be value free, or so most in economics would hold. Whether what people do or do not do is good or bad, right or wrong, is of no significance. All that counts is what can be observed and measured, not blamed or praised, right, wrong, or any such moral or ethical evaluations. Economists study their field hoping to come close to the natural scientific perspective. The field is, then, for most mainstream economists, a descriptive and explanatory science, not one that is concerned with values or norms.[7]

There are numerous other interesting aspects of what is widely regarded as scientific economics. We will concern ourselves only with how economists tend to understand being scientific and with their concern with being value free. With their ideas on these two issues, could ethics be applicable to economic life, to commerce?

As noted, two perspectives cannot be fundamentally incompatible and yet be both accurately used for understanding the same domain of reality. Yet it appears that ethics and economics cannot be reconciled. Ethics assumes that human individuals are *free to choose* and that objective standards of values can be identified. Economics sees human behavior *driven by certain interests or preferences,* causes or variables that explain individual and market behavior and, indeed, enable us to predict human affairs.

We must be content here with considering just one way that this apparent conflict might be resolved. If a resolution is at least not very difficult to imagine, it would seem that both ethics and economics can be respected, studied by all concerned.

First of all, need we conceive of economic man as economists insist in order to have a science of economics? Individuals might be free to choose their values—what they regard as important to do, what they in fact will do—without having *had to make* their choices as they do from the start. One's desires or preferences may be chosen, cultivated, developed, and changed. They may be open to criticism. "You have enough shirts, you shouldn't buy another." or "That is the worst album I have ever heard, why on earth did you buy it?" Even production might be criticized—"You should not try to make money by printing pornography or producing and selling cocaine, even if the economic benefits are great." So what "drives" people to do what they do may be up to them to a large extent—their values, their preferences, their concerns, their beliefs. And they could change these and choose to do so when that is justified.

Yet, once one has settled down with one's values and preferences, one's actions could be predicted with fairly good success. As an adult, one's values, tastes, preferences, commitments, and ideals tend not to change rapidly. And prediction can be made on the basis of knowing these—we often know what music, movies, foods, mates, or political candidates our friends will like without insisting that they had no say about the matter.

One of the choices many people make is to engage in successful commercial endeavors. The social science of economics can be based on this fact: *People want to prosper in life, and once they have chosen to do so, they will often act sensibly, reasonably, rationally — that is, efficiently — to achieve their ends. They will inform themselves as best as they can; they will seek out good deals; they will bargain when they can; they will aspire to become productive.* So a choice that could be free — an individual *might not have made it,* but it was up to him or her to do so — can prompt the individual to pursue a fairly predictable course.

So while ethics presupposes freedom of choice, economics presupposes rational behavior under market conditions. When individuals embark upon seeking prosperity or economic advancement, they freely choose to do so and their behavior then is open for systematic study. So it need not be thought that economic thinking and behavior exhaust how we should study every aspect of life. Economics is rather the study of market or commercial activity; there need be no conflict between ethics and economics. Ethical theorists, too, must accept that however free we are, when we freely commit ourselves to certain goals, we are likely to act predictably. This, in turn, takes nothing away from our human dignity and sense of responsibility.

Role Ethics

Ethics, as we noted earlier, arises in response to the very general question, "How should I live my life?" But there are many areas of human life that can be usefully considered. And when we want to learn how to carry on in these roles, we are, in fact, concerned with a somewhat more specialized area of ethics. For instance, in the role of parents, we may raise rather special questions; so too in the role of friend, colleague, spouse, or professional. In each of these roles we might have use for fairly distinct ethical guidelines.

Consider, for example, that as friends we relate to people differently from how we would as colleagues. The norms governing such behavior are fairly specific. In a friend's home we are free to do certain things, like help ourselves to something to eat, which would be unethical to do in a colleague's house when our host has stepped out. As parents, we are responsible to our children as they are to us in special ways that we would not be to other people's children. One can go wrong in these different roles and it is useful to know how to carry on properly, suitably.

One's profession is one of the roles one has in life, or one of the fairly distinct activities one is involved in, and here too it is useful to inquire as to how one should carry on, as to its special set of rights and wrongs, dos and don'ts. In fact, when one reads books on parenting, this, in a way, is reading about the ethics of parenting. Aristotle, the great Greek philosopher, spent many pages of his most famous book, *Nicomachean Ethics,* on the topic of friendship. Today, books advising lovers on the best way to interact are books on role ethics. This is so even when they are couched in therapeutic language.

So the general field of ethics can be divided into branches according to the roles most of us play in our lives. One such role we play is that of a worker or professional. And within this division, there are further subdivisions focusing on the special characteristics of different professions. That is where the various fields of professional ethics arise: medical, legal, political, athletic, educational, and of course, business ethics.

Let me note here that much of this is disputable among reasonable people, and much is being disputed. But the account here is not unique or esoteric. The sciences are all subdivided — e.g., physics, into hydrophysics, astrophysics, neurophysics. If a practical science or applied science such as ethics is at all possible, in many respects, we can expect it to be similar to other sciences. Ethics is also different, since exploring it is to explore something extremely important to oneself, namely, how to conduct oneself as a good human being. Few sciences are so directly relevant to us all, although psychology comes very close, as do some of the other sciences. It is also of far more general concern than any other discipline: every adult human being must face up to its principles and be accountable for how well he or she has done.

One further note. Merely being able to explain ethics, even to identify sound ethical principles, does not guarantee actual ethical goodness, moral excellence, or the discovery of "truth."

Ours then has to be one of many accounts of the nature of ethics: being free to choose, we need to establish guidelines on which to base our good choices. Ethics is the field in which we search for a sound theory of such guidelines and, if this theory is identified, its answer must be very general in scope — applicable to all human beings in some measure — internally consistent, at least to a very large degree — and not suicidal. Different ethical theories have been put before us to choose the right standard by which to guide human conduct. Before we discuss some prominent ethical systems, mention must be made of one controversy surrounding business ethics.

Is Commerce Ethical?

We are all legitimately concerned with commerce, at least to some extent, just as we are with law, science, medicine, or art. There are some who deny this, who are suspicious of commerce and business, who think that seeking economic advancement, engaging in competitive enterprise, is morally wrong. However widely believed, this is not right, anymore than other prejudices are. The profession of business fulfills a proper human objective, namely, securing economic well-being for people.

Because of our special talents, inclinations, and opportunities, and because of the unique skills demanded from professionals, human beings take up different careers, professions, and vocations in life. Business is one of them.

It must be noted that one of the most prominent social-political viewpoints — Marxism — has no room for business ethics. If Marxism is true, the kind of society that is hospitable to business — capitalism — is merely a temporary and distasteful stage of humanity's progress toward communism, the fulfillment of humanity's collective potential. There is, furthermore, no choice about this for individuals. It will happen, though the precise schedule may be uncertain. What is crucial is that under Communism, the profession of business — and indeed commerce itself — will be absent. People will work just for the love of work, with no desire for profit.[8]

This idea is worth noting, but we cannot discuss it in detail. There are other social-economic theories that are inhospitable to commerce and the profession of business, but Marxism is the most prominent. The others, at least, confront the idea of the moral legitimacy of business with arguments, but Marxism sees the notion itself as merely part of historical development needed to bolster capitalism for the time being.

Here we must simply reject the Marxist view, although some of the essays in this volume will discuss certain features of it in some detail. We will now look at a number of ethical systems.

Ethical Systems

Anyone writing on ethics has taken on a very testy task. In most fields, the discussion of issues is carried out from the viewpoint of widely accepted theories. In some, notably the natural sciences but also in mathematics, archaeology, and economics, there is a reigning theory, and it is treated as the best or most up-to-date framework for such discussions. This is so even when the theory still has problems or invites doubts.

In ethics, a reigning theory exists only in the sense of what may be somewhat widely believed and acted on. We see the evidence for this in how people act, judge each other, and appraise various institutions through drama, newspapers, commencement exercises, speeches, and other vehicles by which we express such judgments. At the same time, many other civilized people hold modified versions, even seriously conflicting ones, as better ethical systems. In short, there is far more overt evidence of theoretical conflict about ethics than about other fields. Ethics has such a wide scope of applicability and generates so many more personally significant opinions that its controversies are usually well known.

In what follows, we will consider some of the main ethical theories, but only to become familiar with them. We will not defend one as the best, though not all are equally good theories. But that is not our concern. After a description of some major ethical systems, I will simply mention what I regard to be the best theory we have available. But this will be no more than an attempt to explain to the reader that authors do have their own choices in these matters — they do not stand apart from the debate and remain neutral.

Hedonism

The central principle of hedonism is that each person lives a morally good life if he or she acts so as to maximize personal pleasure and minimize personal pain. This doctrine gained its most formidable philosophical defense from Jeremy Bentham (1748–1832), the English jurist and philosopher. One does not often find this ethical position defended, but there are implicit endorsements of it throughout our culture. An explicit endorsement of it was found in a series of essays in *Playboy* magazine, written by Hugh Hefner in the mid 1960s.

Hedonism gains its main strength from the belief that whatever we identify as the ultimate good or purpose in life must be something verifiable, something we can detect by way of the senses. Otherwise the definition of "goodness" will be meaningless and no guidance will be provided for us by means of such a definition. Pleasure is, in turn, simply detected, something everyone can notice, even measure. So, considering the matter realistically, it makes the most sense to conclude that we should guide ourselves by reference to whether what we do enhances our pleasure.

However one might regard this to be a shallow view, it does have its strong point in that it is clear, uncomplicated, and empirical. With all the attempts to define "goodness" and to determine standards for pursuing it (which would then be our principles of morality) having met with difficulties, perhaps we should accept hedonism as the right answer to our central ethical question, "How should I live my life?"

Utilitarianism

Here the answer given to the question of ethics is somewhat less personal. Utilitarians advocate that we should conduct ourselves in such a manner as to promote the greatest happiness of the greatest number of people (or, in some cases, any sentient beings). This idea of the greatest happiness of the greatest number is not simple. It still rests on some of the same considerations that give hedonism its intellectual appeal. Happiness for most utilitarians is interpreted to mean pleasure, but pleasure in a broader sense than hedonism uses the term. For the hedonist, pleasure is a strictly physical or physiological experience. Pleasure for the utilitarian can include also psychological, sometimes even spiritual sensations or experiences. The greatest happiness for the greatest number would amount to the widest distribution of pleasure, good feeling, or even well-being, to the greatest possible intensity or extent. From this, it becomes clear that utilitarians urge us to maximize the overall well-being of society — the general welfare. Thus, utilitarianism is an ethical system that is often invoked in support of the politics of the welfare state, including one of its decision-making tools, social cost-benefit analysis.

The idea is that while hedonists are correct about pleasure being detectable, they fail to note that pleasure can be more or less simple. Furthermore, if pleasure is *the* good, it should be maximized not just for oneself but for all, regardless of whose pleasure it is. So the moral responsibility of every person is to promote the general welfare — i.e., overall pleasure or happiness — even if this may mean at times that the person's own welfare must be disregarded or sacrificed, or even if some people's choices must be overridden. The crucial task is to promote overall well-being. It is hoped, of course, that this will not require extensive displeasure, unhappiness, or hardship for particular individuals.

Two types of utilitarianism have become prominent. Act-utilitarianism urges that each of our actions promote the greatest happiness of the greatest number. Rule-utilitarianism urges that general principles that guide our actions should help promote the same end (although admittedly some particular actions may fail to do so). Rule-utilitarianism is usually taken to be the more successful ethical theory. Here again the influence of a certain idea of what would be an adequate definition of "goodness" can be felt quite strongly. Only if observations will serve to identify what counts as good can an ethical theory have a chance of success, and it is believed that observation can establish whether some policy or action advances the general welfare. (This accounts for the proliferation of statistical studies meant to assist those who engage in the social engineering that goes along with administering the welfare state.)

Egoism

This view, to be distinguished sharply from egotism (which means indulgence in vanity or conceit, that is, a concern with one's self-image or appearance to others), states that each person should act so as to promote his or her self-interest. Egoism requires that one aim at benefiting oneself first and foremost.

As with other ethical systems, this view also has its variations. The different egoist systems vary on the basis of their assumptions about the human ego or self. Put briefly, egoism based on a very narrow conception of the self will have a subjective or personal idea of the human good, whereas egoism based on a robust conception of the human self will adhere to an objectivist or impersonal idea of the human good.

Subjective egoism rests on two initial beliefs. First, each person is entirely unique—being called a human being is merely a matter of convention, habit, or custom without any realistic basis for it. Second, anyone would be in the most favorable position to tell what will enhance his or her welfare, which, at any rate, is just a matter of what one likes, prefers, or desires.

The first belief comes from a well respected philosophical idea that reality does not contain firm, inherent differences, and it is the observer's mind, not reality, that is the basis of differentiating things as one or another kind of something. By this view, reality contains no distinct apples, which are inherently different from oranges, or human beings, which are inherently different from apes. It is observers who impose on reality these distinctions and differences. Accordingly, in the last analysis, when we strip reality of these imposed distinctions, each individual is unique, too, standing isolated and separate from everything else. And each individual (person's) self-enhancement is then a matter of what suits it best, that is, what it likes, prefers, desires. In other words, the standard of self-interest is purely subjective, dependent on what the individual takes for being a value or in his or her best interest.

In a way, this view gains its strength largely from the failures of others who try to argue for objective standards of goodness or rightness. But as an ethical position, this view faces difficulties since it does not seem to answer the question of ethics, "How should I live?" in a way applicable to all those who presume to ask it, namely, human beings. Still by some accounts, it is the only plausible ethical system, since it offers at least some guidance, if only one's subjective feelings or desires, for what one ought to do.

The objective egoist position is derived mainly from the view that we are all in possession of a definite human nature and that living so as to succeed as a human being is what amounts to living a morally good life. We are human individuals. To be good as such we must succeed at living in terms of certain objective, knowable standards. Both what we are, human beings, and who we are, namely the individual one is, must be paid attention to in trying to answer the question "How should I live?" For example, that we are social or language-speaking or rational beings would bind us to certain standards for aspiring to excellence. So would the fact that one is the individual person one is, a writer, or a certain age, of a given nationality, with certain talents.

These two types of egoism are not often enough distinguished, and indeed, egoism is often confused with egotism. Both types of egoism may sanction certain actions, attitudes, and institutions, but both may also conflict with each other concerning some others. Both seem to suggest that a community should prize individual liberty and concomitantly, a free market. But while the subjectivist egoist has little or nothing to say about business ethics (do whatever promotes the satisfaction of your desires would seem to be the end of it), the objectivist egoist proposes a fairly elaborate code of conduct. It should also be noted, however, that most moral thinkers do not favor either form of egoism. And because, nevertheless, much of what goes on in the world of commerce exhibits egoistic motivations, the world of commerce is often regarded as inherently amoral or even immoral.

Altruism

This is the most widely known ethical system. Most people even equate altruism and morality. (A prominent volume of essays in business ethics and public policy, for example, refers to "a purely altruistic or moral motivation [as we commonly use the term 'morality']."[9])

Altruism holds that the morally right way to live is to serve others, at least when they are in need. This is virtually common sense. Commencement talks, Sunday sermons, newspaper and magazine editorials and features, advice from teachers, political rhetoric, and many other sources of ideas about how we should live advocate what amounts to some variety of altruism.

The essence of the view is that the primary responsibility of each person is to enhance the welfare of other people, especially of those who fare rather badly in the world. This view may also be divided into at least two versions. The former is perhaps best labeled a subjectivist, the latter an objectivist type of altruism.

If the individual is regarded to be the best or only judge as to what is to his or her benefit, then altruism requires of each of us that we do for others what they want us to do for them. Then other people's wishes, wants, desires, needs, and so forth, as communicated to us by them, would constitute the guide we need to conduct ourselves morally or ethically. Service to others would then mean submission to other people's demands. This would be the subjectivist conception of altruism. If altruism is correct, one attractive aspect of subjectivist altruism is that it precludes paternalism or prescribing for others what is good for them.

On the other hand, objectivist altruism takes it that there are objective, independent standards for judging what is good for people. In doing good for others, we need to consult such standards, not just ask others what they want from us. Indeed, at times we may be required to do something for others that they might not want to have done for them and may even resist. We find such cases in social programs that impose certain requirements on those being helped, for example, what welfare clients may or may not spend their funds on. An especially clear case of such altruism is involuntary mental hospitalization or psychological/psychosurgical treatmemt. While the patient often resists such treatments, those administering the aid see themselves capable of identifying what is, in fact, good for the patient, as well as their duty to impose the treatment.

Altruism gains its appeal mainly from the idea that human beings are innately antisocial, noncooperative, or greedy. In a way, the economic man idea, which proposes that people act to acquire wealth or satisfy themselves as a matter of instinct or inclination or drive, finds its normative match in altruism: to offset the impact of such a drive, an ethics of altruism is deemed necessary to enhance social cohesion, civilization, or general decency among human beings. Even though we are firmly predisposed to advance our own private interests, as intelligent, rational beings we can figure out that such a course, as a general policy, is morally callous or insignificant in the long run. We need for ourselves a system of guidelines or duties that will motivate us to counteract our innate drives. This system prescribes that we consider other people first, leaving our drives and inclination to take care of our own well-being.

On the matter of our natural inclinations for selfishness, both types of altruism agree. What they differ about is the issue of whether any objective standard of right conduct can be identified. Often altruists will urge that we serve humanity, thereby of course fulfilling our duty to serve others, but they will not be precise about whether objective standards for rendering such service are available. Karl Marx, when he was a young man, put the point well:

When we have chosen the vocation in which we can contribute most to humanity, burdens cannot bend us because they are sacrifices for all. Then we experience no meager, limited, egoistic joy, but our happiness belong to millions, our deeds live on quietly but eternally effective, and glowing tears of noble men will fall on our ashes.[10]

How we are to "contribute most to humanity" is a crucial question, and altruism answers it either by way of a complex theory of human nature and development or leaves the matter to subjective demands expressed by others, to be fulfilled by the moral agent.

As we will see in this work, altruism is an ethical system that serves as the moral base for political ideals, legislation, and political movements. For example, the nineteenth-century French thinker, Auguste Comte, who coined the term "altruism" in the context of his system (which urged the eradication of self-love in favor of love of Society) also advocated socialism.

Ethics in Brief

Many more attempts at devising ethical systems could be detailed. We will mention a few only in one or two sentences, which will suffice to indicate the main theses of these less prominent yet seriously proposed ethical alternatives.

Stoicism states that although we should strive to be happy and fulfilled, we should seek this goal by not desiring anything at all. That way we will never be disappointed, disillusioned, or unhappy. Stoicism holds that we should seek full happiness, and the best way to do this is to disassociate ourselves from temporal, fleeting pleasures, joys, delights, and values. A detachment from everything in the world and the resulting inner peace is what a life of virtue and happiness consists of.

Epicurianism, despite its reputation, is not the same as hedonism but focuses, rather, on a higher sort of happiness, associated mainly with the mind. The reasoning here is somewhat similar to Stoicism's argument, namely, that the worldly pleasures are not under our own control, while the joys of the mind are. The view is a version of subjective or hedonistic egoism, and urges that everyone should pursue his or her long-range higher pleasures in life. But contrary to widespread impression, Epicureanism does not urge the pursuit of gourmet food, sensual thrills, or aesthetic joys. Rather, it counsels that we should attain inner peace and freedom, the basic ingredients of true pleasure.

Asceticism, like Stoicism, prescribes self-denial, but not for the sake of personal happiness. Rather, Asceticism requires such self-denial and self-discipline mainly for reasons related to religious convictions and goals.

Christian ethics, which most people in our culture are taught so that morality and religion are quite firmly linked in the minds of most people, is based on the teachings of Jesus and Moses, as recorded in the Old and New Testaments of the Bible. Its essence is obedience to God's Commandments. The main idea is for an individual to live by a code in order to fulfill his spiritual needs. This involves considerable self-denial in one's earthly existence, the sacrifice of oneself for the well-being of those in need, humility of spirit, and doing one's duty in the service of God's will. All of this will then enable one to reach spiritual happiness in an everlasting afterlife.

Christianity, like other major religious movements such as Islam, Judaism, and Hinduism, is now fragmented into innumerable denominations, each having its own set of edicts. In the last analysis the crucial question pertaining to religiously based ethics is whether one should rest one's moral beliefs on faith or on rational understanding. This question would have to be answered even before one accepts the particular ethical code of a given religious creed.

Common-Sense Ethics

In the foregoing description of various ethical systems, the several moral principles of virtues supported by these systems were not discussed. Instead

I focused on the central principle of the various systems and on why this idea was thought to be of primary importance for guiding human conduct.

But ethics for most of us is largely a matter of numerous moral principles or virtues, such as honesty, justice, generosity, prudence, dependability, thrift, trustworthiness, charity, courage, honor, temperance, moderation, frugality, diligence, loyalty, and so forth. These virtues spell out what we should do in various areas of our lives so as to live an upright, decent, good life. Vices, such as betrayal, cowardice, lying, cruelty, greed, laziness, rashness, or inconsiderateness indicate what we should avoid in our effort to live ethically.

Virtually all ethical systems tend to agree on these virtues and vices. But they differ about the order of priority and the arguments in support of the list. Both hedonism and altruism would urge that we act courageously, justly, and generously. But hedonists would stress that courage is more important than, say, generosity, whereas altruists might reverse this order of importance. Furthermore, the two positions would defend these ideals for different reasons. Hedonists claim that abiding by these principles will maximize one's pleasure, while altruists hold that it will benefit others or society.

It should not be very surprising that all ethical systems would include virtually the same list of moral principles. In any field, the ordinary facts being explained and dissected are roughly the same, regardless of which theory is put forth as the best way to do this. So the basic ideas as to what it is to act morally right and wrong do not vary much in ethics either. Not a lot of debate goes on about whether honesty or justice or courage are virtues. Rather it is the order of importance of the various virtues (and vices) that counts most, according to the theory at hand. The virtues and vices are the ordinary objects, as it were, of ethics, just as rocks, trees, ice, or water are the ordinary objects of natural science. When we wish to explain and understand in considerable detail these "objects" so as to manage our lives more skillfully, we discuss and organize them in special disciplines of study.

Of course, different ethical systems may also define some of the virtues and vices differently. For example, justice may be construed as respect for everyone's basic rights, or as the treatment of everyone in an evenhanded fashion, or giving everyone what he or she needs. In some ethical systems, prudence is taken to be a primary virtue, yet in some systems, prudence carries no moral significance whatsoever. According to some systems, the responsibility one has toward other people or society would be the result of having chosen to be a member of society, while for others, such a responsibility is primary, apart from any prior choices one has made. In some people's view, these responsibilities are to be fulfilled as a matter of personal conscience, but in the view of others, they should be made a matter of public policy, enforced by the government. (Here is where some writers conceive of ethics, including professional and especially business ethics, as publicly enforceable edicts, something to be implemented by law and not left to be a matter of the good will of the acting agents. That is how many professional ethics discussions focus mainly on existing or proposed public policy.)

As we focus on the ethics of business, it is natural to assume that in normal circumstances people will be guided well enough by observing the usual moral principles or virtues. Being just, prudent, honest, courageous, moderate, will suffice in most cases for leading a morally decent life in the world of commerce. But in more difficult cases, where one may find that it is not possible to act so as to satisfy several moral virtues — in short, where there seems to be a conflict of moral principles — it will become important which moral system is actually binding upon people, which is correct. It is with such an answer in hand that one can hope, as a thinking person, to confidently determine the proper order or priorities among the several moral virtues that we should ordinarily practice in life. This is especially true when we turn to the subbranches of ethics, the professional ethics of business, law, medicine, education, citizenship, and the military.

If my loyalty is called for by ordinary, common-sense standards of right and wrong, as well as my honesty, but I cannot practice both, how do I tell which to abide by? Suppose that my best friends are threatened with persecution if I answer the question "Where are your friends now?" truthfully. To choose how to act rightly — i.e., to determine which virtue is applicable — is to have confidence in some basic ethical system as against others. In short, my choice should depend, ultimately, on the best answer to the question "How should I live my life?" Of course, we often gain the confidence from knowing that most members of our culture chose one certain way and not another. But that itself is often the result of the confidence of at least some thoughtful people — novelist, philosophers, playwrights, columnists, ministers, among others — concerning the rightness of the ethical system they practice and preach.

In the end, all ethical problems require solution on the basis of the best answer to this very general question, including the problems we face in our roles as parents and professionals, and those we face in some particular profession, for instance in business. Business ethics is secondary, ethics in general is primary. This means that some branch of ethics, as some branch of a science, cannot contradict, at heart, the general frame of reference that the correct ethical theory provides — or which the correct general scientific theory provides.

As to which ethical system is right and why, that question is difficult to answer briefly, if at all. Many formidable thinkers have offered answers, some of which I have summarized. But it might be asked, if it is so difficult how can ordinary people — e.g., those engaged in commerce — be held responsible to live by an ethical system?

While difficult and controversial, ethics is an inescapable subject. Its central question just will not vanish. There is evidence of that throughout human existence. One's own questions, "What should I do?", "How should I act?", or "What is right?" are inescapable.

It seems reasonable that any diligent, conscientious attempt to consider the question will amount to at least the start of responsible conduct. Different people will, of course, find different levels of such diligence suitable for themselves. There is no formula we can just lay out, but neither is the matter arbitrary. A serious, decent try at facing up to our responsibilities to seek solutions to moral problems, a confidence that we can and should succeed, in normal circumstances, would seem to be something everyone can embark upon; it is something we can ask of any person. Quitting the task, letting others do our thinking about the problems, relying on prejudices or preconceptions, not admitting we have ways to go to succeed, all betray something that would be a failure on the part of a human being. When we speak of human dignity, something that must be granted for everyone, it is this that seems to be at issue, namely, a willingness to come to terms with our vital role in governing our own lives.

Let me conclude by stating that I take objective egoism as the best system. We are human individuals, each of us, and our task is to succeed and do well at our own lives. It is for the sake of living our own lives successfully that we require guidance from an ethical system. The virtues embedded in such a system would, then, have to be ones that make it possible for us to reach success in various departments of living; honesty would steer us right in our communication and thinking; justice in our relationships with others would enable us to treat others fairly; courage would require that we stand up for what is important to us; integrity would require that we never lose sight of our values, our virtues for the sake of convenience or laziness; generosity would require that we consider the plight of those who are unfortunate and, if deserving, share with them our fortunes. Most of all, however, this egoistic ethics would require of us to be rational, thinking beings, not led by flights of fancy, despair, elation, and other emotions not under the guidance of good sense. Our emotions are important but not as the means by which to guide ourselves through life — although now and then we might have to rely on them, when there is no time for thought. Still, whenever possible, we should think clearly and organize our lives accordingly.

All this is very general indeed, but some of it will emerge in the course of considering the ethics of commerce. Not all who write on ethics agree with this line of thinking, but quite a few do. But in either case, what is crucial is what makes good sense, and that needs to be explored at greater length than we can treat in this introductory chapter. For the time being this is the most that I can do to spell out in general terms how one should live one's life.

Ethics, Law, and Public Policy

In matters of morality, what comes first is the very broad question, "How should I live my life?" More specialized questions concern how one should act in a given area of human life—as parent, friend, colleague, citizen, or kin. The answer to the second set of questions would have to depend partly on the answer to the first question and partly on the special feature of the role in question. In other words, if hedonism is the correct ethical theory, then to learn how to act properly as a parent, one would have to know the facts of parenthood and the ideals and edicts of hedonism. And when one wishes to learn how one should act as a professional, again, one would need to know what the general ethical system requires of one, as well as how these requirements apply to one's professional life.

Since most ethical systems agree about the general virtues by which we should all live, precise knowledge about just which ethical system is correct would not ordinarily be necessary. It is well enough known that people should be honest, and if they lie, especially to those close to them, this is pretty much evidence of their misconduct in human relationships. It is also well known that courage is a virtue, and if a parent fails to protect his child from danger, it is clear enough that such a parent is not carrying on his parental role in the most responsible fashion.

Apart from ethical guidelines, there are also the laws of one's community, which one is generally expected to obey. A law-abiding person is thought to be at least somewhat decent and good. But there are bad laws, bad legal systems, and even some systems that are legal in name only. How ought one to act in the face of this? What is the proper relationship between ethics and law? That is one of the vital issues to be covered in this book. At this point, we need only raise the issues and leave the discussion to the author who will address them (Professor John Hospers).

As to public policy, this comprises all those government programs and activities by which governments aim to serve the public interest or welfare. Depending on the system, a government may be legally authorized to carry our many or very few programs under the rubric of public policy. Thus, in a totalitarian system there is no limit to what constitutes public policy, since government is involved in all of what goes on in a community. In a constitutional democracy, on the other hand, public policy is checked by constitutional restrictions on the powers of government. The First Amendment to the United States Constitution curbs the powers of government so that it may not restrict religious practices, citizens' ability to speak out, and freedom of assembly.

Sometimes a system of law has an unjustly broad public sphere, sometimes an unjustly narrow one. In either case, the citizens of a community might find themselves morally opposed to their government. In the former case, citizens would have to cope with broader than justified governmental activity. In the context of commerce, that would usually mean government regulation that is beyond proper governmental authority. In the latter case, citizens would have to cope with some kind of lawlessness — for example, by some kind of vigilante action. Whenever a community develops an underground economy, sometimes because government has unjustly expanded its powers and morally legitimate commerce must be hidden from it, it lacks suitable legal measures to cope with the violation of rights. That is when private organizations begin to carry out legal functions, i.e., usually without due process accorded to violators. Here law fails to apply where it should. (Chapter 7, on government regulation, will consider some of the details of public policy in relation to commerce.)

Remaining Issues

In the preceding preliminary discussions, I have tried to address some of the topics that first confront someone coming to an examination of business ethics and commerce-related public policy. What is ethics? How does it compare to economics, the social science wherein commerce is studied? What scope does ethics have and what are its various subdivisions? What are some prominent systems and theories of ethics? What should ethics be understood to involve for ordinary citizens not specializing in moral philosophy — i.e., what is the common sense of ethics? What problems may face us in the relationship between ethics and law, and between ethics and public policy?

All of these questions are touched on in greater detail and with a sharper focus in the rest of this work. But the background provided here will enable one to be prepared for a better understanding of those more detailed discussions.

A final point should be noted about ethics in general. However much one carefully reads articles or listens to lectures about ethics, morality, standards of right conduct, ultimately the matter is in the individual's own hand, unless he or she is a prisoner or slave or is severely incapacitated. The crucial feature of ethics is, after all, personal responsibility to do well at living a human life. That is not something that can be implanted or programmed into people, but must be a matter of the individual's own choice and will. Whether a person is indeed making the choice to act rightly and what this means is just what ethics and its various branches, including business ethics, ultimately attempt to clarify.

Notes

1. Karl Popper, *Unending Quest* (Glasgow: Fontana/Collins, 1974), p. 194.
2. While various fields of interest may differ about numerous matters — method of study, unit of measurement, degree of precision required — they cannot contradict

each other. Reality is not hospitable to contradictions, which is why no court testimony or theory containing a contradiction is even considered.

3. Gary Becker, *The Economic Approach to Human Behavior* (Chicago: University of Chicago Press, 1976), p. 5.

4. George Stigler, Lecture ii, Tanner Lectures, Harvard University, April 1980. In Richard McKenzie, *The Limits of Economic Science* (Boston: Kluwer-Nijhoff Pub., 1983), p. 6.

5. Milton Friedman, "The Line We Dare Not Cross," *Encounter* (November 1976), p. 11.

6. Economists are not always reluctant to admit to this charge. See Gerard Radnitzky and Peter Bernholz, eds., *Economic Imperialism: The Economic Method Applied Outside the Field of Economics* (New York: Paragon House Publishers, 1987).

7. There are exceptions, of course, as one can see from the existence of such scholarly journals as *Economics and Philosophy* and *The Review of Social Economics,* among others.

8. The relationship between the business society, conceived as a pure, free-market capitalist system, and Marxism, is fully discussed in T. R. Machan, ed., *The Main Debate: Communism versus Capitalism* (New York: Random House, 1987).

9. Tom L. Beauchamp and Norman E. Bowie, "Ethical Theory and its Application to Business," in T. L. Beauchamp and N. E. Bowie, eds., *Ethical Theory and Business* (Englewood Cliffs, N.J.: Prentice-Hall, 2nd edition, 1983), p. 16.

10. *Writings of the Young Marx on Philosophy and Society,* eds., Lloyd Easton and K. Guddat (New York: Anchor Books, 1967), p. 39.

Part
I

BUSINESS
ETHICS

1

MANAGERIAL ETHICS

DOUGLAS B. RASMUSSEN

Management "is a process or form of work that involves the guidance or direction of a group of people toward organizational goals or objectives."[1] The manager is the person who performs this work. The functions of a manager can be divided into five categories: (1) planning—deciding what objectives to pursue and how to achieve them; (2) controlling—measuring performance against objectives and taking corrective actions; (3) organizing—grouping and assigning activities and providing the authority to carry out the activities; (4) staffing—recruiting, selecting, and training; and (5) motivating—directing behavior toward the achievement of objectives.[2]

A manager is normally distinguished from an entrepreneur. The entrepreneur is the person who conceives the idea or service the organization is going to produce, starts the organization, and builds it to the point where additional people are needed. The manager is the individual who is hired to perform the basic management functions. The entrepreneur, of course, must perform many, if not all, the managerial functions. Yet, it is important to note that a *manager* is usually understood to be the person who has been employed by others (the entrepreneur) to perform the work called "management".

Ethics deals with the question of how persons should conduct themselves. Managerial ethics, then, is concerned with the question of how a manager (or an entrepreneur as manager) should conduct him or herself so that the organizational goals and objectives are achieved in a manner consistent with the principles of conduct that ethics dictates.

There are two areas to which ethical principles can be applied to managerial conduct: first, to the objectives or goals chosen for the organization, and second, to the strategies, tactics, and policies employed for the attainment of these objectives or goals. Therefore, managerial ethics can be divided into two parts—management goals, and management strategies, tactics, and policies.

Management Goals

Within a free market society, it is generally thought that the primary goal of a business organization is the attainment of profit. Though businesses often consider other objectives (service to customers, employee needs and well-being, assistance to the needy) it cannot be denied that the attainment of profit is the overall and guiding objective of the business organization. Thus, the first question that managerial ethics should consider is whether or not it is ethically proper to make the attainment of profit *the* objective of a business firm. This is a most important question today, for it is sometimes said that the pursuit of profit ought not be the primary and dominant goal of a business firm but rather must be balanced by concern for customers, employees, or society. In order to see what the standards for proper managerial conduct might be, we need to understand what is meant by "free market society" and "profit," and what ethics has to say about such a society and goal.

The Free Market Society and Profit

The terms "free market society" are not solely descriptive. They signify a set of economic and social arrangements that presupposes a certain ethical perspective. For example, "Murder Incorporated" would not be regarded as a business firm in such a society but would instead be viewed as criminal that ought not and must not be allowed to operate. Similarly, the term "profit" does not mean merely a return on an economic exchange that is over costs; it also involves a certain type of exchange — namely, a free or voluntary exchange. In order to understand the ethical perspective from which the terms "free market society" and "profit" derive their particular meaning, we should consider the notion of "individual rights."

A free market society is a society based on the recognition of individual rights. "Individual rights are the means of subordinating society to moral law."[3] They determine what matters of morality — what *ought* to be, are to be matters of law — what *must* be. The view of rights that a free market society is based on is one that holds that every person has the right to life and its corollaries: liberty and property. These rights are rights to actions — that is, the right to take all the actions necessary for the support and furtherance of one's life, and the right to the action of producing or earning something and keeping, using, and disposing of it according to one's goals. To have a right in this sense morally obligates others to abstain from physical compulsion, coercion, or interference. Such actions may only be taken in self-defense and only against those who initiate physical compulsion, coercion, or interference. The right to life also morally sanctions the freedom to act by means of one's voluntary, uncoerced choice for one's own goals.[4] Thus, the activities of producing and exchanging goods and services in a free market society are both protected and governed by this conception of individual rights.

When the foregoing conception of individual rights is followed, an economic exchange is a voluntary one in which only the judgments of individual buyers and sellers determine the price of a good or service. A (the student) deals with B (the teacher) because B has something (knowledge of a certain field) that A values, while B deals with A because A has something (money) that B values, and when each values what the other has more than what he has, when the student values the knowledge the teacher provides more than the money he has, and the teacher values the money the student has more than what he could be doing if he were not teaching the student, an exchange takes place. The difference between the value A and B respectively attribute to the good or service the other possesses and the value they attribute to the good or service they are willing to give up is expected profit.[5] Given that the principle of individual rights is followed,[6] an economic exchange in a free market society is not to be legally prohibited nor is the result of this exchange—profit or loss—to be legally altered. There may be judgments about the morality of the exchange that are negative, for instance, that some or all of the members of the exchange have a set of values that ought not to be followed, but rather changed, i.e., the student ought not to value obtaining knowledge of a certain field or the teacher ought not to value money. Either one or both ought to do something else, or some or all of the members of the exchange ought to reflect more carefully on what they believe their values direct them to do and, as a result, not engage in the exchange. Perhaps the student's values do not really require that he pursue the knowledge the teacher provides. Yet, as long as the foregoing conception of individual rights is followed, such moral judgments are not the concern of the legal code of the society.

Ethics, the Free Market Society, and the Pursuit of Profit

Within the legal framework of a free market society, is the managerial decision to make the attainment of profit the overall and guiding objective of the business firm ethically justifiable? Are the principles in terms of which the legal framework of a free market society developed (that is, the foregoing account of individual rights) ethically justifiable? The answers to these questions cannot be discovered by managerial or business ethics alone. These questions require the more fundamental disciplines of ethics and political philosophy. The standard for proper managerial conduct cannot be derived independently of those ethical principles that determine how human beings ought to live their lives and those political principles that determine the ethical principles by which human beings must live their lives, that is, be a matter of law. The standard for proper managerial conduct must be in accord with what the principles of ethics and political philosophy advise; it cannot contradict the overall frame of reference that the more basic disciplines of ethics and political philosophy provide.

Leaving aside the problems[7] that could be raised regarding the viability of normative disciplines, ethics can be understood as being concerned with whether a person is succeeding at the task of living as a human being. Since we are living things, the consequences of the actions we take can make a difference to whether we do well or not as human beings, and since we are capable of thinking about and choosing the actions we take, this concern for doing well as human beings is something about which advice can be given and principles formulated. Ethics is the enterprise that attempts to formulate the principles by which human life is to be lived.

The aim of ethics so conceived is to enable the individual person to do well as a human being. The Greeks called this "eudaimonia," a state of well-being achieved by a process of self-actualization and characterized by maturation. Though "eudaimonia" is usually translated as happiness, this is misleading if not qualified. Happiness should not be understood as simply the gratification of desire or even the long-run gratification of desire; rather, it is the satisfaction of *right* desire — the satisfaction of those desires and wants that will lead to successful human living or, as some philosophers call it, "human flourishing."

The sort of success that doing well as a human being involves is determined by the nature of a human being. As Tibor R. Machan has noted:

The happiness of a human being is not, therefore, a state of sensory pleasure, although such pleasures are also necessary for a successful human life, since man is not *only* a rational being but an animal with the biological capacity and need for sensory experiences as well. Instead the happiness or successful life of a person must involve considerations that *depend* upon his conceptual capacities. Man must be a success *as* a rational animal. He must live in such a way that he achieves goals that are rational for him individually but also as a human being. The former will vary depending on *who* he is. The latter are uniform and pertain to *what* he is; to his humanity — his goal as a human being must be to do best what is his unique capacity: live rationally.[8]

Most simply put, happiness for a human being requires that one live intelligently, not acting from impulse and habit, but from knowledge and understanding. However, it must be realized that such a way of life is not merely a matter of employing intelligence or reason to achieve whatever ends one happens to desire. Rather, living intelligently or rationally prescribes or determines the ends themselves — the ends one needs to desire — and these ends in turn constitute the overall end of human life, that is, living intelligently or rationally.

Living intelligently or rationally involves first and foremost attending to the world conceptually. Conceptually attending to the world is a *method* of using one's mind. It is no part-time affair and involves more than forming a few simple abstractions or using a few words. Rather, conceptually attending to the world requires that one identify the world by means of concepts — viz., one notes similarities and differences, grasps relationships, and makes integrations so as to expand one's knowledge into an ever-growing sum. This, in turn, involves that one ask questions, discover answers, make inferences, and draw conclusions. This method of using one's consciousness demands a commitment to a state of full and active awareness in every aspect of one's life in all of one's waking hours. Conceptually attending to the world is a way of life.

There is nothing passive or automatic about conceptualizing. Focusing one's consciousness in order to understand the what's and why's of the world requires effort — effort to initiate and effort to maintain. Without this effort, conceptualization would not exist. Perceptual or sensory awareness may be produced in us by those features of the world that possess sensible qualities, but "there is nothing in nature that forces generalizations, classifications, theories and ideas upon us."[9] Furthermore, conceptualizing is our unique and only way of dealing with the world. We do not automatically know what will benefit or endanger us; we do not automatically know what values we need. We must, therefore, use our minds if we are to discover the values we need and the virtues by which to attain them. Yet, whether we do so or not is up to us.

It should be obvious that people exercise the effort necessary to maintain this conceptual state of awareness in varying degrees and many times act blindly from impulse or habit without knowledge and understanding. Yet, what may not be so obvious is that exercising the effort necessary to conceptually attend to the world comes in many forms: in seeking clarity as opposed to vagueness; in respecting reality rather than avoiding it; in persevering in the attempt to understand instead of giving up; in remaining loyal in action to one's convictions as opposed to being disloyal; in being honest with one's self rather than being dishonest; in allowing self-confrontation instead of self-avoidance; in being willing to see and correct mistakes as opposed to maintaining error; in being open to new knowledge rather than being close-minded; and in being concerned with consistency, coherence, and evidence instead of being unconcerned.[10] The question of whether one will conceptualize or not is not simply a matter of whether one will engage in explicit reasoning. The question is more fundamental than that. It is a question that is present in all the problems and issues that make up a person's life.

The question of whether one will conceptually attend to the world is also present in the question of whether one will recognize that it is through productive work that human beings sustain themselves, control their environment, and find fulfillment. It is by use of one's mind that one not only discovers the values necessary for human flourishing but also attains them. Productive work, then, is an exercise of one's fullest potential—a potential that can only be attained by the fullest use of one's mind.[11] Productive work is not the unfocused performance of the motions of some job. It is the pursuit of what is sometimes called a "career." Yet, what matters here is not someone's level of ability or the scale of one's job. Nor does productivity require that one produce what the economists call "consumer goods." The intellectual or artist can be as productive as the businessman. Rather, what matters is that the work be equal to one's actual capacity, that it allows one to develop lifetime interests and goals and requires serious education and training. If one is to live intelligently or rationally, accepting responsibility for being productive is required.

Living intelligently or rationally also involves the recognition that human beings must learn how to use and control their desires. Human beings are not computers. Human beings take actions to attain ends, and it is through the desire for a specific end that an action occurs. Our desires move us toward objects of apparent benefit and away from objects of apparent harm. Yet, our desires can be mistaken. They can direct us toward something that is not, in fact, beneficial or away from something that actually is beneficial. The solution to this problem is, however, not to deny one's desire and attempt to live without passion. Rather, one must discover what the true goods of human life are and strive to harmonize one's desires with one's knowledge of these goods. Aristotle counseled that we develop our desires so that when confronted with situations calling for action, our desires will move us toward what is actually good and away from what is actually bad. David Norton has expressed this ideal well.

The eudaimonic individual experiences the whole of his life in every act, and he experiences parts and wholes together as necessary, such that he can will nothing changed. But the necessity here introduced is moral necessity, deriving from his choice. Hence, we may say of him interchangeably, "He is where he wants to be, doing what he wants to do," or "He is where he must be, doing what he must do."[12]

The intelligent or rational human life is characterized by the cultivation and exercise of moral virtue whereby one comes to consistently desire those courses of action that one's knowledge and understanding dictate and is not deflected by anger or fear or greed or lust or envy or pleasure.

To live intelligently or rationally, to act from knowledge and understanding, involves even more than has been stated. It involves the following: the recognition that the responsibility for thinking is one's own (independence); a refusal to substitute the opinions and wishes of others for one's convictions (integrity); the practice of identifying persons for what they are and treating them accordingly—never granting the unearned or failing to grant the earned (justice); a realization that facts, whether material or spiritual, are ultimate and cannot be faked (honesty); an appreciation that life is not guaranteed but is conditional and thus is the basis for a common bond with others (benevolence); and a commitment to the development of oneself, specifically, to the development of the desire to make of one's character and life all that it can and should be (pride). Successful human living is no easy matter, and regrettably few people live as well as they should.

One of the major, if not *the* major, consequences of failing to live intelligently or rationally has been noted by psychologists and moralists. Many people suffer from insufficient self-esteem. In its most extreme form, inadequate self-esteem leads to self-alienation, mental illness, and even death. People have a fundamental need for a sense of efficacy and worth. Since conceptually attending to the world is not an automatic process and since we cannot guarantee that our efforts to know the what's and why's of the world will succeed, we need to have confidence in our ability to know the world and feel that we are right in our method of dealing with it. Yet,

if we default on the responsibility of thought and reason, if we turn our backs on reality and facts, thus undercutting our competence to live, we will not retain a sense of worthiness. If we betray our integrity, if we betray our moral convictions, if we turn our backs on our standards, thus undercutting our sense of worthiness, we do so by evasion; by the refusal to see what we see or know what we know, we commit treason to our own (correct or mistaken) judgments, and thus do not retain our sense of competence.[13]

Self-esteem does not require infallibility or omniscience. In fact, it is precisely because we are not infallible or omniscient that we have such a need for self-esteem. Yet, self-esteem does require the conviction that we are capable of dealing with reality — that we are competent at using our mind to deal with life's opportunities and difficulties. "Self-esteem is the reputation we acquire with ourselves."[14] We may be able to cheat others in garnering their respect, but self-esteem is much more difficult, if not impossible, to cheat. Self-esteem is attained to the extent we take on the responsibility of living intelligently or rationally. We have within our power the ability to make our own soul — to make our life a joy or a living hell. Such is the glory and misery of our species.

What then does the foregoing account of ethics have to say about the managerial decision within the legal framework of a free market society to make the attainment of profit the overall and guiding objective of the business firm? Is it ethically proper to make profit *the* objective of a business organization? Yes, provided one realizes that trade is not the only way that one can deal with others and that money is a means of exchange, a tool, and not an end in itself.

There is nothing wrong in dealing with others by means of trade. It is a relationship that is based on the mutual judgment that an exchange is to the advantage of each. It is voluntary (it is consistent with individual rights) and respects the judgments of the other person. Further, it does not preclude other ways of relating to persons, e.g., love and friendship.

Money is, of course, a medium of exchange that facilitates trade; and when the supply of money is not inflated by the government and individual rights are not violated, we know that those who have made money have succeeded in offering goods and services that others want. In such a situation, it is not only the case that there is nothing morally wrong with the pursuit of profit; it, in fact, indicates the presence of many of the moral virtues discussed earlier. To earn a profit in the free market requires that one not only know his values but relates them to other values and ranks them accordingly. Moreover, one must act at the appropriate time so as to sell what he values less for what he values more. The entire process is most difficult and requires that a person take responsibility for one's life—viz., discover who and what one is, produce what is one's talent to produce, and from these fashion a fulfilling existence.

Yet, it remains nonetheless true that many people forget that money is a tool and spend a lifetime pursuing it without knowing why. They confuse a means with an end and one day discover that their life is quite empty. As Ayn Rand noted:

Money will not purchase happiness for the man who has no concept of what he wants; money will not give him a code of values, if he has evaded the knowledge of what to value, and it will not provide him with a purpose, if he has evaded the choice of what to seek. Money will not buy intelligence for the fool, or admiration for the coward, or respect for the incompetent.[15]

One must understand not only what money is and what it will do, one must also know what it isn't and what it will not do. Learning this, as well as how to earn and use money, is a primary ethical concern. Thus, there is nothing ethically wrong in making the attainment of profit the overall and guiding objective of a business organization *if* one understands that money is only a tool, and trade is but one way of dealing with others.

One might, however, object that it is ethically better to deal with others out of a motive of love and friendship than from a motive of profit. After all, don't we all prefer that someone deals with us for our own sake and not for what they can obtain from us? Indeed, one of the things involved in loving someone is that one is concerned with the well-being of the other person for that person's sake and nothing else. Yet, this objection forgets that love and friendship are close, personal relationships and, by their very nature, are precluded from being extended to everyone. One cannot profess love and friendship for every person one deals with and continue to mean what is normally meant by these terms.[16]

It may, of course, be that the foregoing objection is really only an elliptical way of saying that dealing with others for the purpose of making a profit is a way of using people – of treating people as means and not ends. This charge is, however, not accurate. When one engages in trade, one is dealing with others on the basis of one's own judgments. The trade takes place precisely because the parties involved regard it as advantageous. Thus, the participants in the trade are treated as ends, because the exchange respects their judgments. They remain moral agents throughout. Still, it is true that when one deals with someone else for the purpose of making a profit, one treats the other person as a means. Yet, it is not exclusively so. One also treats the other person as an end, for the trade would not occur without the person's decision to participate.

Though trade only occurs when there is agreement to participate, is agreement sufficient to ethically justify a trade? Are there not times when people buy or sell something they ought not to? Certainly, almost everyone can recall times when they acted rashly and purchased or sold something without engaging in sufficient thought, and regretted it later. Moreover, it is certainly possible for people to make a trade on the basis of values that are not, in fact, good for them. What people think is a real good can turn out to be only an apparent good. Thus, there is more required to ethically justify a trade than merely the fact that the persons involved have agreed to it. Trades can be ethically evaluated and found wanting.

It is, of course, very difficult for an observer to be in a position to have sufficient knowledge of the circumstances and details of a trade (e.g., the values of the parties involved) to be able to ethically evaluate it. Yet, it is nonetheless possible, and such evaluation can be most helpful. Often, others can see errors in our thinking or flaws in our system of values that we cannot. Indeed, even our judgment as to whether a trade is profitable or not can be changed by a realization that we have failed to note something or have accepted values that are, in fact, not good for us. Ethical criticism of the trades people make can and should be made. It allows people the opportunity to improve themselves.

There is, however, another matter. Suppose that one is in a position to adequately evaluate a trade and suppose further that the trade is based on values that are not conducive to the human flourishing of some (or even all) of the persons involved, should this trade be allowed? Or, is this trade something that must not occur, that is, something to be legally prohibited? According to the theory of individual rights presented in the account of a free market society, such a trade should be allowed if no rights of the participants, or third parties, are violated.[17] Even though a trade may be something that is ethically wrong for some or all of the participants to engage in, the trade ought not be legally prohibited. Individual rights provide the criteria for determining what matters of morality (that which ought to be) are to be matters of law (that which must be). This theory claims that the coercive force of law should only be used to protect individual rights, not to try and make persons moral. Yet, is this theory of individual rights (the basis for the legal framework of a free market society) justifiable?

Human flourishing requires that one live intelligently or rationally. This way of living is an ongoing, self-directed process. The process is not automatic and can only be initiated and maintained by the effort of the individual person. No one can do the thinking for another person. One can offer advice, give orders, and even require actions, but one cannot make someone else understand.[18] Self-directedness or autonomy is the *exercise* of one's reason and intelligence and is the central necessary feature of human flourishing. It is the activity that makes this way of living what it is; for without it none of the virtues that constitute human flourishing could exist. Individuals, then, cannot be what they ought to be without doing so by their own deliberate choice and in light of their own understanding. One cannot claim to be living intelligently or rationally if he is not the author of his own actions, if they have been forced upon him by others.

Persons may, of course, fail to exercise the choice to do what they ought to do, or their understanding of what they ought to do may be erroneous. As was noted earlier, the process of living intelligently or rationally is no easy matter. Many times, we allow our desires to overwhelm us, fail to keep our mind focused, or simply make a mistake. Successful human living cannot be guaranteed. Yet, if individuals are ever to have an opportunity to flourish, "the choice to learn, to judge, to evaluate, to appraise, to decide what he ought to do in order to live his life must be each person's own. . . . His moral aspirations cannot be fulfilled (or left unfulfilled) if he is not the source of his own actions."[19] Respect for the autonomy of the person is required because autonomy is inherent to the flourishing of each person.[20]

The autonomy of a person can only be respected if others abstain from initiating physical compulsion, coercion, or interference against him. Such intrusions into personal autonomy are caused by others[21] and are something they could refrain from doing. Such actions represent a type of behavior that must not occur and thus should be legally prohibited. The claim that individuals have the right to life, liberty, and property indicates the conditions that must be enforced if living a morally commendable life in the company of other human beings is to be possible. Individual rights are principles that acknowledge that persons are ends and not merely means and may not be used for attaining other ends without their consent. Individual rights recognize that human beings are individuals, that the life of each person is the only one he has, and no one may be sacrificed for others. Individual rights, if followed, preserve the essential human dignity of persons.

Individual rights provide the ethical basis for the protection of the autonomy of a person. They do not, however, guarantee that a person will make ethically appropriate decisions or that he will even want to accept the consequences of his decisions once he realizes what they involve. In a free market society it is, then, not at all uncommon to hear someone say that they made a "bad deal" or that the other person "took advantage" of them. Indeed, many times, one discovers *after* a trade has occurred that he did not fully appreciate or understand what the trade involved or that he did not sufficiently consider the alternatives. In some cases, it may even be true that the other party in the trade had good reason to believe that you had not sufficiently considered what the trade demanded or what other options existed. Depending on the circumstances, it may or may not be the case that the other party in the trade had an ethical obligation to tell you of its implications or about the existence of other alternatives,[22] but it is the case that you did not have a right—a legally enforceable claim—to this information.

To claim a right to information from the other participant in the trade requires a violation of individual rights. In such a situation, physical compulsion or coercion would be imposed on the other party in order to obtain the requisite information or, more likely to penalize him, e.g., in the form of a monetary fine for not providing it. In general, to claim a right that others provide you with goods and services—be it higher wages, education, health care, housing, or whatever—means that physical compulsion or coercion is to be used on others in order to obtain the demanded goods and services or, as is more common, to obtain the economic means by which to provide these goods and services, e.g., taking some of the money that one has spent their time earning. To claim such a right means that the autonomy of others is to be denied, that their essential human dignity is not to be respected, and that they are to be treated as merely means.

Some thinkers would, however, disagree with the foregoing, because they believe that failing to provide others with the goods and services they need for living well already constitutes a denial of the autonomy of those in need, and so they hold that using force to obtain the required goods and services from others is merely a rectification of previous rights violations. For these thinkers,[23] rights are "welfare rights." This view of rights is, of course, in conflict with the theory of individual rights, and the debate between these conflicting views is a major issue in political philosophy. A thorough examination of the issues involved in the debate cannot be discussed at the present time, but the following objection to "welfare rights" can at least be noted: unless it is already assumed that a person has the right to the goods and services others have produced, it does not seem correct to say that not providing the person with the goods and services he needs violates his autonomy. No one is doing anything to make the person act against his own judgments or values; no one is taking any action designed to impose by physical force or its threat their will on the person. This is not to deny that the person may not be in a helpless situation or that we are even ethically obligated to help him, but this is to deny that the nonperformance of certain activities requested by the needy person abridges his autonomy and that he has a right to the performance of these requested activities. The welfare conception of rights seems to confuse circumstances that force people to be in need with people who use physical force or its threat to obtain values from others. It confuses the "coercion" of *events* with the coercion of *people*.[24]

Ought a trade that is based on values that are not conducive to the human flourishing of some or all of the persons involved be legally prohibited? If the individual rights of the participants and those of third parties are respected, then the answer to this question is "no." There may be complications and difficulties regarding whether fraud or negligence occurred or even some question about whether the property someone possesses is rightfully owned, but unless there are issues of this sort[25] for the legal system to examine (and a case for an investigation would have to be made), there ought not be any legal interference with trade. Others who find a trade ethically unjustified may not violate the rights of the parties involved, and the legal system should not allow such interference.

As long as individual rights are respected, those who find a particular trade morally offensive, e.g., purchasing pornographic literature or attending pornographic movies, may use any measures to persuade the parties involved to refrain from such trades. These measures could be anything from trying to persuade the buyers of pornography of how it can harm their character and warp their understanding of sex to social ostracism, picketing, and economic isolation of the seller of pornography by refusing to engage in any other exchange with him. Such measures cannot guarantee that such undesirable trades will not occur, but they can be effective.

Management Strategies, Tactics, and Policies

Given that the objective of a business firm is the attainment of profit, what does an ethic of human flourishing have to say about the strategies, tactics, and policies a business manager might employ in order to obtain a profit? In this context the most important thing an ethic of human flourishing holds is that all attempts to coerce, defraud, or otherwise violate the rights of persons are legally as well as ethically objectionable. The business manager is, therefore, required to refrain from any and all rights-violating activities. If the business manager engages in rights-violating activities, he/she is subject to criminal prosecution. Though this prohibition summarizes the business manager's legal obligations, it does not limit his/her ethical obligations. The business manager has five managerial functions to perform—planning, controlling, organizing, staffing, and motivating—and these are to be performed in accordance with the moral principles human flourishing require.

Without knowledge of the details, knowledge that sometimes is only available to the participants in an activity, there is very little specific ethical advice that can be given. Yet, the business manager does have ethical obligations.

First, the business manager has an obligation to be just in his/her dealings with other persons, should identify persons for what they are, and treat them accordingly. For example, when considering employees for promotion, she ought to promote those who have performed well and have shown promise as opposed to those who have not. The manager ought not advance friends simply because they are friends and should not allow irrelevant factors to intrude. Complex and difficult decisions ought not be made in an arbitrary way. Intellect must be the guide in determining what should be done so that the manager, after gathering all the relevant information, can know why one person is to be promoted instead of another.

Second, the business manager ought to be honest in his dealings with others. He should not evade the distinction between what is real and unreal in an attempt to gain what is of value from others.[26] For example, when making the annual report to the owners of the firm, he ought not deliberately misrepresent or distort facts and figures to make his performance as a manager look better than it actually is. Neither should the business manager, in cooperation with other managers in the firm, or with subordinates, guide or direct the company in activities that are personally lucrative but not in the best interests of the company. In such a case, the manager might claim that his policies are designed to make the firm prosper when actually they are only directed for his personal interests. Finally, the business manager should not assume that just as the players know that bluffing is expected in poker, so everyone knows that lying is expected in business. This is not true. Moreover, not everyone has agreed to the lying-is-okay-in-business rule; even if they did, it would still be contrary to what successful human living calls for. One needs to live in accordance with what the facts require and not in accordance with what others have been led to believe. The rules for doing well in human living are not, like the rules of poker, conventions. Though there may be problems and situations that are unique to business, there is no special type of ethics only for business. After all, business managers are human beings, and the requirements of good human living apply to them as much as to anyone else.

Third, the business manager ought to accept responsibility for what she has to do and should not attempt to push the responsibility on to someone else. She should be independent and apply her own mind to the tasks she faces. The manager should not, for example, put off making decisions when they need to be made or simply follow past practices or judgments of others. She should proceed by her own judgment and show initiative and a willingness to consider new policies. Sometimes it is said that one of the difficulties in business today is that managers spend most of their time trying to avoid blame for problems instead of trying to solve them. How accurate this claim is is difficult to say, but it remains nonetheless true that the business manager needs to accept the responsibilities of her position and deal with them by means of her own judgment.

Fourth, the business manager ought not sacrifice his fundamental convictions and values for the sake of what the owners of the business firm expect. If maintaining his position with the firm requires that he engage in activities or sanction policies that are in conflict with his fundamental convictions and values, e.g., he is expected to find "call-girls" for business associates or cover up others' gross incompetence or negligence, then he ought not, given no other alternative, retain his position with the firm. He should, of course, be sure of his facts and values and not merely react to something he does not like. He also should make sure there are *no* other alternatives. For example, is there a possibility that he could extricate himself from having to be a part of the objectionable activity or from having to sanction the objectionable policy; or, if this is not possible, might he be able to meet with the owners of the firm to attempt to convince them to change their expectations? Attempting to convince the owners to change their minds could, however, be the step by which he loses his job; it is difficult to say. As a last resort, could he go to the media and "blow the whistle" on the company's activities and policies? It may be that he *has* no other alternative — he must either do what he finds morally reprehensible or give up his position. The problem may also be compounded by financial and familial commitments. Sometimes there are no easy choices. Nonetheless, he cannot live a fulfilling life or avoid alienation if he must sacrifice his fundamental convictions and values and live a life that is not really his own.

Fifth, the business manager should find his work fulfilling. The work should be within his capacity and not overwhelm him. Further, he should not be a manager simply to advance within the firm or to make more money. Rather, he should be in the position of a manager because it represents a challenge to him and offers an opportunity for the full, creative use of his mind. The business manager should only remain in his position if, indeed, it turns out to be fulfilling. He must neither allow himself to be overwhelmed in a position that is beyond his ability to handle nor stifled in a position that is not sufficiently challenging. It is, however, not easy to determine what one's limitations are or to know one's unique potential, and it is very easy to tell oneself that things will get better tomorrow. While things do sometimes improve, it is nonetheless true that there are too many managers who are in positions for which they are not suited. Instead of discovering and developing their unique potential, what David Norton calls one's *daimon*,* business managers are seduced by the money, power, and

---

Daimon is a Greek word. It is used here to signify an innate standard for excellence that a person has just by virtue of being that very individual person.

perquisites of the managerial position and forget, or in some cases never know, what it is that can make their life unique and exciting. The Greek exhortations, "know thyself" and "become what you are," are as appropriate today as they were when Socrates enunciated them.

None of the foregoing observations about the difficulties of finding fulfilling work are unique to business managers. Indeed, the problem may be much worse in academe. Rather, the point of these remarks is to show that managerial ethics must be aware of the self-referential character of these considerations. Thus, the question for managerial ethics is as much a question of whether there is any understanding by management of what fulfilling work is[27] and what it may personally require of them as it is what management can do to allow people to find fulfilling work. Finding fulfilling work is something the individual must do for himself. He must discover his *daimon* and strive to attain it. Yet, without an understanding of what fulfilling work is, it is most doubtful that there would ever be any appreciation for why someone might not accept a management position or why someone would leave a managerial post for a more specialized area of work with the firm. Instead, such a decision would be considered as a sign that the person did not have ambition. Further, a failure to appreciate what fulfilling work is locks both management and employees into a "vertical" conception of what success within the firm is. They believe that the way one succeeds at work is by being promoted to a managerial position. Needless to say, for some people this creates an incentive not to be too good at one's job. It also limits management's ability to discover and use the most productive persons at the various jobs.

Sixth, the business manager needs to be benevolent. He should at all times remember that his job is defined by the different ways he interacts with people, and people are complicated creatures with many motivations and needs. Considerateness, compassion, kindness, and generosity should as much as possible characterize his dealings with others. Yet, this is not the end of the matter, for, as a manager, he can make his good example a policy and direct employees within the firm to deal with others in like fashion.

Show concern and courtesy not only to our customers, but also to fellow employees and everyone else we deal with—salesmen, the Post Office, United Parcel Service, and the trucking companies. As well as creating a favorable image for our company, a friendly atmosphere will create a happier place to work.[28]

This is a directive from the employee handbook of a mail order sporting-goods firm and illustrates how management can try to make virtue a company policy. Of course, such a policy may seem trivial in comparison to all the ethical questions and difficulties present in today's business world. Yet, a moment's reflection on one's own work experiences should indicate that benevolence is a most important policy for a firm to adopt.

Seventh, the business manager has an obligation to make sure that customers get what they pay for—products that work and are not dangerous as well as service that is efficient and helpful. The business manager has to see to it that the performance of the company will be such that people will want to continue to do business with his firm and recommend it to others. The reputation a business acquires in the market place may be its most precious asset. By doing everything he can to satisfy his customers, the business manager will not only establish a good reputation for the firm but will increase the likelihood of the firm's prospering, and thereby fulfill his obligation to the owners of the firm.

It should be realized that the manager of a business firm has many people depending on her: the customers count on her to make decisions that will allow them to purchase quality goods and services; the owners count on her to make decisions that will allow the company to grow and prosper; the workers count on her to make decisions that will allow them to maintain jobs and develop their skills; and the community counts on her to make decisions that will allow the community to be preserved. Today's newspapers bear witness to the effects of poor managerial decisions on communities. Thus, it is incumbent on the business manager to know as many of the what's and why's of her job as she possibly can.

Overall, the business manager should be committed to: knowing the facts, being fair in his dealings, remaining honest with himself and others, maintaining his convictions and independence, accepting his responsibilities, being open-minded, discovering new and better ways to succeed, respecting the rights of others and defending his own, fostering kindness, considerateness and generosity, and seeking self-knowledge and personal growth. In short, the business manager should try and perform his managerial functions as a rational, intelligent human being.

Beyond the ethical obligations that have been discussed, is there anything else that can be said about the strategies, tactics, and policies a business manager uses to perform his functions? Two things can be said: an encouragement and a warning. First, business managers are in a position to create an environment within the firm that takes the foregoing ethical considerations seriously, and they should do so. As David Vogel has noted: "In the final analysis, it is up to the managers of each company to establish and enforce the standards and norms under which their employees seek to advance their interests and those of the firm."[29] The creation of a business environment that takes an ethic of human flourishing seriously could play a most important role in the moral development of persons. Second, if the business manager is not to have his liberty to engage in trade for the sake of profit denied, he must appreciate the ethical basis on which it rests— individual rights—and not advocate or support governmental actions that violate the rights of others, e.g., tariffs, quotas on imports, subsidies, and price supports. Though such policies can lead to greater profits, they destroy the foundation upon which the moral defense of his own liberty rests. Principles are two-edged swords: if they can be ignored when they benefit you, they can also be ignored when they do not benefit you. The business manager needs to be concerned with what an ethic of human flourishing implies. Ideas have consequences.

Notes

1. Leslie W. Rue and Lloyd Byars, *Management: Theory and Application* (Homewood, Illinois: Richard D. Irwin, 1983), p. 9.

2. Ibid., p. 11.

3. Ayn Rand, "Value and Rights," in John Hospers's (ed.) *Readings In Introductory Philosophical Analysis* (Englewood Cliffs, N.J.: Prentice-Hall, 1968), p. 381. Much of what is said in this essay has been influenced by Rand's thought. For appraisals, both pro and con, of Rand's philosophical efforts, see Douglas J. Den Uyl and Douglas B. Rasmussen (eds.), *The Philosophic Thought of Ayn Rand* (Urbana and Chicago: University of Illinois Press, 1984).

4. Ibid., pp. 381–82. See also Eric Mack, "Individualism, Rights, and the Open Society," in Tibor R. Machan's (ed.) *The Libertarian Reader* (Totowa, N.J.: Rowman and Littlefield, 1982), pp. 3–15.

5. There are two vantage points from which a person can judge his actions—*ex ante* and *ex post*. When a person is trying to determine what to do, when he is considering alternative courses of action and the consequences of each, his position is *ex ante*. When he is considering the results of his past actions, his position is *ex post*. Thus, when one voluntarily purchases a good *ex ante,* there is an expected gain or advantage; yet *ex post,* one might discover that he was in error and that if he had to do it again, he would not purchase the good. See Murray N. Rothbard, *Man, Economy, and State,* Vol. I (New York: Van Nostrand Company, 1962), p. 238.

6. Fraud is a way of violating individual rights—specifically property rights. "Fraud involves cases where one party to an agreed-upon exchange deliberately refuses to fulfill his part of the contract. He thus acquires the property of another person but he sacrifices either none of the agreed-upon goods or less than he had agreed upon." Ibid., pp. 157–58. The person who engages in fraud acquires the property of others on terms to which they did not consent. Fraud constitutes an indirect use of force. Fraud is, however, not merely breaking a promise (which is generally a moral wrong but not a rights violation); for there needs to be a contract—a legally sanctioned agreement. Yet, to be even more precise, fraud involves the deliberate acquisition of another's property by misleading the other person into exchanging a good or service for something you have no intention of exchanging. A refusal to fulfill a contract, but without the intentional misrepresentation of a material fact, constitutes a breach of contract and is usually remedied, as the lawyers say, by applying the law of damages.

7. The problems could be expressed as the following questions: Is there ethical knowledge? How does one derive a normative judgment from a descriptive judgment: Does human life have any goal or end beyond what a person chooses? Do people have any rights beyond those that a government recognizes? Does law have any moral foundation? For approaches to these questions, see Henry B. Veatch's *For An Ontology of Morals* (Evanston, Ill.: Northwestern University Press, 1971); David Norton, *Personal Destinies* (Princeton, N.J.: Princeton University Press,

1976); Tibor R. Machan, *Human Rights and Human Liberties* (Chicago: Nelson-Hall, 1975); Douglas B. Rasmussen, "Essentialism, Values and Rights" in *The Libertarian Reader,* pp. 37–52 and id., "A Groundwork For Rights: Man's Natural End," *The Journal of Libertarian Studies* (Winter, 1980): 65–76; Eric Mack, "How to Derive Libertarian Rights," in Jeffrey Paul's (ed.) *Reading Nozick,* (Totowa, N.J.: Rowman and Littlefield, 1982), pp. 286–302; and Ayn Rand's "Value and Rights" in *Readings In Introductory Philosophical Analysis.*

8. *Human Rights and Human Liberties,* pp. 74–75.

9. Ibid., p. 74.

10. See Nathaniel Branden, *Honoring The Self* (Los Angeles: Jeremy P. Tarcher, 1983), pp. 24–25.

11. See Douglas B. Rasmussen, "Ethics and the Free Market," *Listening* (Winter 1982): 77–88.

12. *Personal Destinies,* p. 222.

13. Branden, *Honoring The Self,* p. 28.

14. Ibid., p. 29.

15. Ayn Rand, *Atlas Shrugged* (New York: Random House, 1957), p. 411.

16. To say that we cannot profess love and friendship for every person we deal with, does not, however, imply that one's dealings with others must be inconsiderate or hateful. There is much middle ground between these extremes. Indeed, Aristotle's discussion of "friendship" in Book VIII of the *Nicomachean Ethics* indicates how there can be such a middle ground. "Friendship" for Aristotle has a much wider connotation than it does for us. According to Aristotle, even commercial associations are regarded as "friendships," but the words "harmony" or "good will" better express what Aristotle has in mind.

17. It can at times be very difficult to determine when a rights violation occurs. It is, for example, not merely a matter of causing (assuming that can be established) another person harm. J. Roger Lee argues that simply because an activity is harmful to another person does not, by itself, require that government ought to prevent the activity. He notes twenty-two meanings of "harm," and distinguishes between harms that constitute rights violations and those that do not. "Choice And Harms," in Tibor R. Machan's and M. Bruce Johnson's (eds.) *Rights and Regulations* (Cambridge, Massachusetts: Ballinger Publishing Company, 1983), pp. 157–73.

18. If it is argued that erroneous moral beliefs can be charged through compelling behavior and thus coercion has a pedagogical function, it should be noted that in such an instance the change in moral belief would not be something for which the person was responsible. It would, therefore, not be *self*-actualizing. For a comprehensive discussion of the relationship between self-directedness or autonomy and human flourishing, see "Economic Rights Versus Human Dignity: The Flawed Moral Vision of the United States Catholic Bishops," in Douglas B. Rasmussen and James Sterba, *The U.S. Catholic Bishops and the Economy: A Debate* (Social Philosophy & Policy Center, Bowling Green State University, 1987).

19. Machan, *Human Rights and Human Liberties,* p. 119.

20. "The same proposition which a person must invoke (and which it is rational for him to invoke) to justify his pursuit of his own well-being, in contrast, say, to his pursuit of the greatest good for the greatest number, viz., that the function of each person's activity, capacities, and so on is to be employed by that person in his living well, shows that a person would be unjustified in bringing it about that another's activity is not directed by that other person." Eric Mack, "How To Derive Libertarian Rights," *Reading Nozick,* p. 291.

21. See Eric Mack, "Bad Samaritanism, and the Causation of Harm," *Philos-*

ophy and Public Affairs 9 (1980) and id., "Negative Causation and the Duty to Rescue," in Edward Regis, Jr.'s (ed.) *Gewirth's Ethical Rationalism* (Chicago: University of Chicago Press, 1984), pp. 147–66.

22. It is, however, possible for someone, e.g., a lawyer, to sell his knowledge of what the law takes the implications of the trade to be, and there are advisors and counselors, not to mention numerous consumer magazines, that sell information about alternatives to the good or service one is considering buying. A deliberate refusal to inform you of relevant information or a deliberate misrepresentation of the facts for which you contracted would, in these cases, be fraud.

23. John Rawls, *A Theory of Justice* (Cambridge, Mass.: Harvard University Press, 1971); Alan Gewirth, *Reason and Morality* (Chicago: University of Chicago Press, 1978); and A. I. Meldon, *Persons and Rights,* (Berkeley, California: University of California Press, 1977).

24. See Jan Wilbanks, "Free Enterprise and Coercion," *Reason Papers* 7 (Spring 1981): 1–19.

25. See J. C. Smith, "The Processes of Adjudication and Regulation, A Comparison" in *Rights and Regulation,* pp. 71–96, for a discussion of the distinction between criminal justice and civil justice as well as the advantages of a system of civil justice over governmental regulation.

26. This is not to say that one ought at all times and in every situation tell the truth. For instance, if one knows that someone is looking for your friend in order to harm him, you would not be obliged to tell him where your friend is. Neither does it seem to be the case that everyone is entitled to the unabridged truth when they ask you a question, "How are you?"

27. These observations raise, of course, the topic of alienating work. See J. Roger Lee's essay, "The Morality of Capitalism and of Market Institutions" in Tibor R. Machan's (ed.) *The Main Debate: Communism Versus Capitalism* (New York: Random House, 1987), pp. 84–110, as well as his essay in this volume, for a discussion of a person's obligation to avoid alienating work and how markets are devices for avoiding alienation.

28. Armand J. Prusmack, "The Austad Company," *Phillips Case Narratives* II (1981): 5. This is a publication of the C. W. Post Center, Long Island University program on value decisions in business.

29. David Vogel, "Could an Ethics Course Have Kept Ivan From Going Bad?" *The Wall Street Journal* (Monday, April 27, 1987): 24.

2

THE ETHICS OF ADVERTISING

Buyer Beware—Seller Take Care

DOUGLAS J. DEN UYL

Introduction

With the possible exception of used-car dealers, perhaps no other area of business has been the subject of so much criticism as advertising. To be told that you have the "ethics of an advertiser" would generally not be considered a compliment. Furthermore, this negative attitude about advertising is not restricted to the "general public" or to "anti-business" groups. My experience with business administration students over the years has convinced me that they have no higher an opinion of advertising than most others, unless they specialize in that area. I suspect that much of the negative attitude stems from whatever truth is contained in the cliché "familiarity breeds contempt." We are all so familiar with advertising that we believe ourselves to be experts on the subject and are ready to find fault with ads that do not measure up to our own ideas of what ought to be done. Moreover, the volume of advertising we are exposed to makes us think that there is a massive conspiracy to sell us things we do not really want or need.

The precarious image of the advertiser makes the ethics of advertising both an interesting and necessary subject of study. Unlike most discussions of this subject, we shall only briefly touch on public policy issues. This will come primarily in the second section of this chapter. In the third section, we shall discuss the context appropriate to the ethics of advertising. Next we shall consider the question of truth in advertising, and finally, we shall look at some of the rules the advertising industry uses to regulate itself. This will help us see how the general theory is put in practice. First, however, we need to understand what advertising is.

I wish to thank Rudy Moeller, Sr. of Fessel, Siegfriedt & Moeller, Emery F. Lewis of McCann-Erickson, Charles Adams of the AAAA, and J.B. Searles of the Commerce Department at Bellarmine College for providing me with helpful information and advice. The views expressed should in no way be seen as necessarily reflecting the opinions of these individuals or the organizations they represent.

42

What Is Advertising?

Definition of Advertising: Definitions of advertising vary, but the most common definition runs something like this: advertisements are "paid, nonpersonal communication forms used with persuasive intent by identified sources through various media."[1] Notice that this definition is probably narrower than an ordinary understanding of the concept would imply. The definition would exclude from qualifying as advertising such things as placing a sign on your front lawn announcing a garage sale. The definition nevertheless serves well as a definition of the *business* of advertising even if it does not cover every conceivable form of advertising. And since our topic here is business ethics, this definition is perfectly adequate.

A number of key terms appear in this definition. First, advertisements are *paid for.* This term indicates both that advertising is a business and that moral judgments relevant to the business world in general will also be relevant to advertising.

Secondly, advertising is *nonpersonal.* Advertisements are not like announcements or information one passes to someone in particular. They appeal to unknown individuals. Therefore, whatever ethical standards apply would probably differ from those used in giving information to friends, colleagues, or acquaintances.

Third, advertising is a *form of communication.* It attempts to transmit a message about a product or service and sometimes an idea (as in "advocacy advertising"). It can be said, therefore, that advertisements *represent* something; and this representative stance is what gives rise to the issues of truth in advertising.

Used with persuasive intent is a key phrase in the definition. Everyone understands that advertisers are trying to persuade us, but not everyone understands the ethical implications of this concept. We shall discuss these implications in more detail.

Finally, the phrase *by identified sources through various media,* although complex, can be treated as a single unit here. One knows for whom the ads are speaking whether one receives the message from print or electronic media. But for our purposes, the delivery system and the source of the advertisement are not of special interest.

With a preliminary account of the nature of advertising behind us, it is now possible to examine some general myths about advertising and the ethical implications that arise from these myths.

Common Myths about Advertising

Many of the ethical objections to advertising are based upon some common myths about what advertising is and how it operates. By exploding these myths, we go some distance towards refuting the more common ethical objections to advertising.

Advertisers Have Bad Taste: Advertisers are often criticized for producing ads that lack both taste and artistic quality. Undoubtedly tasteless ads have been and will be produced. With respect to aesthetic quality, one should keep in mind that advertising does not claim to be serious art, even though some advertisements seem to have more aesthetic appeal than some works of "serious" art.

Although tasteless ads have been and will be produced, the charge that advertisements are *systematically* tasteless lacks more credibility than the charge that advertisements are without artistic quality. If we ignore the subjective elements of "taste," a moment's reflection would indicate that advertisers could not stay in business if their ads were either above or below the tastes of the advertiser's targeted audience. Advertisers must *interest* consumers in the product advertised. Consumers will not be interested if the ads are not properly directed to the tastes of consumers. To indict advertising for being tasteless, then, is a misplaced criticism. It is the culture that "deserves" indictment—not the advertisers who reflect that culture in their ads.

One aspect of the "taste" question often cited by critics is the lack of subtlety exhibited by most advertisements. Most ads seem to "come on too strong." This is seen by some as lack of taste and refinement on the part of the advertiser or manufacturer (or both). It must be remembered, however, that people like what they have been used to and do not change their habits and patterns easily. Therefore, advertisers (a) find some way to capture the consumer's attention, and then (b) convince him or her that it might be worth taking a chance on something new. Subtlety is not an effective way to generate interest in a product or to overcome a potential consumer's habit, laziness, or inattention. But just because an advertisement lacks subtlety or uses gimmicks does not mean that it lacks value or that we are receiving information we do not need. One observer of advertising makes the following useful analogy:

Few motorists navigating a railway crossing wish to collide with a train. They are genuinely grateful for information that a train is coming. And it is a clanging, flashing message that thrusts that information upon them in a way that cannot be overlooked. The desire for information about whether a train is coming, it then would seem, is not sufficient to ensure that motorists would seek out, notice, or heed a clearly visible, but tastefully discreet, signal.

Similarly with advertising. A producer may manufacture a commodity he reasonably believes will please the tastes of many. . . . The producer believes that, after examining the commodity, consumers will purchase the commodity rather than other goods they value less. If the producer is right, there is every reason to be confident that consumers will appreciate information about the existence and nature of the commodity and further information about where they can purchase it.

Yet this is no guarantee that consumers will diligently search out such information. The situation is precisely the same as that of the railway crossing: the desire to avoid collisions does not mean that motorists will seek out a discreet sign warning of the impending approach of a train. The advertiser has to ensure that a certain commodity possesses the quality of being "obviously available." He has to thrust his advertising message at the consumer. Most advertisements are less obtrusive than the clanging, flashing railway-crossing sign, but they are deliberately created to solve the same problem: human laziness or inattention or preoccupation with other matters.[2]

Advertising Wastes Social Resources: Advertising has been criticized as being an activity that wastes resources. The reasoning behind this conclusion is that advertising contributes nothing to the production of the product. It is, at best, dependent or parasitical upon actual production and, as such, "wastes" resources that could have been put to other uses. If all the money spent on advertising, so the argument goes, were spent on producing goods, we would all be much better off.

This argument contains several assumptions; the most important is that advertising contributes nothing to the production process. It may be tempting to think of the "production process" as what it takes to create some physical object or service. However, a more accurate way of looking at production is in terms of what is necessary to satisfy some set of desires or wants. If we look at production in this way, advertising is a part of the production process. People buy goods for more than their use potential. They buy certain goods because those goods project a certain image they, in turn, wish to project to others. Advertising helps to build the image of the product. The consumer who wishes to project a certain image would be unable to do so, if only the physical product were presented.

If we include the informational aspects of advertising, the case is much stronger. Even the simplest product contains unique features or characteristics that emerge when the product is compared to similar products. Different consumers are attracted to different characteristics. Advertising helps to make these characteristics known to consumers and so satisfies the desires of consumers more specifically. Advertising is therefore a part of the production process because, without it, the product would not meet the demands of customers whose reasons for being interested in the product in the first place may vary widely. A good cannot be considered "produced" until it satisfies some need or want. This means that if advertising did nothing else but announce the existence of the product, it would still be part of the production process.

If the money spent on advertising were devoted to other uses, we would actually end up with *fewer choices* and products rather than more. This is because the feedback received in response to advertisements allows the production process to specialize even further in satisfying demand. Most people understand this point, because they understand that competition itself is a means to product improvement and to the introduction of new products. Without advertising, there would be little competition since the information needed to make comparisons would be unavailable.

You may think that there are too many types of toilet paper on supermarket shelves; but this is because you probably have already made your choice of brands. Other people have done likewise, and they may have noticed things about other brands that you do not care about. The plurality of products indicates a plurality of interests and not a waste of resources. Some of these interests may seem trivial to you, but consider how some of your reasons might look to others. In the final analysis, the only workable meaning that can be attached to the question of whether or not resources are wasted is whether those resources satisfy consumer desires or not.

Advertising Creates Desires for Unneeded Goods: One way to try and avoid the lost argument that advertising does not waste resources because it satisfies consumer desires is to say that advertising *creates* the very desires it is thought to satisfy. Advertising, therefore, wastes resources by creating desires for things people do not really need. If there were no advertising, these desires would not be present. Production could then serve basic, not frivolous, needs and desires. John Kenneth Galbraith develops this idea in his book *The Affluent Society,* and his thesis is commonly known as the "dependence effect." Here is how Galbraith describes it:

As a society becomes increasingly affluent, wants are increasingly created by the process by which they are satisfied. This may operate passively. Increases in consumption, the counterpart of increases in production, act by suggestion or emulation to create wants. Or producers may proceed actively to create wants through advertising and salesmanship. Wants thus come to depend on output. . . . This manifests itself in an implacable tendency to provide an opulent supply of some things and a niggardly yield of others. This disparity carries to the point where it is a cause of social discomfort and social unhealth. The line which divides our area of wealth from our area of poverty is roughly that which divides privately produced and marketed goods and services from publicly rendered services. Our wealth in the first is not only in startling contrast with the meagerness of the latter, but our wealth in privately produced goods is, to a marked degree, the cause of crisis in the supply of public services.[3]

Galbraith's thesis has two parts: (1) wants come in two basic types — legitimate and illegitimate; and (2) private sector advertising moves people away from more important and necessary goods, particularly public goods such as mass transit. These two features of Galbraith's theory are supposed to be connected by the concept of a legitimate want — that is, without pressure from advertisers, we would want more public goods and less of the useless private ones we have been pushed into desiring. A legitimate want would be one present in the absence of the advertising or other productive processes that go into creating them. Presumably without the presence of such productive processes we would be left with a few easily identifiable desires.

The distinction between legitimate and illegitimate desires is discussed in detail by economist Friedrich Hayek.[4] It implies that any want that is not natural is a created want. This means that any desire beyond food, shelter, clothing, and sexual opportunity are created or "unnatural" and hence illegitimate. As Hayek points out, desires for Mozart, Aristotle, Goethe, Einstein and the like would also be illegitimate. And I might add that the desires to believe in Galbraith's theories and buy his books would be illegitimate too. Almost all our desires are "unnatural" is the sense of being culturally "created" or influenced. Galbraith must either be advocating the reshaping of society according to *his* values or the reduction of society to the most primitive level of production. If advertising creates wants, it does so in the way that almost all our wants are created — by pointing to things that we would like to have if we knew about their existence.

The other side of Galbraith's thesis is that advertising moves us away from more important goods to less important ones. In Galbraith's case, this means that public sector goods come to be preferred less than private sector goods. Yet, if advertising is as powerful as Galbraith says, then this problem could be solved by advertising public goods and services. Such advertising has been and is being done, but it has not been able to generate enough interest among consumers to turn things like unprofitable mass transit systems into money-makers. The reason is that, given a voluntary choice, people would rather drive their own private automobiles than ride a public bus. Furthermore, it is by no means obvious why another public bus is more important than a new brand of toilet paper. If satisfying desires is the standard — wherever those desires come from — it would seem that a better case could be made for the toilet paper. Lastly, thousands of new products are introduced *with advertising* every year. Most of these fail. Public projects, on the other hand, almost never fail because citizens are forced to contribute to their "success" by paying taxes. If it is undue influence that worries Galbraith, I'll take my chances with the advertising industry.

Advertising is a Means by which Corporations Exert Excessive Economic Influence: This myth can be broken down into three basic categories. The first is just a further extension of the last myth. The second is the idea that advertising causes a rise in the price of products. And the third is the thesis that advertising creates "barriers to entry," that is, firms that advertise heavily make it more difficult for new competing firms to enter the market.

Advertising and Corporate Power: Galbraith's thesis implies the following: (1) that the intensity of advertising will be positively correlated with the rate of sales growth (since advertising creates wants); (2) that the intensity of advertising is positively correlated with the stability of the firm (the more intense the advertising, the more likely the firm will be to stay in business and have a secure market share); and (3) that more money will be spent in advertising for "useless" or luxury items than for basic goods.

It turns out that each of these three implications of Galbraith's position are false. Economist Harold Demsetz has tested for the first two positions. He found that the correlation between intensity of advertising and sales growth was often negative![5] In general, no empirical evidence could be found to support the thesis that advertising systematically increases sales growth. Demsetz also found that no evidence could be found to support the second position.[6] Some firms that have intense advertising retain a stable market share, but others do not. The same can be said for the reverse. Competition, changing tastes, and the quality of the product have more to do with stability than does advertising. The third proposition was tested by economist Robert Ayanian.[7] He took such "useless" or luxury items as candy, paper products, TVs, and compared them to "necessary" goods such as food and drugs. If Galbraith's thesis were correct, one would expect that advertising intensity would be greater for the "useless" goods than for the "necessary" goods. Ayanian, however, found that precisely the opposite was true. More dollars were spent advertising the most needed goods rather than the least needed goods. In fact, food and drugs were the most advertised products.

If these findings are accurate, why do corporations spend millions on advertising? After all, if advertising does not create wants, such large expenditures would not be needed. Some of the reasons why advertising campaigns are undertaken can be found below in our summary of the conclusions of economist Yale Brozen. In general, however, advertising has more to do with interesting consumers in one's own products versus one's competitors' products than it does with creating wants in the first place. And in the case of the introduction of new products, expenditures for advertising campaigns usually come *after* market research has been done to let the company know if consumers will be interested in the product. But as we noted above, even with market research and intensive advertising, many new products fail anyway.

Advertising and Prices: Common sense supports the idea that advertising raises prices because, after all, someone must pay for the advertising, and certainly the manufacturer will pass that cost on to the consumer. This common sense argument has validity, but its power comes from assuming that the cost of a product is the same as its price. Economists, however, define "total cost" as the price of the good plus the "search costs." Search costs refer to the expense incurred to find out about the product. Because advertising gives consumers information about goods, it lowers the search costs to consumers. Advertising can, therefore, have the effect of lowering total costs. Moreover, it can be argued that consumers value advertising, even though the cost of advertising may be added to the price of the product. If this were not the case, firms could cease from advertising, lower their prices, and drive their competitors out of business.

There are also reasons why advertising may lower the price of a product.

Since advertising is the manufacturer's link to the consumer, advertised products are more likely to be changed in response to changes in market demand. A firm may see an increase in demand for its product, allowing it to lower its prices before its competitors (or with its competitors). Moreover, it is even possible for economies of scale to offset the cost of advertising, if, *because of advertising,* the firm has enough sales, and if it can achieve efficiencies elsewhere in the production process.

These remarks are theoretical, but the case need not rest on theory. Empirical studies have been done confirming the conclusions that theory suggests.[8] One of the most well known of these studies was done by economist Lee Benham. Benham compared the price of eyeglasses in states that regulated optometric advertising versus those states that did not. He found that the average price of eyeglasses in states with restrictive advertising regulations was $37.48. In states where advertising was permitted, the price was $17.98. These studies, and the theoretical reasons behind them, have now become so evident that even the FTC has allowed deregulation of advertising in occupations that formerly had restrictive rules (e.g., the legal profession).

Barriers to Entry: Some have argued that advertising restricts competition by making it more difficult for firms to enter the market place. The reasoning behind this assertion is that firms that advertise gain loyal customers, making it difficult for new firms to attract customers away from established firms. Economist Yale Brozen has examined this argument and found it to be lacking in both logic and empirical evidence.[9] Brozen draws the following general conclusions from his research.

1. New products are advertised more heavily than old. This suggests that advertising is used to gain entry into a market rather than hold a market share.

2. There is less customer loyalty in markets with intensive advertising than in markets with less intensive advertising. Advertising is used to create disloyalty to products rather than hold it.

3. Brands with the largest market share advertise less than those with smaller market shares. This suggests the same conclusion as the first point.

4. More intensely advertised brands within a market tend to be more uniform and of higher quality. Higher quality goods are advertised because buyers are more likely to repeat their purchases with higher quality goods than with lower. If advertising held customers rather than gained them, one would expect to find lower quality goods advertising as intensely as the higher quality.

5. Goods whose quality can be examined by observation are advertised less frequently than goods whose quality requires some experience to determine quality. Since consumers must purchase the latter type of good to

determine quality, advertising must be more intense and informative. If advertising simply created loyalty, both goods would be advertised with equal intensity.

Conclusion: Much of the ethical case against advertising is based upon the idea that advertising is either harmful to society or a superfluous waste of resources. We have seen that, in general, advertising is neither. Given that advertising is a legitimate and socially beneficial business practice, the interesting ethical issues will arise within advertising, rather than from outside it. To those issues we now turn.

Advertising and Ethics in Context

There are two main areas of advertising that call for ethical analysis: (1) the ethics of persuasion, and (2) truth in advertising.

The Ethics of Selling Through Advertisements: It is important to realize at the outset that any analysis of an ethical issue must treat that issue in its appropriate context. There are, of course, some moral rules that apply to all contexts (such as not violating human rights); but beyond the limited number of principles that could apply to every context, appropriate ethical analysis must consider the nature and purpose of the subject analyzed. This is why we must return to our definition of advertising and spend some time on the key concepts of that definition and their ethical implications. As a reminder, the definition of advertising used earlier ran as follows: advertisements are paid, nonpersonal communication forms used with persuasive intent by identified sources through various media.

The Duty to the Manufacturer: The first key term of our definition of advertising is the word "paid." Since advertisers are paid to deliver a message, their principle obligation lies with the manufacturer and not the consumer. In making this statement, I am assuming that everyone has the same obligation to respect basic human rights and that no question of rights-violating actions are involved. Given this assumption, when the advertiser agrees to do work for the manufacturer, that advertiser incurs an obligation to represent the interests of the manufacturer. The reasoning here is exactly the same as reasoning you might use when hiring a lawyer — the manufacturer wants his side of the case told. Once the lines of obligation are seen in this way, it becomes clear that advertisers are under no obligation to emphasize aspects of a product that may be "inferior" to those of a competitor. Indeed, it would violate the trust the manufacturer has given the advertiser to suppose that advertisers should act in someone elses interest beside. the manufacturer's. Any complaint about advertising being biased ignores the context and nature of advertising. Of course it is biased; it is supposed to be, and legitimately so.[10]

How an advertiser represents a manufacturer may bring up some questions of truthfulness, which we shall analyze. At this stage, however, we can point out that the standards of truthfulness applicable to advertisers will be less exact than those applied to, say, scientific research. Advertising does not and never has presented itself as *impartial* analysis. Given this context, the standards for appropriate behavior would not be the same for advertising as for science. Advertisers can legitimately convey opinion and not just incontrovertible fact. For example, when you advertise your used car, you might claim that it is mechanically sound. Most people who make this claim have not had exhaustive tests run on their car. They "feel" that their car is in good shape and convey that information in their ads. Moreover, those who read your ad will consider that it is *you* making the claims about your car. Opinions and perceptions are also a part of the advertising business, although (as we shall see) the standards in this industry are higher than what you and I impose on ourselves.

Ethics and "Nonpersonal" Relationships: The next key concept in our definition of advertising is the concept of "nonpersonal communication forms." Notice that the term here is "nonpersonal," not "impersonal." Advertisers often try to give their ads a "personal touch." The fact remains, however, that advertisements are directed not to specific individuals, but to classes of individuals (depending on the marketing strategy). To many, this lack of personal identification is further evidence of the "dehumanizing" nature of our society. Of course, such critics direct their lectures and books to "nonpersonal" audiences; and however much one laments the lack of personal identification, there is no possibility of avoiding it in many aspects of our daily lives. Advertisers are not the only persons who make nonpersonal appeals. We all do in one way or another. Indeed, as I write this I have no idea who will or will not read this article and be influenced by it in the future.

What needs to be said in this context is that the ethics of nonpersonal relationships are not the same as personal ones. When dealing with friends, family, and sometimes even acquaintances, the ethical standards are more rigorous than in nonpersonal relationships. There are histories built up with your friends and family, and there is more of an expectation that you will consider their interests in your dealings with them. With people you do not know, however, the standard is no less important, although it is more general. Your obligation (again apart from respecting basic rights) is to show respect for persons. This means you should treat others as free and responsible agents who can think and act for themselves. You are under no obligation to defer your interests to theirs, nor are you obligated to direct their attention to things you consider faults or weaknesses. To do the latter is to take a paternalistic attitude towards the person you are dealing with. Honesty is your principle obligation, and that is all that others can and generally do expect from you.

For example, suppose you plan to sell your car. If the potential purchaser were your brother, you probably should point out those things that you consider to be defects of your car. This is because you have had a long standing personal relationship with your brother and know his tastes and interests. On the other hand, if you are selling your car to the public-at-large, you may legitimately assume that the individuals who are prospective customers know how to buy a used car, and you may emphasize those features of your car that you believe will be most attractive without giving equal emphasizing to its faults. Of course, you must be honest if a customer chooses to ask about something you did not emphasize, but it is up to them to decide what they care and do not care about when they examine your car.

Some moralists have tried to argue that the seller must inform any prospective buyer of all the qualities of a product, especially the negative ones.[11] This argument depends on two questionable assumptions: (1) that you *can* provide such information, and (2) that the interests of others should be of equal or greater value than your own. The first assumption is false. A 60-second television spot could not possibly live up to this requirement. Indeed, even in the selling of your own car, there are so many factors to consider and so many divergent interests among buyers that the first assumption is not reasonable here either. Yet even if it were possible, it is not required because the second assumption is false. If their interests were of equal or greater value than your own, you would be required to sell at a price much closer to what they would like to pay than what you would like to sell for. Moreover, the costs imposed upon you to find out their interests are, by this assumption, in principle, unlimited.

What people often fail to distinguish when they assert something like the second assumption is that there is a difference between considering the interests of anyone acting reasonably and prudently and simply considering their interests. It may be that you have to inform customers about matters that a reasonable person acting with due caution could not be expected to discover for themselves. That is very different, however, from saying that their interests must be equal to or supersede your own. Furthermore, what "due caution" means will vary from context to context. In the case of the used car, a consumer has a right to expect that the mileage shown on the odometer is actual (unless informed otherwise), because he or she has no other way to verify it. But if the meaning of "prudence" and "due caution" includes having a mechanic check the condition of the car for the buyer, then the seller may not be obligated to describe certain mechanical problems (although lying about them, if asked, is a different matter). One is surely not obligated to point out that your type of car rides less smoothly than others you have driven.

All this is a way of showing that advertisers are unfairly accused of underhandedness when they use selective emphasis in presenting a product.

Since the advertiser is obligated to serve the interests of the manufacturer, and also since his message is nonpersonal, selective emphasis is both morally permissible and practically necessary. It might also be noted that the biblical principle of "he who is without sin cast the first stone" is applicable here. All of us use selective emphasis daily. When we put on make-up, or dress a certain way, or grow a beard, or talk a friend into a blind date, we are emphasizing certain features and hiding or de-emphasizing others. The next time you hear someone complain about selective emphasis or demand that advertisers tell the "whole truth," ask them if they mentioned all their business failures and rejections the last time they applied for a job!

The Ethics of Persuasion: The other side of "nonpersonal communication" is the communication side. Since the ethical aspect of communication is primarily concerned with truth, we shall defer discussion for a moment and move on to the last major conceptual component of our definition — persuasion. As advertising executive John O'Toole points out[12] critics of advertising often forget that advertising is a form of salesmanship. Its purpose is not to be objective, but to be persuasive. As we noted above, applying standards of objectivity to advertising that would be appropriate for scientific research would be a misapplication of those standards. What is needed, therefore, are standards that are applicable to a context of *persuasive* human interaction.

Some see all forms of selling as either immoral or ethically suspect. Much of the suspiciousness about selling is due to the negative evaluation of selective emphasis. Selective emphasis requires that the consumer take responsibility for his or her own actions. This means that selling presupposes that consumers act with reasonable caution and prudence. If this assumption is removed, then someone else (e.g., the state) will step in to determine how one should choose. It is unfortunately common today for people to want to transfer the responsibility of making choices to someone else; but there is no moral requirement that this be so. Individual freedom also implies individual responsibility for one's actions, and selling takes place within a context that assumes individuals can judge for themselves how to use their own resources. Salesmanship is a legitimate activity if the assumption is legitimate.

Some have argued that people are not so rational and prudent as the assumption would apply. For example, the reason that there is so much government regulation of advertising is that the FTC has, more or less, taken an "ignorant man" approach over the years.[13] Under the "ignorant man" theory one adopts the perspective of the least informed and most gullible members of society and then regulates on their behalf. There are both theoretical and practical problems with this attitude. Here are a few examples:

1. The "ignorant man" attitude amounts to a redistribution scheme. The better informed and/or more prudent members of society are subsidizing the less informed or more careless members through the many costs of government regulation.

2. People tend to act according to the standards expected of them. If one assumes people are ignorant and helpless, they will tend to behave ignorantly and helplessly.

3. The "ignorant man" attitude always carries with it paternalism — the idea that someone must tell the "ignorant" what to do and how to behave. Freedom of not just advertisers, but also other consumers is restricted to the extent that paternalism becomes public policy.

It is undeniable that many people are both ill-informed and careless in their choices; but *nothing* follows from this, morally speaking. Others are not obligated to remove that ignorance or to make such people more careful. Nor is it a necessary moral truth that one sacrifice one's own resources, so that these others may be "improved." Such judgments may seem harsh, but it is fallacious to assume that morality is *defined* altruistically, and that such judgments are the only ones consistent with individual freedom of action and judgment.

On the other hand, the "reasonable man" assumption does not operate from the perspective of the most informed and independent members of society. The nonpersonal nature of advertising imposes a constraint upon regarding people in this way. Since ads are pitched to anybody, it is something like the *average* person acting with due care and caution that must be the standard. There is obviously room for flexibility and change, as well as reasonable disagreement, about the nature of this "average" person. Nevertheless, the principle of respect for the independence and integrity of persons remains constant, whatever the variation of details.

It may be argued that treating consumers as reasonable and independent is idealistic, but not realistic. After all, who can withstand the onslaught of giant corporations spending billions to get you to buy their products? Are we not helpless in the face of such pressure, so that real independence of judgment is lost? These rhetorical questions assume that the consumer's relationship to advertising is analogous to a person's exposure to political propaganda in a totalitarian state. However, there are significant differences between the two cases. In the totalitarian state one is forced to listen to the propaganda. In our own country one may leave for a sandwich or turn off the TV if one does not want to listen to the ads. Even more important though is that in the totalitarian state, *only one message is transmitted.* When corporations devote resources to advertising, they do so in the face of competitors doing likewise. Not only are there competing messages for similar goods (e.g., Coke and Pepsi), but also for substitute goods (e.g., soft drinks versus orange juice). Unlike propaganda, the competing messages dilute the effect of any one message; and since advertising helps create a competitive environment and increases choice, we probably have more freedom and opportunity for independence of judgment than without it. Perhaps what is being complained of is really not lack of choice and independence at all. Perhaps it is having *so many* choices that causes some to want their choices to be made for them. However, there is no moral requirement that the freedoms of some be limited so that choosing is easier for others.

Truth in Advertising

Around the turn of the century, advertisers could say just about anything they wanted to about a product. It did not matter whether what they said was "true" or even whether it had much to do with the nature of the product. Patent medicine sales are a case in point. At this stage in history, there was confusion about the relationship between advertisers and the makers of the product. As time went on, however, people began to realize that advertisers were the voice of the manufacturer. And once the direct connection was made between advertiser and manufacturer, questions of fraudulent misrepresentation (truth) legitimately arose. If I claim my hair tonic will grow hair, then it had better grow hair or I have defrauded you. Advertising, therefore, at least partially sets the terms and conditions of a trade or contract. If claims or promises are made that are not fulfilled, the consumer has handed over his money under false pretenses, which is fraud.

The problem today is not the same as it was back then. The state has a legitimate role to play in prosecuting fraud. Yet it is not fraud *per se* that is at issue today, but whether or not the ads are "deceptive" or "misleading." Advertisers are required to back up any factual claims with evidence, and this means that it is not direct falsehood that is being debated. Part of the problem is that "false," "misleading," "deceptive," and "misrepresentative" are all used interchangeably and are interpreted either intuitively or in terms of the "ignorant man" standard. The following list contains some of the situations that have been called "false," "misleading," "deceptive," or "misrepresentative" by both moralists and the general public.

1. Deliberate falsification of the nature of the product.
2. Selective emphasis of a product's virtues.
3. A deliberate attempt to arrange claims about a product (none of which are false in themselves) in such a way and with the hope that the consumer will arrive at a conclusion that is false about the product, but favorable to the seller.

4. Same as number 3, except that the consumer will arrive at true conclusions about the product, but only selective truths about the product.
5. Making claims for a product that the producer believes are true, but have not been backed up with evidence.
6. Making claims about a product that are "true" and not intended to be misunderstood by the consumer familiar with the type of product it is, but that might be misunderstood by the general public or a new consumer to the product area.
7. Same as number 6, except that the ad might be misunderstood by someone familiar with the product area.
8. Out-of-context and/or selective use of published test results that favor the producer.
9. Puffery (exaggerated claims used to build image; e.g., toothpaste giving one a sexy smile).
10. Giving the impression that one "needs" a certain product when one does not.

Obviously there is a wide difference between these descriptions even though all of them have been used at one time or another to label advertising as "deceptive." We therefore need to sort out some of these descriptions to determine the various moral problems they raise (or do not raise).

From the preceding list, little comment is needed for numbers 1 and 10. We have agreed that fraudulent representation should be prohibited, and we have also agreed that the Galbraithian worry about advertising creating wants is a bogus issue. Number 2 (selective emphasis) was discussed earlier in this chapter. The same thing could be said for number 4 (drawing selectively true conclusions) insofar as number 4 looks like number 2. But if 4 begins to approach number 8 (out of context test results), more might have to be said. And number 9 (puffery) can be dismissed also, since image-building is a legitimate part of advertising.[14] Even the FTC allows puffery. With respect to number 5 (unsupported claims), we have already noted that factual claims require supporting evidence under current law and regulations. This requirement seems plausible, since without some objective evidence one could claim almost anything for a product. It should be noted, however, that factual claims must be backed by evidence, not proof. Advertisers are rightfully not required to prove beyond reasonable doubt that their claims are true. To ask advertisers to do more than this would be to require that they become independent consumer research firms — something that is clearly outside their competence and function. The items remaining on the list are numbers 3, and 6 through 8.

Number 8: By itself, number 8 (out-of-context or selective use of test results) could go either way. On the one hand, an advertiser would be acting legitimately if reference is made in an advertisement to a reputable study without mentioning other studies that did not turn up evidence that was as definitive as the one mentioned. On the other hand, to claim a product generally alleviates some discomfort when all the test results show that only a small faction of individuals with a special metabolic constitution found relief, is clearly misleading to even a prudent and careful consumer. This implies that not all selective usages of information are necessarily "out of context" usages. Such matters must be decided on a case by case basis.

Numbers 6 and 7: Numbers 6 and 7 go together as a pair. Number 6 concerns making true claims, but ones that could be misunderstood by one not familiar with the product or service. The situation envisioned in number 6 is one of advertisements being targeted to specific audiences, e.g. financial executives. Since finances can be complicated, a person from the general public or a newcomer to the field might be mislead by an ad targeted at professionals. Here the advertiser should consider where the ad will be carried and who is likely to read it. For example, ads in trade journals would pose no problem, even if some members of the public at large or those without much sophistication happen to stumble across the ad and are mislead by it. It would be unreasonable to expect advertisers to have to worry about every possible person who might be mislead by an ad targeted for a particular group of people. Exceptional cases, therefore, need not be an ethical issue; but the more general one's audience, the more careful one will have to be in describing a product or service.

As for number 7 (making true claims that might be misunderstood by someone *familiar* with the product or service), consider a television ad for a new car that sells for $7,000. The advertisement claims that you can have this car for $140 a month. Both claims are true, but someone watching the ad might conclude that one pays $140 a month until the $7000 dollars (minus the downpayment) is paid off. In fact, however, the total one will pay is $9000, if one chooses the low downpayment plan of paying $140 a month. Today most such ads on TV contain the total costs in small print at the bottom of the screen. Such additional information does not seem to be ethically *required,* since any reasonable person of adult age knows one pays more on a monthly basis through financing than if one simply paid cash.

Herein lies the dispute between the argument in defense of the "reasonable man" standard and the FTC's adherence to an "ignorant man" standard. Failure to mention the total cost in the ad does not, contrary to the thinking of many, *imply* that the final cost is therefore $7000. On the other hand, if the ad were phrased so that any reasonable person was lead to believe the final cost would be $7000, then there would be a problem of the ad being misleading. Again, a case by case assessment, *under the "reasonable man" assumption,* would be necessary to decide such issues.

Number 3: The most common cases of "misleading" or "deceptive" advertising have to do with number 3 above — arranging claims that are not false in themselves in such a way that a false impression is given. Consider the following hypothetical case written up in a business ethics text for student discussion:

Your company sells only in the state of New Wyoming. State law does not prohibit marketing your cola in "giant quarts." A quart is a standard measure, so a giant quart is the same size as an ordinary quart. A survey done by your firm indicates that 40 percent of cola buyers think that a giant quart is larger than a regular quart.[15]

Let us assume further that your company markets the cola with the "giant quart" label, hoping to influence the 40% of consumers who fail to compare labels on volume. Clearly this situation fits the principle described in number 3.

Before discussing this example, a distinction should be made that has been tacitly assumed all along. Even if we decide that your company's behavior was less than ethical, it does not follow that the company's actions should be legally prohibited. This is especially true where the consumer has adequate information to judge the claim for himself or herself. But number 3 *could* represent cases where the message is fraudulent even though nothing untrue was said. Here state interference would be relatively noncontroversial. An example might be brochures for sales of land that pictured lakes, pools, and developed communities where none exist. Furthermore, although the brochure does not say such structures do exist, it does contain phrases like "you will enjoy all the conveniences when you move in." In other words, it is possible for a fraudulent message to be transmitted by other than strictly verbal means.

But our purpose here is ethics and not public policy. Within the confines of ethics itself a further distinction is needed. This is a distinction between what is morally *required* and what is *promotive* of moral values. To retain some connection with ethical theory, let us call the first element the deontological (or obligatory) component and the second element the teleological (or perfecting) component. In our labeling case, your company is not *required* to refrain from using "giant quart." This is because (a) the phrase does not contain a falsehood, and (b) because consumers have the information available to determine if "giant quart" is any different in volume from "quart." But if we turn our attention to the teleological component, our judgement should be different. Clearly the purpose of the phrase is to take advantage of the gullible. Such tactics do nothing to promote the values of honesty and a trustworthy attitude between buyer and seller. Indeed we might say of this company what we sometimes say about individuals—the approach is "shadey."

Should the company refrain from using the phrase "giant quart?" If we consider only the phrase itself, the answer would be yes; but other considerations may be applicable as well. Since companies have binding obligations to their owners to keep themselves viable, sacrificing a significant share of the market by refraining from using the phrase may conflict with that obligation. The teleological principle demands that less deceptive phrases or methods must surely be considered; but if employing these requires significant sacrifice to the firm, the alternatives can be abandoned (especially since the deontological component has not been violated). Nevertheless, the teleological component implies that these extenuating considerations be present. If the extenuating circumstances are not present, the corporation faces some form of legitimate moral censure.

A less complicated but more common example of a situation that some claim would fall under number 3 has to do with so-called "endorsements." If a famous person is hired to advertise a product but does not use it, is that not an example of refraining from saying something false, but leading the consumer to draw a false conclusion favorable to the seller? Consider the case of singer Michael Jackson promoting Pepsi. Jackson is reputed to be a "health food" advocate. It is unlikely that he drinks Pepsi or any other soft drink. When asked about this by the media, a spokesman for Jackson said that Jackson *would* drink Pepsi if he were to drink any soft drink! Is this sort of "playing with words" ethical?

To answer this question some distinctions must be drawn. There is a difference between promoting a product, endorsing a product, and giving testimonials for a product. What Michael Jackson is doing for Pepsi is promoting the product. If one watches the ads, Jackson never says that Pepsi is the best soft drink of all the ones he drinks (testimonial), nor does he even say that he recommends Pepsi to others (endorsement). All we see is Jackson at a concert singing a version of "Billy Jean" with lyrics indicating that Pepsi is the choice of a "new generation." The Jackson/ Pepsi campaign, therefore, is legitimate.

On the other hand, if Jackson were to give a testimonial without using the product, that would be improper. Endorsements fall somewhere in between. Assuming the endorser does not regularly use the product, the closer the endorsement comes to being a testimonial, the less legitimate it is. If the endorsement is more like a promotion, then the activity is less objectionable or unobjectionable. To recommend the use of a product simply because one is being paid to do so (and with no indication or claim that one uses it oneself regularly) is "shadey" and creates the cynicism towards advertising the industry wants to avoid. But there may be other reasons for recommending that others use the product, even though one does not use it oneself. Suppose, for example, that a wheelchair company had hired Jackson to endorse their product and provided some evidence to indicate that their wheelchair was the best on the market. Surely no one would find that endorsement objectionable. Like many issues, reflection indicates that the question of "endorsements" is not subject to simple solutions.

One final point, often forgotten, should be mentioned in this context—

price. A few years ago, consumer advocate David Horowitz was on the Johnny Carson show. He was complaining about a "deceptive" ad for a child's fortress. The ad claimed that for only $5 one could buy a fortress. Horowitz noted that children's fortresses generally cost over $100. He sent in $5 and received a table cloth with a picture of a castle on it that was to be placed over a card table. Maybe the most gullible member of society would have expected a wood-framed fortress, but surely anybody else would have understood the message the price of the product conveyed. And let us not forget that *consumer* greed is a part of the marketplace also. Some people may be so incredibly gullible or ill-informed as to expect a wood-framed fortress for $5; but one suspects that many of those who sent in their $5 thought they were taking advantage of a misguided manufacturer who did not properly price his product.

Sometimes moral judgments cannot be as "hard and fast" as people would like them to be. We have shown that advertising must be understood *in context*. A whole range of values constitute a part of any business decision. Decision makers will have to weigh all of them if responsible decisions are to be made. Moral rules are necessary components in making responsible decisions; but the use and employment of such rules is not self-explanatory or beyond interpretation. What we need, then, are a good set of reasonable rules to help guide decision making. To that task we now turn.

Ethical Standards in the "Real" World

Many students often become impatient with ethical theorizing. Such theorizing seems abstract and difficult to apply in the so called "real world." Moreover, ethical theory often fails to give easy answers to complicated questions, making it difficult for some to know how to behave in certain situations. What is interesting about advertising is that the practitioner of the art suffers no lack of guidelines or rules of ethical conduct. Over 20 national groups have codes of ethics on advertising practices.[16] These groups include advertising associations, special industry groups, media associations, and trade associations. In addition, many individual firms have their own codes of advertising conduct. There are, of course, laws about advertising as well; but we shall briefly concern ourselves here with voluntary industry standards. This is to avoid having to enter the debate about government intervention in the market and to give some idea of how the industry looks at itself.

From a theoretical point of view, much of what is contained in these codes would fall under the heading of "teleological" concerns. In other words, the codes are designed to promote honesty and truth in advertising and go beyond what may be minimally required. Consider, for example, this statement made by the Pillsbury company about advertising:

Our policy thus demands a belief and conviction that we can have honesty and good taste in our advertising, and, at the same time, achieve a level of creativity and credibility unattainable with advertising that reflects lower standards. We truly believe that high ethical standards for advertising are totally consistent with goals in the area of share of market and profit before taxes. (See Appendix 2)

Cynics may argue that all industries have ethical codes, but nobody pays any attention to them. As we shall see below, this is not true of advertising. It should be remembered, however, that these codes are formulated with the recognition that advertising is a business. The codes do not call for the self-sacrificial behavior of advertisers — only responsible and considered behavior within a profit-oriented environment.

To avoid having to describe in full the many details associated with advertising codes of conduct and processes of review, I have included some appendices at the end of the chapter. The first appendix contains the "Standards of Practice" of the American Association of Advertising Agencies. The second appendix contains the advertising policy of the Pillsbury Company. In the third appendix, a flow chart is provided showing the National Advertising Review Board's mechanisms of self-regulation. And finally, the code of ethics in the controversial area of political campaign advertising can be found in appendix 4. These appendices are designed to give examples of rules of ethical conduct in four main areas: (1) industry-wide rules, (2) rules for a specific firm, (3) rules for a controversial issue, and (4) procedures for monitoring compliance.

In the early seventies, the American Association of Advertising Agencies, the American Advertising Federation, the Association of National Advertisers, and the Council of Better Business Bureaus established a National Advertising Review Council. This council in turn created the National Advertising Review Board (NARB) to consider complaints about advertisements and to establish procedures and rules for such a review. The board of the NARB consists of individual advertisers, representatives of advertising agencies, and members of the public. Within the Council of Better Business Bureaus, a National Advertising Division (NAD) was also created. As appendix 3 indicates, complaints directed at the NARB go to the NAD for evaluation. The NAD may dismiss the complaint as unfounded or request changes of the advertiser. If the matter is still under dispute, the advertiser may appeal to the NARB, which selects a five person panel from its members. If a ruling from the NARB goes against an advertiser and the advertiser refuses to change or discontinue the ad, the case is sent to the government.

To give some idea of the kinds of issues discussed and the decisions made, one advertising text offers some sample cases and decisions:[17]

Ads That Were Either Modified Or Discontinued

Allergan Pharmaceuticals for Eclipse suntan lotions claimed the lotion was "the only full line of defense against the sun." NAD considered the comparison of sunscreen lotions with suntan lotions an artificial distinction that gave a misleading impression of the relative effectiveness of available suntan products. Although the company disagreed, the ads were dropped.

Comp-U-Card of America for Money Saver Services claimed customers could save 40% or more on more than 10,000 nationally known products. NAD found that savings of 40% or more could be secured on only a few items and the claim was modified.

Consolidated Foods for L'Eggs pantyhose claimed that L'Eggs pantyhose never wrinkles or sags. Since the ad had finished its scheduled run before the NAD made contact, the company said it would advise the NAD of those claims or equivalent claims in future advertising.

Eastman Kodak for Kodak Colorburst 350 camera claimed its instant camera had the only built-in, closeup lens. Before the NAD's resolution, the claims were permanently withdrawn as a result of a changed marketing strategy.

Advertisers Who Substantiated Their Claims

Best Food's Mazola Oil supported the claim, "No leading oil tastes lighter than Mazola."

Clorox Co. for Clorox Pre-Wash adequately identified a leading competitor to support its claim, "New Clorox Pre-Wash cleans circles around the leading pre-wash."

Royal Crown Cola Co. for Diet-Rite Cola provided results of a nationwide taste test to support the claim, "More people preferred the taste of Diet-Rite than Tab or Diet Pepsi."

Star-Kist Foods for canned tuna fish provided spring water definitions and geological and civil engineering reports, as well as market data, to support claims of "the No. 1 water pack tuna," "half the calories," and "the only tuna packed in natural spring water."

In some of these cases, the advertising industry is much pickier than most of us would probably be. This is because most of us probably notice the advertisement as a whole rather than specific parts. Nevertheless, review of ads is instituted by type of complaint. Someone must find certain phrases objectionable. The advertising industry has claimed in recent years that its standards for honesty are higher than the general public's. These examples lend support to that assertion. In general, advertisements seem to come under careful scrutiny in two main areas: substantiation of claims and misleading phrasing. Regarding the latter, the industry adopts a stance closer to the FTC's "ignorant man" policy than to the "reasonable man" approach defended above. No doubt much of this is due to the sensitivity to criticism advertisers have undergone over the years.

In recent testimony before the FTC, some heads of the AAAA (American Association of Advertising Agencies), NAD, and the NARB discussed self-regulation in the advertising industry. The following, a summary of the disposition of cases before the NAD from 1971 to 1981, illustrates the effectiveness of the industry's self-regulation processes.

Δισποσιτιον	Νυμβερ οφ αασεs
Adequate Substantiation	720
Advertiser Modified or Discontinued	772
Dismissed	323
Referred to NARB by NAD	15
Open	44
Advertisers Who Refused to Comply	0
Total	1,874

These figures do not imply that there are no misleading ads in existence or that the self-regulatory process works perfectly. But any observer of these figures and the process of review itself could not fail to be impressed. As the senior vice-president of NAD noted in his testimony, some of the severest critics of advertising softened their criticism when they observed what is *actually* being done in the industry.

Some may wish to conclude that the high and perhaps overly cautious standards just mentioned are the result of the threat of government intervention. Undoubtedly a freer market would offer the opportunity for some advertising agencies to avoid belonging to such groups as the AAAA. But as we have noted, advertisers do not have much to gain by incurring the distrust of consumers. And it is simply fallacious to assume that in the absence of government regulation all pressures for truth in advertising would disappear. What would disappear would be the "ignorant man" standard, since the burden of proof would fall on the accuser and not the advertiser. This is only to say that, as in life generally, there are people who are unscrupulous and there are those who live by principles. The latter should be encouraged in accordance with the teleological principle that moral values ought to be promoted. Encouragement is not, however, the same as justifying government regulation. The loss of the "ignorant man" standard in a freer market may be worth the gain in less costly goods and personal freedom.

Conclusion

In this essay, we have tried to introduce some of the issues surrounding advertising and some principles useful for evaluating this subject. Ignoring theoretical disagreements over the nature of ethics and the "reasonable man" versus "ignorant man" debate, some may view what has been said as merely a defense of the advertising industry. To some extent this is true; but it is true because many critics of advertising either do not know anything about the industry, are already committed to questionable political ideologies when they examine this area, or are ignoring the appropriate context within which to evaluate the issues. If, on the other hand, one is open-minded, I am convinced that he or she will discover that the advertising industry is more concerned about ethical questions than many other industries. Indeed, one may be surprised (as I was) about the extent to which advertisers carefully consider truthfulness in producing their ads.

Of course, if one is morally opposed to persuasion or if one believes the free pursuit of profits requires lying, then nothing advertisers do or say will be convincing. Advertising is a function of the market place, not of moral philosophy or academic research. In the end, one's moral convictions about a market system will weigh more heavily than any particular issue associated with a specific topic such as advertising, and in reality, our economy still bears some resemblance to a free market system. Working in the advertising field makes demands on one's integrity and raises challenging ethical questions.

Notes

1. C. H. Sandage, V. Fryburger, and K. Rotzoll, *Advertising Theory and Practice* (Homewood, Ill.: Richard D. Irwin, 1983), p. 5.

2. John K. Williams, "And Now, A Pitch for Advertising," *Reason Magazine*, Sept., 1983, pp. 38. An excellent discussion of many of the issues discussed can be found in this article.

3. J. K. Galbraith, "The Dependence Effect," in *Ethical Theory and Business*, Tom L. Beauchamp and Norman E. Bowie, eds. (Englewood Cliffs: Prentice-Hall, 1983), p. 360. The debate between Galbraith and Hayek on this issue can be examined in pp. 357–67.

4. *Ibid.*

5. Cf. *The Attack on Corporate America*, M. Bruce Johnson, ed. (New York: McGraw-Hill, 1978), p. 238.

6. *Ibid.*, p. 238.

7. *Ibid.*, p. 239.

8. *Ibid.*, pp. 182–86.

9. Yale Brozen, "Is Advertising a Barrier to Entry?" in *Advertising and Society*, Yale Brozen, ed. (New York: New York University Press, 1974), pp. 79–109.

10. Some may argue that my claim that advertiser's owe their primary obligation to the manufacturer gives too much power or weight to the advertiser as against the consumer. Since this type of objection might come up again on some other issue, it is best to deal with it here. The idea that it is the purpose of ethical analysis to balance the interests or power of various groups is itself mistaken. Our role is not to devise rules that would give advertisers or consumers more or less power or rights. That view supposes that the ethicist and the social engineer are the same.

11. A similar view is taken by Burton Leiser, "Deceptive Practices in Advertising," in Beauchamp and Bowie, *Ethical Theory and Business,* pp. 334–43.

12. John O'Toole, *The Trouble with Advertising* (New York: Chelsea House, 1981), p. 9ff.

13. An excellent discussion of the "ignorant man" and the FTC can be found in "Reasonable Consumer or Ignorant Consumer? How the FTC Decides" by Ivan L. Preston in *Ethical Theory and Business,* pp. 348–57. It should be noted, however, that the FTC has lessened its adherence to the "ignorant man" position over the years. In the 1940s a strict "ignorant man" position was taken. Since then, puffery has been allowed. The Reagan administration may also further weaken the "ignorant man" standard.

14. For those opposed to puffery, it is important to realize that regulations can sometimes provide incentives for puffery if they are too strict. This is because saying something informational and concrete may subject one to complaint and/or prosecution; whereas describing one's product simply in an "image building" fashion make chances for repercussions less likely.

15. This case can be found in *Ethical Theory and Business,* p. 393.

16. Cf. *Advertising Theory and Practice,* p. 472.

17. *Ibid.,* pp. 473–75.

18. This information, along with the formal remarks made to the FTC, was sent to me by the AAAA.

APPENDIX I: STANDARDS OF PRACTICE, AMERICAN ASSOCIATION OF ADVERTISING AGENCIES

First adopted October 16, 1924

Most recently revised April 28, 1962

WE HOLD THAT a responsibility of advertising agencies is to be a constructive force in business.

WE FURTHER HOLD THAT, to discharge this responsibility, advertising agencies must recognize an obligation, not only to their clients, but to the public, the media they employ and to each other.

WE FINALLY HOLD that the responsibility will best be discharged if all agencies observe a common set of standards of practice.

To this end, the American Association of Advertising Agencies has adopted the following Standards of Practice as being in the best interests of the public, the advertisers, the media owners and the agencies themselves.

These standards are voluntary. They are intended to serve as a guide to the kind of agency conduct which experience has shown to be wise, foresighted and constructive.

It is recognized that advertising is a business and as such must operate within the framework of competition. It is further recognized that keen and vigorous competition, honestly conducted, is necessary to the growth and health of American business generally, of which advertising is a part.

However, *unfair* competitive practices in the advertising agency business lead to financial waste, dilution of service, diversion of manpower and loss of prestige. Unfair practices tend to weaken public confidence both in advertisements and in the institution of advertising.

1. Creative Code

We the members of the American Association of Advertising Agencies, in addition to supporting and obeying the laws and legal regulations pertaining to advertising, undertake to extend and broaden the application of high ethical standards. Specifically, we will not knowingly produce advertising which contains:

a. False or misleading statements or exaggerations, visual or verbal.

b. Testimonials which do not reflect the real choice of a competent witness.

c. Price claims which are misleading.

d. Comparisons which unfairly disparage a competitive product or service.

e. Claims insufficiently supported, or which distort the true meaning of practicable application of statements made by professional or scientific authority.

f. Statements, suggestions or pictures offensive to public decency.

We recognize that there are areas which are subject to honestly different interpretations and judgment. Taste is subjective and may even vary from time to time as well as from individual to individual. Frequency of seeing or hearing advertising messages will necessarily vary greatly from person to person.

However, we agree not to recommend to an advertiser and to discourage the use of advertising which is in poor or questionable taste or which is deliberately irritating through content, presentation or excessive repetition.

Clear and willful violations of this Code shall be referred to the Board of Directors of the American Association of Advertising Agencies for appropriate action, including possible annulment of membership as provided by Article IV, Section 5, of the Constitution and By-Laws.

2. *Contracts*

a. The advertising agency should where feasible enter into written contracts with media in placing advertising. When entered into, the agency should conform to its agreements with media. Failure to do so may result in loss of standing or litigation, either on the contract or for violations of the Clayton or Federal Trade Commission Acts.

b. The advertising agency should not knowingly fail to fulfill all lawful contractual commitments with media.

3. *Offering Credit Extension*

It is unsound and uneconomic to offer extension of credit or banking service as an inducement in solicitation.

4. Unfair Tactics

The advertising agency should compete on merit and not by depreciating a competitor or his work directly or inferentially or by circulating harmful rumors about him, or by making unwarranted claims of scientific skill in judging or prejudging advertising copy, or by seeking to obtain an account by hiring a key employee away from the agency in charge in violation of the agency's employment agreements.

These Standards of Practice of the American Association of Advertising Agencies come from the belief that sound practice is good business. Confidence and respect are indispensable to success in a business embracing the many intangibles of agency service and involving relationships so dependent upon good faith. These standards are based on a broad experience of what has been found to be the best advertising practice.

Source: *1986–1987   Roster and Organization* (American Association of Advertising Agencies, 1986).

APPENDIX II: PILLSBURY'S ADVERTISING POLICY

The Pillsbury advertising policy has its philosophy rooted in the recognition that a commitment to the consumer's rights ("consumerism") is essential to the corporation's well-being.
Among these rights are:

The right to protection against fraud and deceit;
A guarantee of safe and healthful products;
The right to know the attributes of the products;
The right to freedom of selection among product alternatives with clearly defined price-value relationship.

It is our policy that every claim we make regarding the product advertised be substantiated and documented before use.
Pillsbury communications must reflect a sensitivity to consumer knowledge, sophistication and skepticism. More specifically, a working policy should include the following:

1. We must insure that advertising and publicity materials not include "evidence" of any product attribute and benefit, when such evidence is not a true indication of the specified product characteristics. Thus, food products cannot be shown or written about in such a manner so as to exaggerate, misrepresent or in any way incorrectly show the product qualities. This applies to depiction of the product itself, as well as the reported results of any test, experiment or demonstration.
2. We must examine any piece of communication that could have a real or implied, purposeful or accidental, element of fraud or deception. Moreover, it is not good enough to simply look at a piece of advertising for the words or claims used. We must also read between the lines in search of elements which may lead to consumer misinterpretation.
3. We must insure that our advertising be in good taste. It cannot be offensive to any religious, ethnic or political segment. Advertising must be competitive in a positive sense, not derogatory to the products of other companies.

Our policy thus demands a belief and conviction that we can have honesty and good taste in our advertising, and, at the same

---

Source: *Advertising*, William A. Weilbacher (New York, N.Y.: Macmillan, 1984).

time, achieve a level of creativity and credibility unattainable with advertising that reflects lower standards. We truly believe that high ethical standards for advertising are totally consistent with goals in the area of share of market and profit before taxes.

The Pillsbury Company and its advertising agencies share responsibilities for the preparation of labels, advertising and point of sale materials which truthfully and accurately represent the Company's products. In order to accomplish this result and to aid Pillsbury personnel in working with its advertising agencies and other suppliers in the development of its labels, advertising, trade brochures and point of sale materials, the following guidelines for product representation have been prepared:

1. *Source of Products for Pictorial Representation*
   Products which are to be photographed or otherwise pictorialized should be representative of those available to the consumer and should therefore be obtained in representative markets from retail shelves or trade warehouse when possible. When a new product has not yet reached the retail shelves or trade warehouse, a representative sample should be obtained from an actual production run. If a new product is not yet being produced at the plant, a laboratory sample may be used if there will be no material difference in appearance between it and the plant-production product. If a laboratory sample or early production run product is used, the Consumer Service representative having responsibility for the product will obtain a sample from a representative retail market or trade warehouse as soon as it becomes available for comparison with the pictorial representation. If any material difference exists, the Brand Manager and Consumer Service representative will immediately institute a corrective change in the representation.
2. *Preparation of Products for Photography*
   Products should be prepared for photography according to package directions. Any deviation from such directions must be disclosed on the label or in the ad. Implements used should be those which are readily available to the average consumer and the method of preparation should be such that it does not require any professional expertise. The recipe copy on the package and end product quality standards are the sole responsibility of Pillsbury.

3. *Product Pictorial Representations*

The pictorial representation of food products including drawings as well as photography, must be accomplished in a manner which will portray them as they would be likely to appear when properly prepared by the consumer in accordance with package directions. Photography should be achieved without the use of such techniques as deceptive lighting effects, artificial props or special agents (dye, lacquer, etc.) and without retouching the photograph unless full disclosure is made. If any such techniques are believed necessary in order to more accurately portray the product, clearance for the use of same should first be obtained from the Law Department of The Pillsbury Company and the agency. Each photography session should be planned in detail by appropriate representatives from Pillsbury Marketing and/or Consumer Service and the advertising agency. Documentation of the plan and any changes made during actual photography should be made and kept by Pillsbury Consumer Service.

4. *Recipe Advertising*

When photographs or other pictorial representations are to be made of foods prepared according to recipes referred to or contained in advertising, labels or point of sale materials, the foregoing guidelines should apply. In addition, the recipe should be complete and should be identical to that used in preparation of the food portrayed therein.

5. *Advertising Directed to Children*

All pictorial representations as well as the words used in connection therewith which are primarily directed toward children must be carefully prepared and reviewed in order to avoid misconceptions by children as to claims made for the product and misunderstanding of such things as premiums and promotional offers. All plans for such advertising shall be reviewed by the Brand Manager with the Pillsbury Law Department before final preparation thereof.

6. *Procedural Problems*

In the event of any question or problems concerning the interpretation or use of these guidelines, the Pillsbury personnel directly involved should contact the Pillsbury Law Department immediately for clarification. Any differences with the agency as to any such

question will be resolved between the agency legal
department and the Pillsbury Law Department. In no
event should any Pillsbury employee sign any affidavit
or statement concerning the subjects covered by these
guidelines for the agency or any third party without
first consulting the Pillsbury Law Department.

(Reproduced with the permission of Pillsbury Company.)

APPENDIX III: THE MECHANISMS OF THE NATIONAL ADVERTISING REVIEW BOARD: ADVERTISING SELF-REGULATORY PROCEDURES STEP-BY-STEP

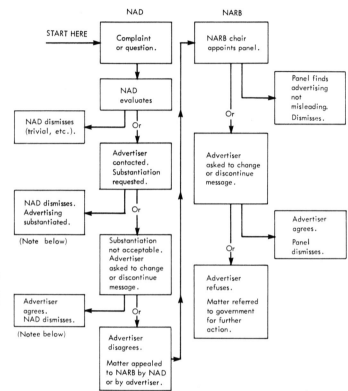

Source: *Advertising Theory and Practice,* C. H. Sandage, Vernon Fryburger, and Kim Rotzoll (Homewood, Ill.: Richard D. Irwin, Inc., 1983).

APPENDIX IV: CODE OF ETHICS FOR POLITICAL CAMPAIGN PRACTICES CODE OF FAIR CAMPAIGN PRACTICES

The advertising agency has become an increasingly important factor in the conduct of American political campaigns. Just as the political candidate must observe the highest standards of fairness and morality in his campaign, so must the advertising agency operate under a code that reflects the finest values of our political system rather than any unethical temptations that arise in the heat of battle.

The advertising agency should not represent any candidate who has not signed or who does not observe the Code of Fair Campaign Practices of the Fair Campaign Practices Committee, endorsed by the A.A.A.A.

The agency should not knowingly misrepresent the views or stated record of any candidates nor quote them out of proper context.

The agency should not prepare any material which unfairly or prejudicially exploits the race, creed or national origin of any candidate.

The agency should take care to avoid unsubstantiated charges and accusations, especially those deliberately made too late in the campaign for opposing candidates to answer.

The agency should stand as an independent judge of fair campaign practices, rather than automatically yield to the wishes of the candidate or his authorized representatives.

The agency should not indulge in any practices which might be deceptive or misleading in word, photograph, film or sound.

Adopted by the Board of Directors of the
American Association of Advertising Agencies
February 22, 1968
Endorsement Reapproved by A.A.A.A. Board July 20, 1982

Endorsed by
Fair Campaign Practices Committee and
League of Women Voters.
Endorsement Reapproved August 12, 1982.

Code of Fair Campaign Practices

There are basic principles of decency, honesty and fair play which every candidate for public office in the United States has a moral obligation to observe and uphold, in order that, after vigorously contested but fairly conducted campaigns, our citizens may exercise their constitutional right to a free and untrammeled choice and the will of the people may be fully and clearly expressed on the issues before the country.

THEREFORE:

I SHALL CONDUCT my campaign in the best American tradition, discussing the issues as I see them, presenting my record and policies with sincerity and frankness, and criticizing without fear or favor the record and policies of my opponent and his party which merit such criticism.

I SHALL DEFEND AND UPHOLD the right of every qualified American voter to full and equal participation in the electoral process.

I SHALL CONDEMN the use of personal vilification, character defamation, whispering campaigns, libel, slander, or scurrilous attacks on any candidate or his personal or family life.

I SHALL CONDEMN the use of campaign material of any sort which misrepresents, distorts, or otherwise falsifies the facts regarding any candidate, as well as the use of malicious or unfounded accusations against any candidate which aim at creating or exploiting doubts, without justification, as to his loyalty and patriotism.

I SHALL CONDEMN any appeal to prejudice based on race, creed, or national origin.

I SHALL CONDEMN any dishonest or unethical practice which tends to corrupt or undermine our American system of free elections or which hampers or prevents the full and free expression of the will of the voters.

I SHALL IMMEDIATELY AND PUBLICLY REPUDIATE support deriving from any individual or group which resorts, on behalf of my candidacy or in opposition to that of my opponent, to the methods and tactics which I condemn.

I, the undersigned candidate for election to public office in the United States of America, hereby endorse, subscribe to, and solemnly pledge myself to conduct my campaign in accordance with the above principles and practices, so help me God.

DATE_____ SIGNATURE _____

Source: *Political Campaign Advertising and Advertising Agency* (American Association of Advertising Agencies, 4th ed., 1982).

3

EMPLOYMENT AND ETHICS

JAMES E. CHESHER

I. The Context and Central Issues

Since human beings must work for their sustenance and comfort, employment is a major part of most people's lives. In modern societies, the greatest number of people who work are employees who provide some skill and/or labor in exchange for a wage. Problems related to employment, then, touch the lives of nearly everyone and are especially significant and pressing when they are of a moral nature—our values as well as our livelihood may be at stake. What are these problems, and how are they to be understood and properly handled? In short, what are the ethics of employment?

Among the many questions and problems that can arise in employment are these: what obligations does the employer have to his/her employees? For example, does the employer have an obligation to insure the health and safety of his employees? What does the employee owe his employer? For example, does he have a duty or obligation to protect the interests of the employer? To what extent ought an employee be loyal? What ought an employee do when his duty to loyalty conflicts with another duty or value? Is it wrong for an employer to hire on a basis other than qualification? Is it wrong for an employer to fire someone "at will"? What of sexism, prejudice, or harassment or exploitation?

A few qualifications and clarifications need to be made before addressing these questions. First, I shall focus on private rather than public (government) employment. Political factors inherent in public employment and problems peculiar to the public sphere require separate, lengthy treatment. Thus, not everything that follows applies to public employment. Furthermore, my discussion will be limited to the moral aspects of employment: government employment necessarily involves often complex legal and bureaucratic considerations, which may cloud or otherwise complicate the moral issues and may not be relevant to private employment. Suffice it to say that not every legal right, obligation, or consideration is a moral one. I assume from the beginning that morality is prior to law. I also assume that employment is not an evil and that the employment relationship is not necessarily an adversarial one, despite apparently common belief to the contrary. Finally, the entire discussion that follows rests on the conviction that understanding and coming to terms with moral problems, though often difficult, is an activity requiring no special training or technical language. What is required is within the reach of normally intelligent and reasonable human beings. This does not mean, of course, that solutions are always easily found or that unanimous agreement will always result. What it does mean is that moral argument ultimately rests on appeal to reasons and principles, neither of which are the special province of any particular group of human beings.

II. The Essential Features of the Employment Relationship

In the Gospel according to Matthew, Jesus tells the parable of the vineyard owner in need of workers. The story goes roughly as follows. A man seeking laborers for his vineyard strikes a bargain with several unemployed men early in the morning. The men agree to work in exchange for a penny each. They begin work and the owner continues seeking workers. A couple of hours later he finds other idle men in the marketplace and tells them that if they work the rest of the day he will pay them whatever is right. They take him at his word, agree to the offer, and go to the vineyard. Several times later during the day the owner makes the same offer, each time securing an agreement. At the close of the day all the workers are summoned. The last ones hired, who worked only an hour, are given a penny each; the next to last also a penny, and so on to the first ones hired who expect to receive more for having worked the longest. The employer gives them each a penny. They complain and feel unjustly treated. He reminds them of their agreement: "Friend, I do thee no wrong; dids't not thou agree with me for a penny. . . . Is it not lawful for me to do what I will with mine own?" And so the story ends. Now, to be sure, Jesus did not relate this parable as a lesson in business management or in the psychodynamics of employment. This biblical tale is an excellent illustration of the essential features of the employment relationship. What does it reveal?

The employment relationship has a clear and definite birth, marked by a voluntary agreement by both parties, each with an interest to be met or an anticipated gain to be realized. There is, then, something contractual in the relationship: the employer agrees to pay the employee a stated amount (or a certain percentage, or some acceptable consideration) in exchange for the employee's services, skill, or labor. Thus the nature, the essence, of the relationship is an agreement of exchange, where each side seeks to gain something, improve his/her circumstances, or satisfy some interest by means of the agreement. Each offers the other something *in trade.*

Of course, not every exchange or trade constitutes an employment relationship. Typically, the employment agreement makes explicit the following terms: rate of pay, days and hours to be worked, description of work to be performed, length of employment, and fringe benefits. Once the employer offers the job and the applicant accepts, the employment relationship begins, and each side is morally bound to the terms of the agreement. This is the employment relationship in its original and essential form, prior to influence from organized labor or legal statutes or regulations. For the purposes of identifying the employment relationship in its essential form, for later discussion, I'll refer to it as the "Primary Instance."

To summarize up to this point, the Primary Instance, as illustrated by the parable of the winemaker, shows that the employment relationship is a voluntary arrangement whereby one party agrees to pay a stated amount or rate for the services, skill, or labor of another party, who in turn agrees to provide the services, skill, or labor, in exchange for the amount of pay offered. Additionally and typically, other terms, such as length of employment, days and hours to be worked, and fringe benefits are also made explicit and agreed to. This description is very general. The particular terms or conditions agreed to in one situation may not be suitable for another situation. For instance, what is to count as a fair or reasonable or attractive rate of pay may vary not only from industry to industry or from place to place, but also from one individual to another, depending on needs, desires, or circumstances. Apart from an actual context, it is impossible to state what terms ought to be made explicit or what the specific limits of the terms should be. Generally speaking, the terms agreed to are determined by what each side has to offer and by the value of those offerings as perceived by both parties. It should be added here that, since the terms agreed to are fundamental to the employment relationship, both employee and employer would benefit from a discussion about the meaning and implication of the terms and anticipate, if possible, future problems that might arise from a misunderstanding of the terms.

A good many disputes that actually occur in employment can be prevented by careful attention at the stage of negotiating and clarifying the terms of the contract. For instance, when the relationship is expected to be of long duration, it would be prudent for both sides to consider terms dealing with pay raises. More generally, it would be good for employment contracts to specify some way of handling employment problems or disputes: how should a complaint or grievance be communicated? Ought there be an arbitrator, and at what point? Again, the kinds of problems that can be anticipated will vary, and the way that problems or disputes ought to be handled will depend on such factors as the number of employees in a company. The point to stress here is that prudence and foresight ought to play as central a role in employment as it does in other areas of life where our welfare is at stake.

Given the essential features of the employment relationship, what can the employee expect of the employer — what is he entitled to? The employee can reasonably expect the employer to meet his end of the employment agreement with regard to specified pay, work schedule, and fringe benefits. An employer's failure to meet any of the original terms agreed to is fundamental and serious and, on its face, is good cause for the employee to take some action, from making an inquiry to demanding redress, to perhaps even work stoppage. The appropriate action to take will, of course, depend upon a number of factors, including the seriousness of the situation, mitigating elements, or any prior agreement about how problems of the particular sort are to be handled.

It might be argued that all of this talk of terms of employment and voluntary agreement is fine in principle and as an ideal, but that in fact no such thing exists. Instead, the actual situation shows the worker to be at a tremendous disadvantage to begin with. More often than not, the terms are dictated by the employer and prospective employees must either "take it or leave it." The employer is the one who has the job to offer, who decides who gets the job; the employer has the capital to spend, the machinery, the building, the "means of production." Talk of "negotiating" terms or of "voluntary" agreement is misleading at best, and straightforwardly false at worst.

Without doubt it is not always the case that prospective employees have power or opportunity to influence the terms of employment. Indeed, the more people compete for a job, the less pressure will be exerted on the employer to alter terms in favor of the employee. Furthermore, the less skill required to satisfy the job description, the more applicants there are likely to be, so that at any given time, we can expect a fairly large number of workers who have little direct and individual influence on the terms of their employment. These are undeniable economic facts of life, but people can, and often do, respond to such facts in a variety of ways, including acquiring skills that are in demand, or moving to more favorable employment areas or industries. To deny that people have options demeans their dignity and altogether ignores the power of individual initiative. Furthermore, to the extent that individuals respond to unfavorable economic conditions by exercising options, they tend to alter those very conditions and to shift the economic balance. In a free society, economics is highly dynamic precisely because people respond to economic realities in various ways. A view that stereotypes the worker as helpless and hopeless (and the employer as a heartless Scrooge) is static, false, and pernicious. This is not to say that exercising options is never painful or difficult, but those who do take the initiative tend more often than not to be rewarded.

That workers are sometimes (and many workers are at any given time) at a bargaining disadvantage is not an essential feature of the employment relationship. According to the Primary Instance, neither employer nor employee has an inherent or necessary advantage. In other words, whenever a disadvantage exists we need to explain it in terms *outside* of employment as such. What is certain to vary from situation to situation or from time to time is the relative bargaining power of each side. Sometimes the employer will have many potential workers to choose from and will then be in a position to get the best for less. That is, supply will far exceed demand and so the cost to the employer — the wage — decreases. At other times, as in the case in recent years with computer technicians and engineers, the demand exceeds supply, and so the wage goes up.

What causes or influences the balance of supply and demand in the labor market has nothing to do with the employment relationship as such. Instead, it is generally an array of forces, conditions, events, attitudes, some of which are the result of deliberate choices by individuals, some not; some that take place or have their effect over a long period of time (such as the influence of education), some that happen suddenly, such as natural disasters. In all events, wherever an employment relationship exists, the terms of the relationship were agreed to voluntarily, if not always happily, and each side to the agreement receives something in exchange for something else.

Far from being a slave/master situation, the employment relationship is grounded in mutual self-interest and voluntarism. Furthermore, though the relative bargaining power of either side may vary from time to time or from place to place, each is autonomous and equal to the other in the central and most crucial respect: the freedom to accept or reject a contractual relationship. In the absence of such freedom, in the presence of coercion or fraud by either side, a genuine employment relationship does not exist, and a corrupt version of it masquerades instead. Again, the point is not whether corruption is possible, for surely it is, but whether corruption is inherent in the relationship.[1] An examination and analysis of the Primary Instance shows that it is not.

To summarize, the employer and employee are independent moral agents attempting to come to terms in a matter that affects their lives, their values, their futures. Each seeks to gain from the agreement; each is free to refuse the terms or to suggest a change in terms; each is morally bound by the terms agreed to. Each acts in his own best interest, but must do so without deception, coercion, or fraud. In these fundamental respects, employer and employee are autonomous and equal. On analysis, the most striking feature of the employment relationship as it comes into being is its moral dimension: human beings making decisions in matters of great importance to them and relating on the basis of commitments freely chosen.

We should note also that not only is the employment relationship not a slave/master one, more importantly, it is not even an adversarial one as common belief would have it. In an adversarial relationship, the principals seek to gain at the other's loss. An adversarial relationship tends towarddissolution and toward the destruction or loss of the other party. The energies and resources of each side are aimed at the diminution of the other. Nations at war, teams on a playing field, sides of a debate, are paradigm adversarial relationships: conflict, tension, and opposition are central. In an employment relationship, each side attempts to gain a value at least cost to itself: the prospective employee seeks the highest wage with least demands on her time or energy; the employer seeks the best worker at the lowest wage. The actual terms that they come to depend upon many factors, some of them totally beyond each others' control (e.g. the cost of housing in an area will influence the wage offered or sought). In general, what emerges in the end is a mutually satisfactory arrangement under the prevailing conditions. That each side seeks to gain a value at least cost to itself does not necessarily lead to conflict. It quite often leads to both sides getting what was wanted. Thus, people's seeking to realize values at least cost to themselves often leads to happy endings, not necessarily to grief, tragedy, or enslavement.

III. The Myth of Employer as Scrooge

Before examining in detail some of the common employment problems and their possible solutions, we need to dispel a fairly widespread prejudice concerning the nature of employers. Most people from personal experience have an idea what it is like to be an employee, but only a relative few have had experience as employers. Judging from the treatment that employers typically receive in television and movie presentations, employers are stereotypically viewed as greedy, uncaring slave-drivers. In this view, the employee's health, safety, and welfare are the furthest things from the employer's mind. No doubt some employers fit this description, and certainly some do not. If we look again to the Primary Instance, we find nothing in the essential features of the relationship that necessitates either the employer or the employee to be uncaring. Each side has an interest at stake to be realized and neither side is more or less likely to exploit the other. To the extent that exploitation occurs, the reasons or causes are independent of the employment relationship as such. We need to consider the *particular* employer who is uncaring, just as we might need to consider the *particular* employee who is unproductive, rather than assuming that "employers" are uncaring or that "employees" are lazy.

Sometimes it helps to be reminded of the obvious. In this case, we need to remember that an employer is a person, someone with needs, hopes, fears, talents, limitations, preferences, values. Employers come in all shapes, sizes, colors, educational, political, economic and social backgrounds. (Indeed, some employers earn much less than some employees). Employers then are faced with the same kinds of problems and have the same kinds of concerns as anyone else. And, as with anyone else, when an employer has to make an employment decision, he is nonetheless a person. Making a decision as an employer narrows the scope and brings forward some concerns rather than others. The logic here is the same as that of someone making a parenting decision or medical decision or personal finance decision. One is not necessarily less of a person when making a business decision than when making a parenting decision. Often, even when making a parenting decision, one has to consider finances or safety or personal tastes. But not always. In making a parenting decision what one *always* has to consider is the welfare of the child. That is precisely why it is called a parenting decision rather than, say, a medical or financial decision. Similarly with an employer. As a business person, the employer's ultimate concern is the welfare of the business. As often as not, the clearest indicator of this is what we call "profit."

As an employer, the businessman's ultimate concern has to do with the health of the employment relationship, which includes concern for worker morale, safety, health, productivity, all of which affect the viability of the business — this is the ultimate concern of the businessman *as* a businessman. It is easy for some to say that the only thing the employer is interested in is profits; in fact, a genuine concern for profit as an indicator of the health of the business necessarily includes a concern for the welfare of the workers who help make a profit possible. An employer who disregards the relevant concerns of his employees does so to his own detriment. This is no more or less true of employers as of anyone else who acts in disregard of the people or things that his values depend upon. That some employers do in fact show little concern for their employees is not due to their being employers. If being a Scrooge were inherent in being an employer, then all employers would be Scrooges. Clearly, some are not. It is safe to assume that under any other arrangement (including a socialist one) those who would have become Scrooges would find little trouble expressing their ungenerous natures. We forget too soon that the sweet and gentle, caring, and generous man that old Scrooge becomes at the end of the story is still an employer, but he has found his heart. Many employers have hearts to begin with. If we keep in mind the simple fact that employers are persons too, we shall be in an excellent position to understand the dynamics of the employment relationship. In particular, we can better analyze some of the pitfalls that employers face, and which are, in large measure, responsible for the prejudice against them.

IV. The Pitfalls of Employment

Hiring

When an employer hires someone, she invariably hires someone *rather than* or in preference to someone else. Unless she does this purely on whim, or the flip of the coin, her decision is based on some reasons, criteria, or standards by which the applicants are assessed. Some interesting questions arise here. Is it morally proper for an employer to hire whomever she wishes, for whatever reasons?[2] If not, then what considerations ought to guide the employer's choice? What place, if any, do the employer's personal tastes, habits, preferences, and biases have in the decision making process? Do prospective employees have any moral (as distinct from legal) rights during the hiring process?

It might be argued, and a good many people have held, that the only consideration that ought to guide an employer's hiring decision is the extent to which an applicant meets the specified job requirements. According to this view, the basic question at the time of hiring is, "which of the applicants is the most qualified?" As a rule, qualifications include relevant experience, skills, knowledge, training, and education. Depending on the position to be filled, certain skills may outweigh experience or education, and vice versa. Here, the employer has latitude and discretion so long as he is guided by the requirements of the job to be filled and the relevant qualifications of the applicant. Following this rule would prevent discriminating on the basis of sex, race, color, or age. In short, hiring on any basis other than job qualification is wrong and unfair.

This view certainly has merit as well as wide support. It seems clear on its face that it is in the employer's best interest to hire the most qualified person. This is precisely what most employers set out to do when they announce a job opening. But suppose that the most qualified person also demonstrates a lack of humor or good will or behaves in an obsequious or overbearing manner or in some other annoying or disturbing way. Depending upon the situation, this may or may not be perceived as serious. But if it were, and if the employer believed that his business would not be well served by this otherwise "most qualified" person, what must he do? According to the rule of hiring only the most qualified, the employer would be morally bound to hire someone he believed would be less of an asset to his business than another applicant, which contradicts the very purpose of hiring someone to begin with.

The problem with the "most qualified" rule is that it overlooks the fact that the employer is hiring a *person* and not just filling a vacancy. Virtually every job and nearly every work place has a social dimension, and an employer must consider qualities and attributes that would be impossible, pointless, or inappropriate to list in a job description. Thus, although it is proper to be guided by the question of which applicant is most qualified, an employer must make this decision in a context that includes more than just a job to be performed or a task accomplished.

To decide from a number of apparently qualified applicants is no easy task and not the kind of problem that can be solved in the abstract.[3] In one case, it may be that "personality" in addition to certain identifiable skills is important; in another case, a woman might be more appropriate; in a third case, special "good looks" is important; in a fourth, enunciation, or tactfulness, or directness, or slenderness are needed. The criteria against which applicants might be measured are indefinite in number and the importance of the criteria will vary from one employer to another, from one locale to another, from one job to another. The employer has to decide whether hiring this or that applicant is in the best interest of the business. Rarely is it the case that a single factor alone is decisive; more often than not, since the work place is also a social environment, all manner of factors not directly related to the actual job to be performed can be important, even if not decisive. For example, whether or not someone is pleasant to be with may be a consideration more significant in one case than another, or to one employer but not to another. It would be impossible to list, much less to rank in order of importance, each and every consideration. We cannot formulate a rigid set of rules or provide a calculus that will guarantee an employer the "best" choice consistent with morality any more than we can do this for any other area of human choice where values and judgment are central.

We can, however, say this much: since the employer's fundamental concern as a businessman is (ought to be) the welfare of the business, he ought to hire the person who, in his judgment, is most likely to do the best job, to perform with the greatest skill, in whatever ways are relevant to the concerns of the business. The employer's hiring policy (and business practices in general) ought to derive from his concern for the business. Thus, when a business decision is at hand, personal, non-business, non-job related considerations ought to be subordinated to the primary, business considerations. Again, this holds as well for doctors, mothers, waitresses, artists, teachers, policemen—in short, it holds for everyone who has commitments. This is part of what is involved in someone's having integrity: keeping faith with one's commitments. Making decisions, the uniquely human activity that makes morality possible, is something that each of usdoes throughout life. *Moral* decisions are those that involve the welfare or rights of a human being. Thus, morality applies to all persons regardless of their particular circumstances. That is, morality applies to persons *as persons*. It follows that there can be no moral obligations that apply to only some kind of persons but not to others. So, there can be no *special* moral obligations for an employer over and above those he already has by virtue of being a person. If, when faced with a business decision, moral considerations are relevant, the employer must act in accord with morality. This is another way of saying that moral principles take precedence over any and all other principles or considerations. As a person, an employer has the fundamental obligation to avoid violating the rights of others, and in turn enjoys the right to freedom from violation by others.[4]

A consequence of this moral fact is that an employer may not hire or reject whomever she wishes for whatever reasons she might have: there are limits here. Those who hold to the view that employers have total (moral) freedom to hire and fire base their position on the fact that the employer has property rights, i.e., the business is her property and thus she can dispose of it as she wishes. If she doesn't want a particular person or kind of person as an employee, that's her business and no one else's. It is no different from her having the right to let or refuse into her house whomever she wishes, and surely no one denies her this right.

Having the right to dispose of one's property has its moral boundaries, as do other rights and freedoms. It is a mistake to say that, since the employer has property rights, he may do anything he wishes where his business is concerned, including violating someone else's rights in the exercise of his own. Rights cannot conflict this way: people's hopes, goals, wishes may, and sometimes do, come to odds, but their rights do not. To say that an employer has property rights is simply to say that if anyone has the right to hire or fire, the employer does, but his having that right does not ever free him from moral constraints.

When an employer seeks an employee, he does so to serve an interest. The range of possible interests here is wide: he may want to fill a vacancy, or to create a new position, or to increase production, or to decrease his own work load, or to have some companionship during business hours, or to impress a prospective client with his work force, or to perform a business experiment to test a theory of production. None of these reasons is, on its face, unworthy, immoral, or unprofessional. The interest to be served will, to some extent, determine who will be hired. The context within which an employer acts is business and, as such, his fundamental concern ought to be the welfare of the business. An employer's non-business interests may, at times, override his business interests—he is, after all, a person—but to the extent that personal considerations preempt business ones in just those areas where the welfare of the business is at stake, he is failing as a businessman. Such is the case, for example, when he is called upon to make a careful, intelligent, professional decision such as hiring someone. What this means is that, though all sorts of considerations may come into play, including the employer's personal tastes, whims, or biases, *as a businessman,* he is morally obliged to keep non-business considerations secondary and subordinate to the business ones. That this is a moral matter relates to certain commitments that one makes in choosing business as a profession.

To choose business (or any other field) as a career or as a way of life is to commit oneself to the means required to sustain that choice. Thus, it is a contradiction for an employer to choose that which clearly undermines or threatens the welfare of his business.

All of this may be true, but still, isn't it obvious that the employer has an obligation to treat all of the applicants equally and to be fair to all in his hiring practice? After all, this is the least that anyone can expect. As persons, we deserve fair and equal treatment. If anything is a fundamental right, surely this is.[5]

If the right to fair and equal treatment is a fundamental human right, then it applies to all persons and obligates everyone, not just employers. Does it obligate everyone? Consider how our lives actually work and the various and frequent times that we discriminate: seeking out (or avoiding) a particular salesperson; contributing to a charity or supporting a cause; compiling an invitation list for a party; choosing a restaurant for dinner; sending a birthday card; hanging up on a prank caller; getting married. It simply makes no sense to say that I have violated someone's right to fair and equal treatment by not inviting them to my party. The right to fair and equal treatment is a legal, Constitutional right, not a fundamental human right. It is based on the understanding that justice requires such treatment. In other words, any society whose *legal* processes do not apply equally to all its citizens is, to that extent, an unjust society.

There is a more fundamental respects in which we are equal: our rights to life, liberty, and the pursuit of happiness. These rights, listed in the *Declaration of Independence*, are *natural* as well as legal rights. That is, they derive from the nature of being a person and the requirements of living as a person in society. It is in this sense that all human beings are "created equal" and, in this sense, that we remain equal throughout life. Each person has an equal claim to these rights solely by virtue of being a person. That these are *natural rights* means that wherever and whenever persons exist, they enjoy the moral protection of these boundaries: a violation at this level is not only improper, it is immoral. However, that they are rights obligates each of us to the other only insofar as we must refrain from violating the rights; we are not further obligated to assist one another in the realization or exercise of those rights. I am not morally bound to provide you with the means of sustaining your life, nor are you so obligated toward me. If I were so obligated, then my right to liberty would be abridged—I would not be free to make efforts to sustain my own life—which results in a contradiction. Further, a person cannot be obligated to do the impossible: I *cannot* assist any and everyone in the exercise of his rights. To say that a person has a right to work cannot mean that he has a right to a job, since this would require that someone *else* be obligated to provide him a job, which is absurd. The right to work means, rather, that a person has the right to seek work and to do work without interference from others.

An employer does not owe the job to anyone at all, much less to anyone in particular. It follows from this that his hiring someone—no matter what his reasons—is not a violation of the rights of those not hired. This does not mean that an employer is free to lie, deliberately mislead, or otherwise be careless with the applicants, anymore than he (or anyone else) is free to lie, deliberately mislead, or be careless with people in other aspects of life. If an employer denies someone a job on grounds other than lack of qualifications, he has not violated the applicant's rights, though he may be blameworthy for other reasons. For example, if Jones refuses to hire Smith because Smith is black (or white, or a Catholic)—that is, if Jones acts out of prejudice, then he is blameworthy. His being morally accountable here has nothing to do with his being an employer and nothing to do with anyone's right to work. Rather, the wrong lies in being prejudiced, in *categorically* denying the worth of an individual because he/she is a member of a group whose attributes one disapproves of.

We must be careful here, since it is not always clear whether someone is acting out of prejudice. Is it bigotry, for example, if Jones refuses to hire an alcoholic or someone obese? Couldn't this possibly be a case of *protest* rather than bigotry? Or assume that Jones's business is located in and depends upon the trade of a community predominantly white (or black) and strongly opposed to interaction with blacks (whites). Is Jones acting from prejudice if he refuses to hire a black applicant? Suppose he has good reason to believe that hiring a black (or a white) will result in a dramatic, perhaps fatal, drop in sales? And how is this different in principle from hiring an attractive receptionist rather than a homely one? In certain cases the employer's conscience may be taxed and his reserve of courage tapped. To the extent that the welfare of the business is at stake, he may be drawn by prudence or economic necessity to act in one way rather than another. He is not, regardless of the circumstances, morally obligated to hire anyone at all, much less someone in particular, or of a particular kind. What he cannot do and still remain within the bounds of morality is categorically rule out blacks or whites "in principle." Refusal to hire a black (or a white, or a homosexual, or a woman, or a Catholic, or . . . *ad indefinitum*) is prejudicial and morally reprehensible only if, regardless of the circumstances, one holds them to be less as persons, less worthy of human respect, less deserving of the rights inherent in personhood.

It may be that the employer is not prejudiced in refusing to hire a black but instead is acting on her judgment that hiring a black would threaten her business. Some may respond that, in such a case, though the employer may not be prejudiced, she is nonetheless a coward. Again, this may or may not be true, for we can easily imagine a situation where hiring the black (or white) was foolhardy, even reckless. Besides, we must remember that the employer's livelihood is at stake here: she clearly has a *right* to that, and no one has a right to the job that she is offering. Finally, and most important, even if the employer does act cowardly in this case, that does not constitute *moral* failure. The issue is whether she has an obligation to hire the black (or white) or whether she has violated anyone's rights in refusing to do so. The answer to both is "no," since no one has a *right* to the job at all.

Health and Safety

Once hired, a worker can expect his employer to meet all of the terms agreed to. Some have argued that, in addition to what is specifically dictated by the contract, the employee can reasonably expect and has a moral right to protection from health and safety hazards while on the job. Isn't it obvious, so the argument goes, that the employer should provide such protection since the employee is working for him, under his orders, direction, or supervision and, more often than not, is working at the shop, store, factory, or field owned by the employer. Furthermore, the employer is typically in a better position than an employee to know about matters of health and safety peculiar to his industry or place of work.

At the other extreme, it can be argued that the employer has no obligations whatever beyond those specified in the contract. If anything is obvious, the employee ought to see to his own health and safety. After all, the employee has an immediate, continuous, and natural interest in his own welfare and ought not leave such an important matter to someone else. Besides, employers are less apt to be responsive to employees' needs here, since doing so necessarily costs money and brings down profits.

It is certainly true that employees work under the direction, command, or supervision of their employers. It is also true that they usually work at a place owned by the employer. But these facts do not establish any special obligation on the employer to provide health and safety protection. Having authority over others does not in itself entail being responsible for their health and safety. Nor does someone's working for me on my premises entail my being responsible for them. This does not mean that an employer may ignore health and safety matters concerning his workers or his work place, or that he/she is necessarily immune from blame should a mishap occur. In other words, workers do not have a *moral* right to health and safety protection, though they can make health and safety concerns part of the employment contract; an employer does not have a *moral* obligation to provide health and safety protection, though he may offer certain health and safety terms as part of the employment contract.

There are, however, certain common-sense standards and widely accepted standards of health and safety that workers expect. Given these standards, workers are entitled to (i.e., have good reason to expect) safe and healthful working conditions; employers have a consequent responsibility to provide such an environment or to inform their workers when and where conditions fall below expected standards.

Now, what is considered reasonable depends upon a number of factors, including not only prevailing or customary standards, but cost, availability, and perceived need or value, which may vary from place to place or time to time. Additionally, relative risk has to be estimated and weighed against cost. Without doubt, every worker in an office or a plant would be "safer" if there were a fire extinguisher on every wall and at each door. But, unless special conditions exist (for example the plant manufactures highly flammable products), a demand for such precaution would be extreme and unreasonable. Each trade, industry, and profession has its special risk factors, and it is the shared responsibility of employer and employee to ensure reasonable safety: the employer, because he has both an economic interest in the safety of his workers, as well as a common human interest in the safety of human beings, particularly those with whom one associates; the employee, because it is obviously in his best interest. Again, we must remember that what is considered "reasonably safe" conditions for mine workers is far from what would be considered reasonably safe conditions for school teachers. That there might be disputes within a trade or industry about a specific condition does not count against the general view here. Disputes are to be expected, partly because people's values and needs differ. Additionally, most trades and industries are continually being impacted upon by science and technology with new knowledge and new tools that affect health and safety. At what point this new knowledge or technology "ought" to be implemented necessarily depends upon the cost, estimated risk, and perceived gain. Clearly, at *some* point it may or will be evident to most of those concerned that implementation is called for, and that failure to do so is unreasonable and irresponsible. As a rule, however, such changes happen somewhat gradually until they become part of the common or prevailing condition. Again, what counts as safe today, or in this industry, or under these conditions, may be deemed reckless at another time or place.

Organized Labor

That employees tend to see one another as members of a group, as having certain needs and interests in common, is no surprise since people tend to do just that whether they're employees, parents, teachers, or students. The tendency to organize when there is a perceived common need or shared interest to be realized is an expression of the social side of human nature. The organization of labor is generally viewed as a movement directed *against* the employer, but this needn't be so: it can be of benefit to employers as well as to employees. A labor organization can serve as an insurance group, or as a resource or information tool. It can help to promote better relations with management by, among other things, letting management know what the concerns of its employees are, and it can provide a vehicle in the other direction, for letting management inform labor of its concerns. In this way, employees can become more active participants in matters and processes that affect their welfare. It is good for people to feel efficacious, to have influence over matters that concern them, and a labor organization can be an excellent medium for exerting influence.

To the extent that employers sincerely encourage and promote this sense of participation and influence, the employment relationship will thrive and tend toward cooperation and mutual respect. It is through this kind of relationship, rather than the adversarial one, that employees come to see and to accept their responsibility to be dependable, honest, efficient, hard-working. This is the same psychology that applies to families, members of a team, or to any group of people whose destinies are intertwined. Additionally, a labor union can effectively and rationally engage management in a bargaining forum, wherein all parties concerned make known their needs as well as their willingness to negotiate and to come to mutually agreeable terms. As such, bargaining can be a discovery process: wages alone are not the only legitimate terms of trade. Depending on the industry, such things as insurance, overtime pay, holidays, medical leave, promotion, and retirement policy may, to varying degrees, be significant.

If this view sounds too idealistic and optimistic, consider the alternative, which has been the prevailing view for some time. The problem with the adversarial view of employment is that it too rigidly identifies people with their roles. It subordinates the essential to the accidental and as such fosters the very division assumed to be inherent in the relationship. What is essential in the moral sphere is to treat people as persons, entitled to certain rights, and possessed of reason and the capacity to make choices for themselves. This is something that can be done and is being done all the time by people who happen to be employees as well as by people who happen to be employers. It is an insult to assume that, just because a person has a certain economic or employment status, she is incapable of treating others morally. The employment relationship consists of *people*: as such, problems will arise, and when those problems are of a moral nature, those involved (to the extent that they are acting responsibly) will seek a solution by a careful, reasoned, and honest exploration of the relevant facts, feelings, values, and principles. Of course, it may occur that a meeting of minds is not at hand even after discussion and attempts at bargaining. Typically, such an impasse leads to a workers strike.

In its simplest terms, a strike is a suspension of the employment relationship with the purpose of forcing the employer to agree to certain terms out of economic necessity. There is nothing wrong, in principle, with workers agreeing not to work, and there well may be times when a strike is the most effective course of action for workers to take. However, an employer is under no moral obligation to rehire the workers, any more than he was obliged to hire them in the first place. A worker's (or a group of workers') refusal to work, except in response to the employer's failure to abide by his obligations, is a breach of the employment agreement. This does not mean that workers may not have good reason to stop work — they may, for example, be protesting the company's refusal to recognize their organization, or demonstrating a need for better worker facilities. But unless the employer has violated the original terms agreed to, or has acted out of deceit or coercion, a strike (or some form of organized work stoppage) is identical to quitting: it has the logical consequence of relieving the employer of any obligation toward the employee. A violation of the original terms suspends the employment relationship. Additionally, strikers may not forcibly (or with threats) prevent others from working. Doing so violates the right to liberty and threatens the right to life.

By the same reasoning, an employer may not interfere with his/her employees' attempts to organize. The right to liberty entails the right of human beings to associate with one another. This is the most fundamental principle operating in the employment relationship. It is, as well, the defining characteristic of a free society. As such, any law, regulation, policy, or action that contradicts or undermines this principle to the same extent undermines the foundations of the society.

V. Concluding Remarks

Two fundamental assumptions about the nature of morality underlie this essay. The first is that morality cannot be programmed in advance of actual cases. What a person ought or ought not do is a matter that arises in actual and often very complex situations. The possible relevant variables in even similar situations are indefinite in number and render futile any attempt to formulate rules that generalize over all possible cases. Though there *are* answers to moral questions and solutions to moral problems, there are few, if any, *categorical* answers: we never know what interesting twists the future may bring. In the end, there are no shortcuts — we have to think our way through. The second assumption is that the moral problems that arise in the employment relationship are not of a special kind requiring technical or special or expert skill for their solution. In some ways it is unfortunate that our society has developed elaborate and complex legal mechanisms that dictate how certain matters in the employment relationship are to be understood and handled. Of course, rules-making and the institutionalizing of human activities is, to some extent, natural and desirable, but in the area of ethics in particular, that tendency should be strongly resisted, for it robs people of the actual *practice* of grappling with and solving moral problems. These sorts of problems are the kind that people *ought* to solve, for it is here that we uniquely appeal to that which is most human, the combination of reason and values.

What this means is that there are no experts here. Morality may reach very complex proportions, but it is not a technical activity. The direction that we are moving in, toward legalizing, regulating, institutionalizing, and otherwise making abstract an aspect of life that operates well only in the concrete, is literally *de-humanizing* us, taking us from the very thing that makes us what we uniquely are.

Notes

1. For a discussion of the view that the employment relationship is necessarily corrupt, see Karl Marx's essay "Estranged Labor," which appears in a number of collections, including *The Marx-Engels Reader,* edited by Robert C. Tucker (New York: W. W. Norton, 1971).

2. The issue of hiring and firing "at will" has generated considerable debate. For further exploration of this and other employment matters, see the concluding chapter of the book.

3. It is, I think, a failure of understanding to believe that knowledge of moral principles alone is sufficient to making a sound moral decision, as though by the simple application of a formula we could arrive at the correct moral solution to every moral problem. Even when possessed of the knowledge of moral principles, we face the sometimes difficult task of applying them to particular actual situations, since principles are by nature general and abstract. Clearly, not every moral principle applies in every moral situation, and determining which one does apply often requires more than moral knowledge alone.

4. By "rights" here, I am referring to the fundamental natural or human rights to life, liberty, and property, and mean to exclude nonnatural and/or legal rights, such as the right to counsel, or the right to a jury trial. I also mean to exclude some alleged rights that, on analysis, turn out not to be rights at all, but things that are usually highly desirable for human beings to have, such as decent housing. We have a right to seek out, or pursue, decent housing, without interference from others but we do not have a *right* to decent housing, which implies that someone ought to provide it for us.

5. For a discussion of how equality pertains to the treatment of employees, see Henry Shue's "Transnational Transgressions" in *Just Business,* edited by Tom Regan (New York: Random House, 1984).

4

MORALITY AND THE MARKETS

J. ROGER LEE

Introduction

Capitalism is the social, political, and economic system that lets rights to property be transferred by market transactions among private individuals, alone or in groups. Systems of thought that oppose capitalism oppose this way of fixing legitimate property claims and substitute other criteria for the legitimacy of property transfers, or prohibits such transfers altogether.

In either allowing or disallowing market transactions, capitalist and non-capitalist systems either allow or disallow business. Business is a set of organized human activities which take place in markets. So it is appropriate to engage in a general consideration of the morality or immorality of markets and of market institutions, in a business ethics text. Much of what makes for good business or bad business is the suitability of business practices to engage in market activity. But if market activities were essentially bad, that badness would transfer back to the business activities. On the other hand, if it is a good thing for humans to participate in markets, then good business can be good human activity.

In any event, this chapter is a discussion of the morality of markets and of market institutions. Since this is an introductory essay, I shall explain everything that is taken up in the essay. So I start by explaining what markets are and what morality is.

What is morality? The study of morality is an attempt to formulate rational standards that can be used to distinguish between right and wrong action and also between good and bad things. For example, most people think that peace and prosperity are good things and should be pursued. One of the things that any moral theory must do is to come up with a reasonable

This essay is a shortened version (with minor stylistic revisions) of the author's "The Morality of Capitalism and of Market Institutions," in *The Main Debate: Communism versus Capitalism,* edited by Tibor R. Machan (Random House, 1987), pp. 84–110.

proof of why people should or should not hold this and other widely held moral opinions. Such a proof should show a reasonable person that the goodness or badness of these things or the rightness or wrongness of actions associated with these things is demonstrable on the basis of general, plausible principles.

What are markets? A market is a situation in which people can exchange some goods or services for other goods or services.[1] If I place an ad in the local newspaper offering to sell my typewriter and you read the ad, call me, come to my home, and buy the machine from me, then that complex situation of newspaper, people reading it, your phone contact, and the exchange in my home constitutes the market in which we traded.

Other situations are not markets. For example, chaotic situations like battlefields block cooperation and trade. There are areas or times in which there are no people interested in trade; for instance, there is no market for refrigerators on the North Pole.

Market exchanges have to be voluntary. Nonvoluntary exchanges like theft or taxation are not market exchanges. They involve exchange, but not market exchange, because they are forced exchanges.

Utilitarianism and Markets

Utilitarianism is a moral theory about the rightness and wrongness of action. In its pure form, it holds that among the things we can do in any given situation, the right action is the one that produces the most good consequences.[2]

From the time of Adam Smith's *An Inquiry into the Nature and Causes of the Wealth of Nations* (1776) onward, for a century, both critics[3] and supporters of markets agreed that, as Adam Smith maintained in his book of that title, more wealth is realized on unfettered markets than on any known nonmarket alternatives. Even critics of market institutions allowed that that was true.[4]

There are only two alternatives to market economies. The first leaves economic affairs absolutely uncoordinated and disallows trade. Perhaps people produce only for themselves, perhaps for a common pool to which they deposit and take as they will or need. I take it as clear that the most elementary economics shows this alternative to be incapable of producing the greatest amount of wealth, so economics does not show it to have a moral defense on utilitarian grounds. This first alternative to markets may be laudable on nonutilitarian grounds but nonutilitarian considerations are taken up further on. The only nonmarket alternative to this is the case in which markets are suspended, yet economic affairs are coordinated in a nonmarket way. First someone[5] makes a decision about what will be produced and how it will be distributed, and second, that state of affairs is imposed on the entire community.

The Calculation Problem

At the end of the nineteenth century and the beginning of this one, however, some social theorists came to think that the objective of maximizing wealth could be better served by government-administered, boards of central planning who would replace the seeming anarchy of market exchanges with coordinated planning. In this century, such planning boards were established in the Soviet Union and the Fascist states of Germany and Italy. Since then, such boards have been imitated in other European countries, the United States, and in parts of the Third World. Although this theory had a certain short-run popularity, it had an early theoretical refutation in economics, called the calculation problem, and has been found wanting in practice in the countries that have attempted it.

The calculation problem is best viewed as an argument showing that there is a vital problem that a central planning authority trying to coordinate the affairs of an economy by directives could not meet.[6]

The argument proceeds as follows. In the marketplace, particular economic decision makers proceed to their activities on the basis of knowledge that they have of particular factors of need, cost, and availability. Much of the rationality of the economic activities of these individuals rests on this particular knowledge to which they alone have access and use.

The central planners of a planned economy, on the other hand, do not have access to this knowledge of particular circumstances that individuals on the scene have because they are not on the scenes of activity for which they plan. Bereft of this knowledge, their decision making is relatively uninformed and so their economy is relatively inefficient. Consequently, it is impossible for a centrally planned economy to function as efficiently as a market economy — it is impossible for the central planners to plan wisely.

Market prices are important here. Market decisions are effected through and informed by pricing in money, a recognized unit of exchange. Prices are determined by people who, using their knowledge of the market, rank commodities as more or less desirable.

In a centrally planned, nonmarket economy, the decrees of the planning board determine which goods and services will be produced and the prices at which they will trade.

This leads to an important conclusion. *The information used in determining the prices will be only the information available to the plan in the beginning, before the plan is implemented.* Once the plan is in effect, the planners cannot respond to changes in the marketplace that occur as the plan is implemented—i.e. changing desires, relative scarcities, or technology. On the other hand, in a free market, prices will fluctuate in response to changes in consumer preference or factors of production. The prices show changes in the relative values of things. *Central planners cannot use the prices that they themselves have imposed to inform themselves of these changing factors.* Markets are vast information flow networks and central planners remove themselves from that information.

So the problem of economic calculation can be stated thus: in the absence of market prices, how will the planning authority get the information that would have been coded into prices in a market economy?

To the extent that we would try to replace the market in order to impose a vision of the good on economic affairs, we will lose our ability to produce that good because we lose our ability to use the information available to us to coordinate production and distribution.[7] That is the difficulty the calculation problem presents to those who would attempt a utilitarian justification of the suspension of markets in favor of political or community direction of economic affairs for the greatest good. The utilitarian ideal of the realization of the most good probably would not be realized. A utilitarian cannot endorse the planned economy alternative to market institutions.

This does not mean that a utilitarian must endorse markets. There is no good reason to think that markets are ideal vehicles for realizing the utilitarian idea. Ideal utilitarianism requires that the institution that is to be considered right is the one that produces the greatest good for people.

Adam Smith and others held that market economies maximize the *wealth* of nations. But maximum wealth may not be the maximum good. We consider a society wealthy if it contains a large number of the things that *we desire*. But, if we did not desire the good, another society could have more good and yet be less wealthy *from our point of view*. Markets are ideal for providing people with the maximum possible set of *desired* goods and services from among those that are technologically possible to produce and distribute. What markets deliver can be different from what is required before markets are shown to be morally defensible on utilitarian grounds. In markets, utilitarianism requires that the market provides the distribution of the set of goods and services that would be maximally productive of the good in the community. Markets need not do that, and certainly a society like ours shows that weakness when it lavishes money on producers of pet rocks and comic books while leaving artists and research scientists wanting. A free market can deviate from a system that maximizes the production of good states of affairs, since it maximizes the satisfaction of desires.

In summary, utilitarianism does not determine whether markets or their alternatives are morally desirable. Thus, we reach an important conclusion.

If we are to find the moral case for or against market institutions, we must look past utilitarianism to another type of moral theory for the answer to the question, "Which is morally desirable, markets or their alternatives?"

Deontological Considerations of Markets

A moral theory of right action is called deontological if it treats rights or obligations, rather than consequences, as primary in evaluting actions. For example, given a minimal theory of rights, there is good reason for me not to kill some innocent passerby. The consequences don't count in evaluating this potential killing. The human right to life does.[8] There is a justification of market activity of just this sort. It relies on the rights of self-determination of actions.

The Right to Self-Determination

Right now, I am acting to promote my well-being by writing this chapter. I hope to sell first publication rights for money and fame. The time that I am spending securing money and fame is time that I am not spending helping someone else secure their fame or fortune or the minimal requisites of life.

I have a basic moral right to do what I am doing.[9] Generally, there is a fundamental right each person has, to pursue his or her own welfare without also having the obligation to *promote* (other than by not impeding) others in pursuit of their own welfare. The permissibility of my writing this essay is a particular instance of the application of that right.

Let us advance my chapter writing into the future. Suppose, despite my best professional judgment, that there is no market for this work. I will have written it for naught. Would that future development show that I did not have a right to write this essay? Would it show that I may be prohibited from writing it? The answer to both of these questions is "No." I have a right to write and try to sell this essay. It doesn't matter what the consequences are.

This shows an important feature of my right to pursue my own welfare. What I have a right to do is to undertake actions that I judge to be in my best interest. It does not matter if my judgment is correct or not. If my best judgment is that doing "A" is in my best interest and if doing "A" does not conflict with others' rights, then it is morally permissible for me to do "A".[10] People's rights are limited to rights to do only what is the best thing.

The deontological defense of markets appeals to just these rights. It is desirable, given these rights, that there be institutions that maximally allow people to exercise these rights. The deontological case for the free market is that it is such an institution. Because the institution is well suited to allowing people to exercise their rights, it is a good institution.

Personal Flourishing

There is a nondeontological tradition in moral philosophy that comes to the same defense of market institutions as the deontological. It is the personal flourishing tradition, which originated with Plato and Aristotle in the fourth century B.C. In personal moral philosophy, the tradition holds that actions are right if they lead to the flourishing of the person who performs the action. "Flourishing" means that a person will develop all of his or her vital potential. This is a consequence-based theory of right action. It matters whether the consequence is a state of flourishing or not. But this consequence-based theory leads almost immediately to an endorsement of the right of personal direction of one's life, regardless of the particular results of the exercise of that right.

Human beings have a rational faculty, including a practical rationality that plans action. Just as it is important for plants to have good root systems and healthy leaves, so too it is a necessary condition for human flourishing that a person has and uses a well-developed faculty of practical reason. Human beings cannot flourish unless they direct their own actions. Slaves, under the control of a mad scientist who manipulates their behaviors by means of electrodes implanted in their brains, might show the excellence or malevolence of the mad scientist, but none of their own.

In the human flourishing view, the effective use of practical reason is a necessary, but not sufficient, condition for any humans doing any right things. It must be permissible for them to undertake self-directed action — they must have a right to direct their own actions.[11]

No one has a right to prevent people from undertaking right actions. No one has a right to block another's actions in pursuit of their own well-being. In the human flourishing view, if I am prevented from acting for my well-being on the basis of my best judgment of a situation, then I am prevented from acting rightly. No one has a right to treat me that way. The people who do treat me that way are violating their obligations to accept my autonomy so that my rights are not violated.

This is the same deontological rights' claim in interpersonal relations that the deontological analysis gave rise to.[12] Again, since markets are efficient devices for ensuring that societies are arranged to maximize people's being able to act on their best vision of their well-being, then market institutions can be justified on that basis.

Cooperation

There are other lines of defense of markets. For example, cooperation among people is a desirable state of affairs. When we cooperate, you and I work for our own well-being in concert with one another. As a result, our actions to achieve harmonious ends are reinforced by the actions of the other. Consider the following situation. You find yourself with two copies of the same edition of Kant's *Critique of Pure Reason* and I have none but want one. I have two copies of the same edition of *Fanny Hill* and you have none, but want one. Then it would be a cooperative thing for us to trade one *Critique of Pure Reason* for one *Fanny Hill*. Market exchange, trade, is a form of cooperation, and cooperation is a social enhancement of one's ability to act on one's best judgment of what is right for one.

This result agrees with much of our experience; markets *are* cooperative institutions compared to government agencies, for example. Buying a record in a store is a nicer experience than dealing with the Department of Motor Vehicles or the Post Office. Isn't it?

The institution most capable of maximally realizing the ends that people actually have in a community is a market. It allows the production of the maximal set of goods and services desired by the members of the community from among the many alternative sets and distributions of goods and services that are technically possible of production. So, markets are ideal institutions for people to maximize the implementation of their right to pursue their own well-being. That is the deontological case for markets.

Markets are devices for letting people follow their own best judgment of what is good for them. Markets do not interfere with people's opting out of the market to join a commune, if that is their decision. But if people do join such voluntary, cooperative societies, while their action itself is all right, it is questionable that it is defensible as an enhancement of cooperation. By withdrawing from the market to the extent that these communities do, they withdraw from a vast coopertive network.

The Public Goods Problem

Economists have developed a problem for the deontological defense of the market presented above. It is called the problem of public goods, and it has influenced many thinkers, including John Rawls, to despair of the level of cooperation that I have sketched manifesting itself in free markets.[13] Without cooperation, the deontological case for markets unravels, and Rawls and others urge that morality requires that there be some suspensions of markets and that political or constitutional provisions be made to reintroduce cooperation.[14]

A public good is a good that, if provided to anyone, is provided to everyone — for example, a guard patrolling a neighborhood street. If one or two of the five people who live on the street finance the guard, then each of the five benefits equally from the guard in the street scaring burglars away. If any benefit, all benefit.

The problem of public goods is that many people will be tempted to "free ride," to take the benefit without paying, counting on others to pay for the public good. Then, it is feared, the public good will not be provided or will be provided in inadequate supply, because not enough people will pay for their provision. Cooperation breaks down in the provision of public goods on the market, so people are to be forced to pay for the provision of public goods.[15]

Free riders can be morally tolerated voluntarily. If I come across a coin-operated merry-go-round activated by inserting a coin, if I want to ride it, it is irrelevant to me whether or not there are ten other people already sitting on it waiting for someone else to come along and put in a coin so they can ride free. I'll be willing to put the coin in and not care about the free riders. While the free riders may have character flaws or lack feelings of benevolence and cooperation, they in no way violate my rights. So I may tolerate them morally. I may cooperate with them and, in many cases, I will provide the public good.

But then, it is argued, not enough of some public goods like national defense will be provided. Maybe this is so. But it is entirely unclear just how much provision of the public good is to count as enough. And it is essential that the person who is putting the public goods problem forward be able to specify just what this amount is because that person is faulting the free market on grounds that it is not providing enough. Can we really understand the complaint?

Further, the attempt to provide public goods publicly, through the planning and coercion of law, will entail all of the difficulties of the calculation problem. We just will not have the information needed to say how much of what needs to be produced when and where. The perennial political debate over the desirable levels of military expenditure in the federal budget is evidence of this difficulty.[16]

Discussion

It is crucially important to make this distinction among the utilitarian, the deontological, and the personal flourishing kinds of moral justification of the market. This can be seen by a consideration of the famous economist, John Maynard Keynes' attempt to justify interventions in the market.

Keynes. When Keynes comes to give *moral* arguments against market institutions, he argues only against a utilitarian position. He writes:

It is *not* true that individuals possess a prescriptive "natural liberty" in their economic activities. There is *no* "compact" conferring perpetual rights on those who Have or on those who Acquire. The world is *not* so governed from above that private and social interest always coincide. It is *not* so managed here below that in practice they coincide. It is *not* a correct deduction from the Principles of Economics that enlightened self-interest always operates in the public interest. Nor is it true that self-interest generally *is* enlightened; more often individuals acting separately to promote their own ends are too ignorant or too weak to attain even these.[17]

His first sentence is an assertion that rules the deontological case out of court, but without argument. That will not do. Humans do possess rights and they possess them in their economic, market activities, in their choices to buy celery or carrots, as well as in any other context. At the very least we should have a strong argument before we give up this position.

Keynes, of course is right in arguing that self-interested action often is ill-suited to attain its ends. That is a point we noted above, about utilitarianism. For a short time, maybe, more desirable goods and services could be provided in some alternative nonmarket society.[18] That would be impressive on a utilitarian theory that defined rightness and wrongness solely in terms of the production of the good. But if we attend to the deontological defense of market institutions and thus to the rights of the individuals involved, then Keynes' utilitarian critique falls short of the mark of justifying the suspension of the market.

Not all thinkers who criticize market institutions make the mistake of just criticizing the utilitarian defense of the market. There are other problems raised by thinkers who are not prepared to endorse the market and it's attendant justifying feature—freedom of contract. These thinkers challenge the deontological case for markets presented above. Two such thinkers are Karl Marx and Thomas Aquinas.

Alienation.   Karl Marx, in his earlier writings, made an influential critique of the entire project of a worker laboring to produce commodities, which are then to be sold. Marx's charge is that production for the market goes against the very essence of human, conscious producers. He maintained that the process involved alienation. It is unclear that Marx himself might have thought of the moral import of alienation. But it is clear that Marx thought that such alienated conditions could be done away with in the future, in a communist, nonmarket society.

Marx thought that this alienation manifested itself in four ways, all of which spring from a common cause, which is also the first form of alienation.

[T]he fact that the worker is related to the *product of his labor* as to an *alien* object. For on this premise it becomes clear that the more the worker spends himself, the more powerful becomes the alien world of objects which he creates over and against himself, the poorer he himself—his inner world—becomes, the less belongs to him as his own.[19]

Marx fails to point out that this form of alienation or estrangement would exist even without a market or without exchange. If I design a product in the world and make it, then *I* am in the product, in some sense. I identify with it but it is not me. One might think, and Marx does think that this is made worse by the fact that on a market, I then sell the product of my labor or my labor itself.[20] Then the thing that I have made is no longer even proximate to me, is no longer mine. Even though I am alienated, I might have treasured it in some way if it were mine.

The second way that trade on the market is alienating is that the worker's labor itself is sold on the market. Marx maintains that the sort of labor one does for a wage is not labor that fulfills a human nature. He bases this claim on the fact that, with wage labor, "as soon as no physical or other compulsion exists, labor is shunned like a plague."[21] We all know of people who have this attitude toward their jobs. In contrast, some of us have jobs, which we enjoy, at least in part, and find personally satisfying.

Selling labor on the market is thought to be alienating because it involves working under the direction of another. The alienation is intensified, according to Marx, because, in exchange for our labor and for the commodities produced by our work, we receive money. It is characteristic of money that it is absolutely exchangeable. There is nothing distinctive about any unit of money. As a consequence, the money I receive for my labor has none of my personality. So I give up something that has my personality for something that does not, and that is even more alienating. But if money is estranging, the lack of it is also said to be estranging.

Marx is critical of frustrating work: if the result of selling your labor is a money reward but no personal satisfaction, then it is imprudent and not conducive to personal flourishing to sell your labor in an alienating market transaction when alternatives are available.

In fact, not all market exchanges are alienating in this way. I am writing this essay now. That is labor. I will sell first publication rights to the product of this labor for money. But I will suffer no estrangement through this transaction. A cellist arrives in town, plays a concerto with the local orchestra, is paid, and leaves town. Where is the alienation there? Perhaps he does not make close affective ties with any of the orchestra members. But it would have been wrong to count on such during a short visit. The cellist's close affective ties must come from other contexts. But in the case of either type of alienation, it is hard to see any in this case.

Information and alienation. When I was a youngster, I acquired information about which jobs were likely to be alienating and which were not. I then oriented myself to the nonalienating ones. My classmates did not seem to place a premium on whether alienation was involved in their work, some of which paid more than the work that I undertook. I did mind. There was information available and freedom to decide which types of work we would do. I used it to avoid alienation. Had there not been either information flowing about the character of jobs or the freedom to contract as I and others wanted for jobs, it is very likely that I would not have been able to avoid alienation in Marx's first two senses.

Now, and this is vitally important to the topic of alienation and the morality of markets, the requisites mentioned in the last paragraph amount to saying that unless there had been a job *market,* I might not have been able to avoid alienation. Market exchanges, far from condemning one to alienation, offer the possibility of redemption from it. So markets, in general, cannot be held responsible for alienation, only certain transactions can be, and they are avoidable if there is a market.

Alienation and others.   The third type of alienation that Marx lays at the door of the market economy is the loss of a sense of dominion over all of nature, which is properly ours.[22]

The fourth form of alienation, which Marx says results from the market economy, is a failure of a sense of fellow humanness with others and an antagonism among people. A result of capitalist production and distribution causing alienation of the first two sorts, is "the (estrangement of man) from *man.*"[23] Estrangement of the first three sorts show that humans are in strife in the market, or are treating each other in ways that are psychologically distancing.

The *alien* being, to whom labor and the product of labor belongs, in whose service labor is done and for whose benefit the product of labor is provided, can only be *man* himself. If the product of labor does not belong to the worker, if it confronts him as an alien power, then this can only be because it belongs to some *other man than the worker.* If the worker's activity is a torment to him, to another it must be a *delight* and his life's joy. Not the gods, not nature, but only man himself can be this alien power over man.[24]

There is a moral dimension to this form of alienation. One moral requirement is that we be loyal to our own humanness and that requires benevolence toward others. So, if knowing that our employees would be working in alienated conditions, employing them could be a failing of this sense of benevolence and shared humanity. To fail at this is itself to be alienated from the worker as another human being. If the transaction proceeds, then the worker will also be alienated from me because there is little human regard in our relationship.[25]

There are exceptions to this. Suppose the worker says to me "I know that this job is alienating and I appreciate your concern, but I know that this is the best job that I can get for the short run, and so I want it anyway. Just don't expect me to stay on it any longer than it will take me to find different work." In that case, I may concur and employ the worker. That would be an instance of the importance of freedom of contract for treating others as ends in themselves.[26] Moral insensitivity to a prospective employee's job-related alienation means asking another person to live for *our* sake, not for his or her own.

Different thinkers will evaluate differently the implications of alienation for the morality of markets. It seems that Marx either wants to deny that markets are devices for cooperation of the sort we have sketched earlier, or he is denying that societies ever actually have markets. His only case for the first of these two choices is the importance of the first two kinds of alienation. Some market transactions do involve alienation. But importantly, markets are also devices for *avoiding* alienation.

Aquinas and Just Prices

Karl Marx is not the only nonutilitarian critic of the market. Some thinkers revert to a notion of justice that is individual-rights centered, as opposed to social end state centered. Saint Thomas Aquinas, though generally utilitarian in his discussion of markets and morals, gives one nonutilitarian ground for calling profit lawful: "when he [the trader] seeks profit, not for its own sake, but as a reward for his labor."[27] Here the use of the word "reward" suggests a natural order of justice in nature. So much work is entitled to so much reward. Various thinkers have attempted to make this notion precise, but no one has succeeded. Classical economists like Adam Smith believed that labor created wealth as a direct function of time spent. And the last classical economist, Karl Marx used the labor theory of value to underlay his theory of capitalist exploitation. Since the workers in factories clearly work, and since it is not clear to the workers, at least, that the owners of factories, the capitalists, work, then making money from the labor of the workers is exploitation.[28]

It is worth noting that the Marxist moral exploitation theory appeals to this same notion that Aquinas uses. It holds that the capitalist who does not work receives an unjust reward in terms of profit stolen in the form of surplus labor value from the workers who did produce it. Labor itself, regardless of the terms of the contracts people freely enter into to sell it, has a certain morally *required* return.

Those capitalists who are quick to point out the many excellent activities of the owners of industry, accept with the Marxists and Aquinas the legitimacy of this picture of a just fitting of reward with labor. Lucky results are somehow ruled out of moral consideration. And that is unfortunate, because luck plays a big role in business, as in the rest of life.

Subsequent economists have abandoned the labor theory of value and so have abandoned the notion that the economic value of my work and, hence, its proper rate of return is independent of the desires and choices of other people. The economic value simply is what it will fetch on the market and what it will fetch is caused by a complex of factors involving the free choices of trading partners established on the market.[29]

The notion of a correct or moderate price operates as a criterion of justice independent of people freely contracting to do what they want with their labor and its products. The deontological defense of markets above is that markets leave people free to pursue their own well-being on their best vision of that well-being and of its causes. To say that there is a just price independent of and potentially inconsistent with people's exercise of their right to pursue their own well-being on the basis of their own judgment is to make justice incompatible with human rights. At best, this is to put deontological considerations at war with each other. At worst, it is to remove the nonutilitarian concept of justice from its foundation in human rights theory.

The notion of a fair or just price is also imprecise. What is the criterion of moderateness? Profits must first be moderate. But what is the gauge of what is moderate? How could there be a gauge that was not arbitrary? If a person gives incalculable reward to a community whose members gladly pay him or her while thinking that they are paying next to nothing for what they get in return, then 200% profit would not be excessive. But if that would not be, what would be?

One possible answer involves paternalism. We could say that only what is good for you, in fact, should be rewarded, so we will see to it that you only reward the provisioners of good things. When we say that, we adopt the rights and responsibilities of a parent to the person we address — hence paternalism. If we were to treat an individual other than our dependent child in this way, we would be violating that person's right to act on his or her best judgment. This has no deontological justification.[30] Were we to try a more generalized program of such actions to realize maximal good in a community, then we would lapse back into a utilitarian critique of markets and encounter the difficulties we encountered above, including the calculation problem.

Recently freedom of contract has come under a friendlier form of criticism and restriction. I have in mind the doctrine of unconscionability in law.[31] Some contracts have been held not to have been freely entered into despite the beliefs of their parties to the contrary, because features of the putative contract show this absence of freedom. Perhaps the parties had unequal bargaining power. In that case, the stronger power could have overcome the other and there would have been no free consent on the weaker party's part. Perhaps the disparity of compensation in the contract would show that no one would freely agree to such terms.[32]

If it was shown that there was absence of free consent in a particular trade, that would remove all deontological support from that trade. So this part of law is on the right track in its understanding of the deontological justification of market transactions.[33]

Particular Cases

Middlemen

Middlemen facilitate trade and cooperation by coordinating sellers and buyers. I, for example, need a buyer for a typewriter that I have for sale. I would be glad if a middleman came along and coordinated me with a market. If such a person came to me with a buyer, I would be glad to pay him or her for doing this. Stockbrokers, for example, sell stocks and by so doing coordinate would-be investors with firms issuing stocks to raise money for potentially profitable ventures. I only trade with discount brokers. And they charge me only for the execution of orders. This is less than the full-service broker who researches firms and associates me with those firms that are reasonably expected to make profits. Whether this falls within or outside the morally defensible in the market is a question of whether this is an ideal or optimal device for making cooperation possible among people with overlapping purposes.

Speculators

Speculators, a kind of broker, are people who are paid for taking other people's risks. If I am a farmer who has planted enough wheat to garner 100,000 bushels, then it will make some large difference to me whether wheat is selling for $8 per bushel or for $5 per bushel when the wheat is harvested.[34] I plan to handle all of my next year's economic transactions from the income I will get from selling this year's wheat. That income will determine how much I can eat, whether my children will go to a high-priced college, whether I can afford to have my farm machinery repaired (so I can use machinery in the production of hoped-for future income), and even how much of a crop I can afford to plant next year.

If I am a gambler and enjoy risk, I might want to bet the well-being of my farm on the future price of wheat. However, if I am averse to taking risks and enjoy security, as many people do, then I will wish to be rid of the insecurity I have about how much the price of wheat will be when I sell it.

Suppose that my best calculations are that I will need $650,000 in proceeds from my wheat in order to meet my financial obligations and to have a little left for luxuries. $800,000 would be nice. $500,000 would be a disaster; with that income I would have to sell the farm and look for something else to do with my life. Suppose further that I seek security and would like to be out of my risky situation if I could be. It would be nice if I could find someone who would like to buy my wheat for $650,000 now. If I could, I would sell it to that person gladly.

Such persons exist. They are called speculators. They buy "futures contracts" in wheat and other commodities and assets. That is, they assume the risks that others do not choose to hold in the hopes that the future price of the commodity will be greater than the present price at which they buy it. Sometimes it is and sometimes it isn't. That's the risk.

So, I sell to a speculator at $650,000 and get the money that I need, plus security. As this story is told, it is a completely cooperative affair. The speculator and I cooperate. The speculator has taken the risk off my hands. In return, there are no guarantees. But if wheat does sell at $8 per bushel, then the speculator will make $150,000 on my wheat — a profit of 23%.

If wheat does sell at $8 per bushel, then perhaps it was a bad thing for me to have sold it at $6.50 per bushel. The speculator sold me what I desired — security.

If this were to happen, my situation would be the same as that of the person who desired a commodity and enthusiastically paid more for it than it was, in fact, worth to her/him. Critics of the profits of speculators either do not recognize this similarity of cases or they do not agree that the deontological moral defense of market institutions or their rivals, trades on preserving feeedom of action instead of preserving good results.

Agents

Agents are another often disparaged group of businesspersons on the market. Comedian Fred Allen is reported to have said about Hollywood, "You can take all of the sincerity in this town and stuff it in a flea's navel and still have room left for an agent's heart." Agents are frequently ill-thought of. And indeed the agent-client relation in the entertainment industry looks at first almost like a master-slave relation in some of its aspects. Because of a contract entered into years ago, a film superstar who has his/her choice of million dollar roles still has to pay 10% to an agent who no longer has to work to place the client. Consequently, some clients come to see agents as parasites. But this is a mistake.

An agent is best seen as a combination of a middleman and a speculator. The criticisms of the last paragraph arise from just attending to the middleman role. But the agent is also a speculator. In the beginning, the agent works without return for the client, works to get the client known, and works to get the client jobs. But this is risky. It is a risk that was formerly completely born by the client. If all that work and expense come to naught; the client owes the agent nothing. The agent assumes the costs and risks of promotion for the client. The agent, in turn, freely accepts the risk as a gamble that 10% of the client's future earnings will be a lucrative return for the effort spent. Whether this falls within or outside the morally defensible in the market is a question of whether this is an ideal device for making cooperation possible among people with overlapping purposes.

Immoral Trades

Fraud

Even thinkers like Ayn Rand who are optimistic about the morality of markets allow that there are some economic transfers that seem to be voluntary but are immoral. For example, if, by representing myself, I sell you a house that I do not own, that would be immoral. Similarly, I defraud you if I sell you a car, representing to you that it is in perfect condition when I know that it will fall apart within the first ten miles of use, or that the brakes are unreliable. Each of these imagined transactions would be indecent, callous cases of fraud, and Rand and others brand them immoral.[36] A good bit of the basis of the doctrine of unconscionability above is that such unconscionable contracts can be fraudulent. Rand makes a case that fraudulent transactions involve the initiation of force and so are not voluntary. By implication, they are not market transactions. "Fraud involves a similarly indirect use of force: it consists of obtaining material values without their owner's consent, under false pretenses or false promises."[36] The theory may or may not hold up that fraudulent transactions are not market transactions. But whether or not fraudulent transactions are the market exchanges they seem to be at the time that they are entered into, they are immoral.

Here the immorality is in treating another as a means to our ends (acquiring the other's property) without treating the other as an end in himself or herself. We pay lip service to the treatment of the other as an end when we volunteer to meet the other's ends by offering a car in working condition. We then fail to deliver on our promise to do something consonant with the ends of the other in exchange for securing our ends.

It would have been all right if the other had allowed us this result as a gift. In that case, I treat the other as an autonomous person with ends by acquiescing to the other's judgment — even the one to bestow gifts on me.[37] But in cases of fraud, the other has not consented.

Other Cases

There are more controversial examples of immoral trades. One which has a popular following and for which some reason can be given, is prostitution, the buying and selling of sex. It is probably immoral, in some cases at least, to be a prostitute or to trade with them.[38]

Another example is selling drugs when one knows that the consequence of the purchaser using the drug, given their health or state of intoxication, will be instant death. Knowing that others will die if I sell them the drug is good reason not to sell them the drug.

An action such as a trade on the market might be ill-intentioned. I may sell you perfectly good food under the mistaken opinion that it was poisonous and that you will suffer great, unwanted harm as a result of buying and using it. This action clearly is immoral.

Whether any of these immoral practices fall within the deontological defense of the market or not is open to a simple test. The deontological defense treats people having institutions that would allow them to cooperate freely in projects. The simple test of whether or not the *trades* are moral as trades is whether, if the practices were outlawed, a black market would arise in those trades. In the case of prostitution and drugs, the answer is clearly yes. Outlawing prostitution and drug traffic blocks cooperation among people in pursuit of their ends. Conversely, the markets further those ends.[39] On the other hand, outlawing fraud and extortion would not lead to a black market in those practices. So they are not cooperative ventures and do not fall within the scope of the deontological defense of market institutions.

What this shows is that, in some cases, an action can be correct as a trade and incorrect as a failing to care for the well-being of self or of another. Similarly, something can be immoral both as a trade and as a failing to care for another.

There is nothing unusual about this. Many actions are such that if only part of their character is specified, they would receive praise for that part, while if other aspects were highlighted, they would look onerous. If you provide liver transplants for free or at a reasonable fee, that is fine. But if you don't get the consent of the donors, that part of your transactions is wrong. Breaking a promise is generally wrong, but when a friend's life depends on it, that command of benevolence can so override the wrongness of promise-breaking as to make that the right thing to do.

So too with the morality of market transactions. A number of them may be good as market transactions. Yet other considerations, like the care of one's character, may raise negative considerations that outweigh the positive and make a particular act wrong. But not wrong *as a market transaction,* wrong as a failure to take care, or under some other description. To find immoral transactions, we have to look to cases like fraud or conspiracy to violate another's rights of life or property or freedom to pursue one's own ends.

Notes

1. The difference between the words "can" and "may" is important here. "Can" connotes possibility of achievement, and that is the term which I have been using throughout. "May" connotes the moral or legal permissibility of an action.

2. The classical statement of this theory is by G. E. Moore, *Principia Ethica* (Cambridge: Cambridge University Press, 1971), pp. 24–26, 147–48.

3. Karl Marx allowed for values other than utilities to be realized. That is discussed below.

4. Karl Marx and Friedrich Engels for example, writing about the new bourgeoisie market economy said: "It has been the first to show what man's activity can bring about. It has accomplished wonders far surpassing Egyptian pyramids, Roman aqueducts, and Gothic cathedrals; it has conducted expeditions that put in the shade all former Exoduses of nations and crusades. . . . The bourgeoisie, during its rule of scarce one hundred years, has created more massive and more colossal productive forces than have all preceding generations together. Subjection of Nature's forces to man, machinery, application of chemistry to industry and agriculture, steam navigation, railways, electric telegraphs, clearing of whole continents for cultivation, canalization of rivers, whole populations conjured out of the ground — what earlier century had even a presentiment that such productive forces slumbered in the lap of social labor?" Karl Marx and Friedrich Engels, *The Manifesto of the Communist Party,* in Lewis Feuer, ed., *Basic Writings on Politics and Philosophy* (Garden City, N.J.: Anchor Books, 1959), p. 12.

5. I use the word, "someone," because it leaves open all sorts of ways that economies can be centrally directed: by one person with autocratic powers; by a board of such people where the board takes on that power; by a body of regulatory agencies subject to legislative, judicial and administrative control; or it may even be by the people as a whole, determining by majority political vote what will be imposed on people as a whole — so-called economic democracy. And there are probably other possible ways that "someone" may be interpreted.

6. The calculation problem is the difficulty, for centrally planned economies, which was first formulated by Ludwig von Mises in *"Die Wirtschaftsrechnung im sozialistischen Gemeinwessen,"* and developed by Friedrich A. Hayek, in many places, but chiefly in his "The Use of Knowledge in Society." Mises essay is translated and reprinted in F. A. Hayek, ed. *Collectivist Economic Planning* (London: Routledge & Kegan Paul, 1963). This volume collects all of the major papers of Mises and Friedrich Hayek on this topic. References are to this volume unless otherwise noted.

7. This presupposes, innocuously, that the good is not some such thing as universal destruction or universal suffering, or some other thing more likely to proceed from inefficient production and distribution of goods and services.

8. This is not to deny that utilitarians could come up with good reasons, in another style, to support this judgment. They can.

9. It is assumed that I did not have a contractual obligation not to write this paper and that someone else had not copyrighted this paper first, and that I had not promised to do something else at the time. But if anything, including your reading this paper, is ever morally permissible, a similar set of such conditions obtains.

10. In a particularly extreme case like an attempt at suicide, we may interfere with someone because we think that the attempt is not based on the person's best judgment of the situation. But in doing this, we may be wrong. The test is whether, after some further discussion, the other person freely approves of what we did. If the other person says, "I wanted to do it, I still do, and you had no right to interfere," then they are right.

11. Two quick technical qualifications: first, it does not follow that because an individual has a need for something in a particular situation in order to act rightly, that person has a right to the needed thing. But the argument I am presenting is about a necessary condition for any person undertaking any right action, and those elements of universality make the difference. Second, parents have the responsibility

to direct children in order to start the development of their practical reason, and then when it is developed, to gradually let the children go off to lives of self-direction.

12. This style of generation of the relevant rights is attempted by Eric Mack, "Egoism and Rights," *The Personalist* (Winter 1973); Tibor Machan, *Human Rights and Human Liberties* (Chicago: Nelson Hall, 1975c); and Ayn Rand, *The Virtue of Selfishness* (New York: New American Library, 1964).

13. *A Theory of Justice* (Cambridge: Harvard University Press, 1971).

14. In addition to Rawls, see James Buchanan and Gordon Tullock, *The Calculus of Consent* (Ann Arbor: University of Michigan Press, 1962).

15. James Buchanan, *The Demand and Supply of Public Goods* (Chicago: Rand McNally, 1968), chap. 5.

16. For an alternative attempt to defuse the public goods problem for the market, see Tibor Machan, "Dissolving the Problem of Public Goods" in T. R. Machan, ed. *The Libertarian Reader* (Totowa, NJ: Rowman and Littlefield, 1982).

17. John Maynard Keynes, *The End of Laissez-faire* (London: Leonard and Virginia Wolf, 1927), p. 39. Italics and strange capitalizations Keynes's.

18. In point of fact, as the calculation problem shows, a planned economy will be inherently frustrated by information gaps. And so, except in cases of accident, or self-contained small-scale enterprises, situations that a utilitarian interventionist would appeal to are unlikely to occur.

19. Karl Marx, *Economic and Philosophical Manuscripts of 1844* ed. D. Struik, trans. M. Milligan (New York: International Publishers, 1982), p. 108. And, "The alienation of the worker in his product means not only that his labor becomes an object, an *external* existence, but that it exists *outside him,* independently, as something alien to him and that it becomes a power on its own confronting him." (Ibid.) This of course is directly the situation of the slave in the master-slave dialectic at the beginning of Georg Hegel's *The Phenomenology of Spirit.*

20. For a nonmarket form of both of these kinds of alienation, see G. W. F. Hegel, *The Phenomenology of Mind,* J. B. Baillie, trans. (NY: Harper and Row, 1967), pp. 235, 238–89.

21. Ibid., p. 11.

22. "Man is a species being, not only because in practice and in theory he adopts the species as his object (his own as well as those of other things), but—and this is only another way of expressing it—also because he treats himself as the actual, living species; because he treats himself as a *universal* and therefore a free being. . . . The universality of man appears in practice precisely in the universality which makes all nature his *inorganic* body—both inasmuch as nature is (1) his direct means of life, and (2) the material, the object, and the instrument of his life activity. Nature is man's *inorganic body*—nature, that is, insofar as it is not itself the human body. Man *lives* on nature—means that nature is his *body,* with which he must remain in continuous interchange if he is not to die." (Ibid., p. 112). It is not clear that this loss of a sense of dominion is directly a function of market activity except remotely insofar as the division of labor facilitates production for trade. It is clear that Marx thinks that the suspension of the market with the coming of communism with social planning of production will eliminate this form of exploitation.

23. Ibid., p. 114.

24. Ibid., p. 115. It is not necessary to Marx's case that the employer take pleasure in the worker's sorry state in alienated labor. The worker is alienated enough even if the employer is either well intentioned or oblivious to the problems of the worker.

25. It is to be observed that the terms worker and employer can be replaced by the terms husband and wife and a critique of certain sexist marriages results.

26. Again these are the sort of moral concerns that the robust champion of free markets, Ayn Rand, treated seriously. She has the idealized heroes of one of her novels all swear the following oath: "I swear — by my life and by my love of it — that I will never live for the sake of another man, nor ask another man to live for mine." *Atlas Shrugged* (New York: Random House, 1957), p. 1069.

27. *Summa Theologica,* Question 77, Article 4, conclusion.

28. First, it is clear that almost all capitalists work, but it is easy to see how one could miss this fact. The work that the capitalist does is different in kind from that of the factory workers. It involves planning to meet the market, arranging financing, etc. From the outside, it may not look like work, but it is. Second, it is unclear whether Marx attached any moral censure to this situation. See William J. Baumol, "Marx and the Iron Law of Wages," *The American Economic Review* 73 (May 1983): 306.

29. Sidney Trivus, "Dissolving a Muddle in Economics or Dr. Marx Meets Lord Russell," *Reason Papers* 2 (Fall 1975): 7–12, also his "The Irrelevance of the Subjective." *Reason Papers* 3 (Fall 1976): 94–95. Ayn Rand indicated a conception of economic value similar to this, based on the scholastic notion of objective being, but the relation between the cause of something's being of value and the state of its being of value is less clear in her brief indication of the desiderata of a theory of value compatible with capitalism. *Capitalism the Unknown Ideal,* pp. 22–24.

30. We could gamble here and act, hoping that on consideration the affected party would approve our action on reflection. But it is a gamble and the rightness or wrongness of our action will come out of that approval or lack of it. Our action, however, cannot wait. But see Steven Kelman, "Regulation and Paternalism" in M. B. Johnson and T. R. Machan (eds.) *Rights and Regulation: Ethical, Political, and Economic Issues* (Cambridge, MA: Ballinger Publishing Co., 1983.

31. For a discussion of this doctrine see Lewis A. Kornhauser, "Unconscionability in Standard Forms," *California Law Review* 64 (1976).

32. Here the deontological principle that freedom of contract is to be preserved is retained. It is defended in spite of what the results of people's free choices were. Results are only appealed to as evidence for or against the presence of free choice.

33. Whether there are other defects with it as a doctrine of law is a topic that I do not address here. The notion of economic bargaining power is very much more imprecise than I am indicating here. Further, although some courts have been good about this, [*Morris v. Capitol Furniture and Appliance Co.*, 280 A.2d 775 (D.C. Ct. App. 1971)], there is tremendous opportunity for paternalism in particular cases arising out of different interpretations of what is acceptable compensation. I might think that a certain compensation is all right and freely contract for it. A court might have a different assessment of what is worth what and so forbid me to contract here.

34. It makes a difference of $300,000.

35. Ayn Rand, *Capitalism: the Unknown Ideal* (New York: New American Library, 1967), p. 333. See also John Hospers, *Libertarianism* (Los Angeles: Nash Publishing, 1971c), pp. 93–94.

36. Ayn Rand, *Capitalism,* p. 333. There she also treats extortion as indirect use of force.

37. In some cases, it could be wrong to accept gifts. It might be ignoble or a failing in benevolence to see someone deprive themselves for our benefit.

38. I only indicate the salient fact that might make this true in some cases. It can be demeaning to one's sexuality and thus to one's full flourishing to compound the

sexual response with considerations of money and exchange. The psychological consequences of so doing for many people are pretty well documented. Also, the recent introduction of the sexually transmitted viral infection that leads to Acquired Immune Deficiency Syndrome (AIDS) to the human environment can make prostitution unacceptably dangerous to both the prostitute and the client. Ignoring this fact to engage in prostitution would be morally objectionable.

39. I quickly note that cooperation in doing the immoral does not make a justification of doing the immoral. So, although there is a black market for professional murders, that sign of cooperation between A and B who want to have C killed is nothing to the point, as murdering C is immoral on independent grounds. Further it is hard to see the envisioned situation as cooperation among people unless C wants to die, then and in that way.

References

Aquinas, Thomas. *Selected Political Writings*. Ed. A. P. D'Entreves, trans. J. G. Dawson Oxford: Basil Blackwell, 1959.

Baumol, William J. "Marx and the Iron Law of Wages." *The American Economic Review* 73 (May 1983): 306.

Buchanan, James M. *The Demand and Supply of Public Goods* (Chicago: Rand McNally, 1968).

Hayek, Friedrich A. "Socialist Calculation III: The Competitive 'Solution.'" *Economica* 7 (May 1940).

Hegel, Georg. *The Phenomenology of Mind*. Trans. J. B. Baillie (New York: Harper & Row, 1967).

Hospers, John. *Libertarianism* (Los Angeles: Nash Publishing, 1971).

Kelman, Steven. "Regulation and Paternalism" in M. B. Johnson and T. R. Machan (eds.) *Rights and Regulation: Ethical, Political, and Economic Issues* (Cambridge, MA: Ballinger Publishing Co., 1983).

Keynes, John Maynard. *The End of Laissez-faire* (London: Leonard and Virginia Wolf, 1927).

Kornhauser, Lewis A. "Unconscionability in Standard Forms." *California Law Review* 64 (1976): 1151–1183.

Mack, Eric. "Egoism and Rights." *The Personalist* (Winter 1973).

Machan, Tibor. "Dissolving the Problem of Public Goods: Financing Government without Coercive Measures," in T. Machan, ed., *The Libertarian Reader* (Totowa, NJ: Rowman and Littlefield, 1982).

_____ . *Human Rights and Human Liberties: A Radical Reconsideration of the American Political Tradition* (Chicago: Nelson Hall, 1975).

Marx, Karl. *Economic and Philosophical Manuscripts of 1844*. Ed. D. Struik, trans. M. Milligan (New York: International Publishers, 1982).

Marx, Karl, and Frederick Engles. *The Manifesto of the Communist Party,* in Lewis Feuer, ed., *Marx and Engles: Basic Writings on Politics and Philosophy* (Garden City, N.J.: Anchor Books, 1959).

Mises, Ludwig von. *"Die Hirtschaftsrechnung im sozialistischen Gemeinwessen"* [Economic Calculation in the Socialist Commonwealth] in F. A. Hayek, ed. *Collectivist Economic Planning* (London: Routledge & Kegan Paul, 1963).

Moore, G. E. *Principia Ethica* (Cambridge: Cambridge University Press, 1971).

Rand, Ayn. *Atlas Shrugged* (New York: Random House, 1957).

_____ . *The Virtue of Selfishness* (New York: New American Library, 1964).

_____ . *Capitalism: The Unknown Ideal* (New York: New American Library, 1967).

Rawls, John. *A Theory of Justice* (Cambridge: Harvard University Press, 1971).

Smith, Adam. *An Inquiry into the Nature and Causes of the Wealth of Nations* (New York: P. F. Collier and Son, 1901).

Sidney Trivus, "Dissolving a Muddle in Economics or Dr. Marx Meets Lord Rusell." *Reason Papers* 2 (Fall 1975): 1-14.

_____ . "The Irrelevance of the Subjective." *Reason Papers* 3 (Fall 1976): 83-89.

Part
II

BUSINESS
AND LAW

5

ETHICS AND LAW

JOHN HOSPERS

A code of ethics is a set of rules and principles for guiding one's conduct. This code can differ from one person to another. It concerns actions such as keeping promises, misleading people, or lying to them, mistreating animals, helping your family and friends before strangers, and countless other details of life. Only occasionally does law enter into these matters: most people consider murder and theft morally wrong, and the law also holds these acts to be illegal; the law considers them to be not moral wrongs but *crimes*. But most matters of morality are not under the jurisdiction of laws or courts.

Of course, if you believe it is your duty not to pay taxes, or that theft is preferable to honest labor, or that you needn't stop at stop-lights, and you act on these beliefs, then you will run afoul of the law, which will hold these actions to be crimes. But many people flout *moral* rules every day without ever doing anything illegal. The law covers only certain aspects of your life; a code of ethics ideally covers every aspect of life of which you could ask, "Is this act right or wrong?" and "Is this ideal good or bad?" A person can be very bad indeed while yet doing nothing illegal: he may promise marriage to a woman and then renege on his promise. Yet he can't be touched by the law unless he breaks a legal contract.

In contrast to a moral code a code of law includes within its scope everyone in a geographical area: federal law covers everyone in the United States, and California law applies to all persons in California. Moreover, the law does not merely exhort their compliance, it requires it and imposes penalties (fines or jail sentences) for not obeying. Law uses physical force and threat of physical force to make you comply, whereas a system of morality uses only moral persuasion. If the system of morality is based on religion, threat of divine punishment or the hope of eternal reward is an inducement to right behavior.

When you are born into a society, you are subject to its laws whether you want to be or not: if you don't obey its laws, you are punished. But if you

119

violate a moral code, you are punished (if at all) only in "the court of public opinion." If you are unreliable or don't deal honestly with people, they will soon cease to deal with you. That is your punishment, rather than fines or imprisonment.

The Moral vs. the Legal

1.   In some ways, law is less restrictive than morality. Morality is very much "a matter of the heart"; if you have a virtuous disposition and a good character, you can make mistakes and they won't count against you as actions as much as if you did them with evil intent. In morality—most moralities, at any rate—you are just as much to be condemned for your intentions as for your actions. A person who commits adultery "in his heart" is as guilty, according to the Gospels, as he who actually does. This is extremely demanding exhortation, but Christian morality and some other religions hold to it. If you try to shoot someone, but you miss because you're a bad shot, you are as morally guilty as if you hadn't missed; the fact that you missed is no credit to you—you certainly tried to kill someone, and your failure to do so is the result not of lack of will but of lack of skill.

The law handles this matter differently. In law, *there must be an act.* You can be tried for attempted murder (if the attempt can be proved), but the penalty for it is small compared with the penalty for actual murder. Attempted murder is an act; but *intended* murder is not. Under law, we can intend anything we please, but if it doesn't result in an act, we are legally blameless. *Conspiring* to murder is an act that involves planning with at least one other person to murder someone. It is legally punishable as conspiracy, because conspiracy to murder is more than mere intent. An intentional act is usually more heavily punishable in law than an unintentional one—that is the difference between murder and manslaughter; but the question of intention does not arise in law unless there is first an act. In morality there needn't be an act at all.

Suppose a soldier tries to shoot his own lieutenant but misses, and shoots an enemy soldier instead. Morally, he is as guilty as if he had shot his lieutenant; but because he shot an enemy soldier, he is legally blameless. Shooting an enemy soldier in time of war is no offense, and that *is,* however accidentally, the act that he committed. Or suppose you plan to steal someone else's umbrella from the rack at a restaurant; by mistake you take your own umbrella instead. Morally you are guilty—your intention was to steal; but legally there is nothing that constitutes a crime in retrieving your own umbrella.

But if law is less restrictive than morality in judging an act, it can also be more restrictive. In morality, "ought implies can": you cannot have a duty to do something that you can't possibly do. It would be highly desirable to cure all the diseases in the world, but since you can't do that, you have no moral duty to do so. But in law, you are sometimes punishable for not knowing something you could not possibly have known. It is impossible for persons to know all the laws of the county, the state, and the nation in which they live—these laws fill many volumes. It would take most of a lifetime to read them all, and certainly it would be impossible to remember them all. Yet, if you violate even one of these thousands of laws, you are punishable for the violation. Ignorance of the law is not accepted as an excuse. "Ignorance of the law could never be admitted as an excuse, even if the fact could be proved by sight and hearing in every case," wrote Oliver Wendell Holmes[1]. "To admit the excuse at all would be to encourage ignorance where the lawmaker has determined to make men know and obey." If ignorance of the law were permitted, a person accused of murder could say, "But I didn't know, your Honor, that there was a law against murder." And ignorance would then be carefully cultivated: people would purposely remain ignorant so that they could present a plea of ignorance to the court. The rule that ignorance of the law is no excuse, of course, is quite understandable. If ignorance of the law would excuse a person from responsibility, there might as well be no law at all.

When faced with a difficult situation, morality (as a rule) only says of us "Do the best you can—you can't be blamed for failing to do better than your best." But the law sometimes requires more, however unreasonable this may seem. A person who is mentally defective or has a congenital defect, may not be *able* to avoid accidents in which other persons are hurt; but the law of negligence requires such a person to live up to the same standard of "reasonable care" that is expected of everyone else. "When men live in a society," wrote Justice Holmes, "a certain average of conduct, a sacrifice of individual peculiarities going beyond a certain point, is necessary to the general welfare. If, for instance, a man is born hasty and awkward, is always having accidents and hurting himself or his neighbors, no doubt his congenital defects will be allowed for in the courts of Heaven, but his slips are no less troublesome to his neighbors than if they sprang from guilty neglect. His neighbors accordingly require him, at his proper peril, to come up to their standard, and the courts which they establish decline to take this personal equation into account."[2] In other words, their defects make a moral difference, not a legal one.

Negligence law requires that every person live up to a standard of "reasonable care." A woman knocks her head against the hot pipes in a ladies' room of a train; was the company negligent in placing the pipes where they were? Children climb over the railway company's fence and play among the railroad equipment with the result that one of them has an accident; was the railway company negligent, in spite of the fences and warnings? A woman sprains her ankle falling down the subway steps; was the subway company negligent? A donkey grazing on a country road is hit by a passing car; was the driver negligent, or was the owner of the donkey? If the accused party is found negligent, he has to pay damages. The outcome depends on whether the defendant was negligent, i.e., whether he "took reasonable care," i.e. the degree of care a "reasonable person" would take. Workers are supposed to handle cases of Coca-Cola by the handles; a worker instead transports the cases by grasping the bottles by their tops, and one bottle explodes in his hand and injures him; was he negligent, or was the company for not providing sufficient warnings? (*Honea v. Coca-Cola Bottling Co.*, 143 Texas 272, 1944) If a party is found not to have exercised "reasonable care," he pays the damages. Similarly, a conductor is considered justified in expelling a passenger from a bus or train if he reasonably believes the passenger has no ticket. And if one person kills another in the reasonable but mistaken belief that doing so was necessary to preserve his life, he is not guilty of murder.

But not all cases in law are like this. Some cases are decided by *strict liability*. In these cases, you are responsible for the damage even though you took reasonable, even extraordinary, care. Consider the following examples. (1) If a bar owner serves a patron who is under the legal age, his bar may be closed down, even though the patron produced a cleverly forged birth certificate. No matter how careful the bartender was in examining the patron's proof of age, if, *in fact,* the patron was under the legal age, the bar owner is liable. (2) A man elopes with an under-age girl. She says she is over 18, she looks over 18, and her birth certificate says she is 19; but if, in fact, she is under 18, he can be found guilty of "statutory rape," judged by what the facts are, not by what he reasonably believed them to be. (3) If a woman remarries while her husband is still alive, she is guilty of bigamy, even though others have testified to her that they saw the husband die; the facts, not what she reasonably believed them to be, are what counts. (4) A man may take reasonable care, in fact, extraordinary care, in conducting a dangerous activity, such as fumigating other people's houses or raising poisonous snakes. But if an accident nevertheless occurs, he is strictly liable no matter how much care he took. Similarly, if anything drops from an airplane the airline is held to laws of strict liability; the amount of care taken to avoid such accidents is legally irrelevant. (5) A merchant ships a case of corrosive acid from New York City to a city upstate, reasonably believing that the shipment will not leave the state; but unknown to him, part of the shipment is actually made through New Jersey. This places the shipment under Interstate Commerce Regulations that prohibit such shipments without prior permission from state authorities. The merchant is liable without regard to what he reasonably believed. (6) A policeman pursues a suspect with a gun, reasonably believing that the suspect is guilty only of a misdemeanor. The policeman is held liable, since the law permits him to pursue a felon with deadly force but not someone guilty only of a misdemeanor.

Morally, such judgments based on strict liability seem quite unfair. If you do your best, what more can be expected of you? How can you be expected to do more than you can do in the circumstances? It doesn't seem fair that you are held liable for an innocent mistake. Strict liability law, however, ignores such moral considerations. Rather, it views the situation from the point of view of the victim (plaintiff): the victim has suffered damages, and even if they weren't the defendant's fault, as long as the defendant was a cause of the damage, he has to pay. If you were the victim, wouldn't you want to be recompensed for damages, even if the accident was not due to the defendant's failure to take reasonable care? (If, however, the damages cannot be attributed to any human being—if it was the result of tornado, earthquake, lightning, flood—then it was "an act of God" and no one is liable for damages.)

The tendency of the law today is to increase the range of strict liability offenses. Is this in accordance with morality? It isn't if "ought implies can," and you have done the best you can; but if you are the injured party who wants only to receive money for damages incurred, then you may wish strict liability offenses to be extended even further. The trouble is that you never know in advance which you are going to be.

Law as a Reflection of Societal Morality

In spite of these differences between the legal and the moral approach to problems, there are also great similarities. You can infer much about the prevailing morality of a society by examining its code of law. If enough people in a society think a particular act is wrong, they are likely to say, "Pass a law against it." and the prohibition will become law. Enough people in the United States were opposed to the sale and consumption of alcoholic beverages to pass the Volstead Act (Prohibition) and to encourage their legislators to pass a constitutional amendment against the consumption of alcohol; later, enough people felt differently so that the amendment was repealed.

Legal moralism is the name given to any system of law that attempts to impose one code of morality on an entire society or nation. The regime of the Ayatollah Khomeini in Iran is an example of legal moralism that imposes virtually the entire Muslim morality upon every resident of the nation. Legal moralism can be made to work if the vast majority of citizens share the same moral convictions.

It can also be made to work, though with much more internal dissension when the nation is a dictatorship and the people face terrible punishments for refusing to obey. The majority of Russians surely do not *approve* the practice of children reporting to the authorities their parents' antigovernment conversations so that the parents may be shot or sent to labor camps for many years. But the police are so omnipresent, and the punishments so great, that many people who would not otherwise conform to such laws do so out of fear and terror.

By contrast, the United States is a relatively free nation. It is also a heterogeneous society with many races and creeds, a melting pot of diverse cultures and moralities. In the United States, it would be difficult to enact and enforce a moral code that was opposed by the vast majority of the population. The issue would be subjected to wide press coverage, and there would be popular movements to throw out of office the legislators who enacted such unpopular laws.

Thus, in the case of *Griswold v. Connecticut* (1965), the Supreme Court invalidated a Connecticut law that prohibited the dissemination of information and medical advice, even to married persons, as to the means of preventing conception. Connecticut, a mostly Catholic state, had enacted this law, and the Supreme Court declared it unconstitutional. Whether or not to employ birth-control devices, said the court, was for the individuals concerned to decide.

On the other hand, in 1892 the Supreme Court denied the petition of the Mormon Church to continue the practice of polygamy. One might say that "that's the Mormons' business—if they want a man to have more than one wife, who has the right to say he may not?" But the United States has always been a monogomous society—a man can only have one legal wife—and the prevailing morality within the United States disapproved of polygamy; so the law followed the prevailing morality, and the Mormon practice was made illegal.

There are countless examples of prevailing morality becoming law. Most persons don't like to have their privacy invaded and so they approve laws against invasion of privacy. But they also like to read uncensored news; so if a man tries to stop newspapers from carrying reports of his wife's suicide, charging that this is an invasion of his privacy, the newspapers believe that "the news comes first" even when it does invade someone's privacy, and so the law, too, takes this position.

Business and the Law

One purpose of the law on which virtually everyone will agree is to enable people, however diverse their goals and moralities, to live together in peace, so they can pursue their individual goals without constant fear. For this purpose to be achieved, it is necessary to have police to protect individuals from aggressors inside their nation; armed forces to protect the populace from aggressors outside the nation; and courts to adjudicate disputes, so that not every dispute will break out into open warfare.

When it is said that the main function of the law is protection, this means not only protection of life, but also of property. In order to be able to plan their own future, people must be able to possess something they can call their own. If your business requires office equipment and a computer, you must be able to own these things and be sure that they won't be taken away from you—so the law must protect you against theft. If you are a farmer, you must be able to plant crops in the expectation that you can harvest them, without vandals coming on your land and destroying your crops—so the law must protect you against trespass. "Crimes against the person" include assault, rape, mutilation, and murder; "crimes against property" include theft, embezzlement, extortion, fraud, and mayhem.

Many persons would say that providing such protection is the *only* function of the law—that if the law tries to do more than this, it interferes too much with people's lives. Others, however, believe that the law should, for example, protect one from libel and slander as well as from invasion of privacy; that the law should provide housing regulations; building, zoning, electrical and plumbing codes; regulation of foods and drugs; that it should provide payments (out of taxation) for the unemployed; and so on.

Business enterprises cannot flourish in the midst of civil commotion, and gladly pay taxes to protect themselves for the peaceful pursuit of their activities. With regard to the second class of laws, however, businessmen differ enormously—some would approve of antidrug laws, for example, and others would not. But in general, they prefer to have as few laws as possible that interfere with the conduct of their business.

The attitude of the businessman toward "law and order" is certain to be quite positive: he cannot conduct his business except against a background of peace. If there is a crime wave and the police force has to be expanded, he willingly pays to support this. But his attitude toward laws he considers, at best, useless, or, at worst immoral, is quite different, and it is in relation to these laws that he is presented with difficult moral choices. Should he obey the law, willingly or unwillingly? Should he actively oppose compliance and risk fines and jail sentences? Here are some examples of situations involving the law in which virtually every businessman today is forced to take some stand or other:

1. Sometimes a man's business enterprise causes damage to other persons or to their property. For instance, if you own a factory whose smokestacks emit smoke and sulfur into the air, and the wind blows it onto other people's property, it may cause illness and lung damage, and, at the very least, discomfort and annoyance. But to install equipment that would prevent these contaminants from entering the atmosphere would be expen-

sive—it would be much cheaper for you not to install it. What should you do?

Well, you wouldn't want other people's smokestacks to pollute *your* air. You would be annoyed if pollutants from elsewhere blew onto your house or yard. It might be better all round if none of these pollutants were emitted.

But not everyone would voluntarily comply with such a rule; there would always be some manufacturers who preferred to emit pollutants in order to save money and underprice their competitors. So there would have to be a law prohibiting everyone—yourself included, of course—from emitting these pollutants. It would be more expensive for you, but it would also be more expensive for your competitors. Yet such a law would be the only way to enforce everyone's compliance, and everyone's compliance would be desirable, since only in this way could everyone breathe clean, healthful air.

The same considerations would approve any kind of legislation that prohibits one person from damaging another person's property. If one man lives upstream from another and pollutes the water, this would prevent healthful use of the water by a person living downstream, and the person downstream should have a legal case against the polluter upstream.

In other cases, however, the guilty party is not so easy to identify, but what of the thousands of automobiles that are polluting the air? Not one person or organization but millions of car-users together cause the pollution. Should all of them be fined? Should the car manufacturers be fined? Or should every car owner be required to use antipollution devices on his car? The last mentioned alternative is a reality today. Perhaps it is the best alternative. But there are several precautions:

Some antipollution laws cause great nuisance but have very little effect. Most garage-owners will tell you that catalytic converters do little or nothing to prevent pollution; yet they add greatly to the cost of every car. Certain garages are licensed by the state to inspect your car, and others (equally capable) are not.

Inspection requirements easily become political footballs, increasing one's fees but not one's safety if no one is truly accountable for the inspection.

A second problem concerns the level of pollution that is to be permitted. In an industrial society, it is impossible to get rid of all pollution: it costs little to lower pollution by 5%; to lower it 10% costs about five times as much, and to lower it 40% or 45% becomes so expensive that most factories would have to close down to implement such antipollution devices. Besides, much pollution is caused by nature herself and not by human activities. A great deal of information about pollution is overstated in the press. The Santa Barbara oil spill of some years ago was given headlines for months, and it was widely believed that that section of the ocean would become permanently uninhabitable for fish, and yet it turned out not only that the effects had worn off long before anyone thought they would, but that, in some ways, the compounds containing the oil were beneficial—the fish thrived especially well in that area.[3]

(2.) The businessman doesn't want the government with its coercive powers to tell him how to run his business. Yet governmental agencies do just that, and confronted by the coercive apparatus of government, the businessman is not sure what to do. Suppose he, as the owner of a foundry, is fined by the regulatory agency, OSHA (Occupational Safety and Health Act), for an excess of silica dust in his plant. He finds out from a consultant that the dust comes from heavy traffic, which the city has detoured onto an unpaved road running past the foundry. Nevertheless *he* is fined, and the total cost to him is over $100,000. Or suppose the head of a construction firm is fined for a minor violation. The business owner contends that there was no violation; he is determined to fight the judgment. But if he appeals the case, there is a $1,000 per day penalty for each day during which the case is appealed. Since he can't absorb these plus the legal costs, he writes to his senator. Shortly thereafter, the district director of OSHA comes to the plant, attacking him for having written a letter to his senator criticizing OSHA. Swarms of inspectors then descend on the plant, fining him so heavily that he has to go out of business.[4]

Even trying to find out what the regulations are can cost hundreds of dollars to buy the documents containing the millions of words in the regulations. But more and more regulations are passed by the bureaucrats in Washington. You may ask OSHA itself for help in determining how you are to comply, but if you do, the officers will conduct an inspection that could result in a large assessment of penalties against you.

As it did many other regulatory agencies, Congress established OSHA in the name of safety—something no one can deny is important. There already were laws against negligence, unsafe operations, and harm resulting therefrom (some common law, some statute law), and indeed the record of factory safety was hardly improved by OSHA: its main effect has been to create a regulatory bureaucracy that makes and enforces its own rules, costs taxpayers a lot of money, and subjects every business to regulations (often pointless and stupid) that multiply the workload, cause wasted man-hours, and do nothing to increase safety.

It is the same with building codes, fire codes, zoning ordinances, and many other activities now heavily regulated. They all have a valuable purpose—the enhancement of safety. But they easily become politicized and result in a large bureaucracy that drains the economy, preventing money and workers from going into productive activities, and places an extra financial burden on those who do. For example, (a) a city building ordinance prohibits sandpiles near building sites. But it is impossible to build any high-rise apartment building without such sandpiles. So the building contractor does the obvious thing: he bribes the building inspector for not reporting the violation. This practice, of course, increases the cost of all building in the city, without any benefit to anyone but the inspector. (b) A city fire ordinance requires such high standards of fire prevention that more than half the businesses in the city would go bankrupt if they were to follow the ordinance in all its details. So the fire inspector on his monthly visit inspects just one thing: the manager's desk, to see if his monthly payoff check is on it. If a serious fire does break out, many people may be burned to death; meanwhile, the fire inspector is the only beneficiary of the ordinance. (c) When plumbing and electrical codes are too perfectionistic, it is virtually impossible to comply with all their detailed requirements; in many cities, virtually every building in the city could be closed down for violations. Naturally, such ordinances cannot be fully enforced to any great extent: if it were, there would be no legally habitable buildings in the city. But the elaborate codes invite *selective* enforcement: if the officials want to get you for something, they can always enforce the building code to the maximum and close you down, even though they don't enforce it equally.

Is there any alternative to these requirements (all introduced in the name of safety) that have become simply a means of putting thousands of people on the city or state payroll at every taxpayer's expense? "Free market remedies could, most likely, replace the overweening regulatory framework our states now enforce. Building codes and fire codes could presumably be replaced quite easily by private enforced codes drafted by insurance companies. Few developers would construct hazardous firetraps if they knew beforehand that they could not acquire insurance for their buildings. . . . Restrictive covenants that run with the land, renewable at intervals of several decades, could very expeditiously insure that a slaughterhouse will not locate in the middle of Shaker Heights, Beverly Hills, or Boca Raton. If one were so unfortunate as to find one's house suddenly within proximity of a noisome chemical plant, a remedy would lie in nuisance law, for no one has a right to use his property in such a way as to adversely affect another's enjoyment of his."[5]

3. If the businessman is successful, he makes profits. He puts some money in the bank, puts some back into the business for capital investments, which will enable him to expand his operations and hire new workers, and pays some to the government in taxes. Meanwhile, however, he finds that although his taxes have risen, the price of everything he needs to stay in business has risen even more. The reason is not difficult to find: in order to finance its growing expenditures, the government has expanded the money supply; it has simply printed more paper money to cover its massive expenditures. The result, of course, is that the money he has earned is worth less. His expenses keep rising because the government has "watered the stock"—it has made his earnings less valuable, and the money he earns buys less and less. Government needs more and more to run its expanding activities (including the very regulatory agencies that already bedevil his

existence), and even if he makes profits on paper, they are worth progressively less as time goes on. In effect, inflation is just another tax he is made to pay. If people were taxed directly to pay for the added government agencies, they might rebel; so instead, the government inflates the currency, which for all practical purposes is the same as a tax.

The government takes more and more and leaves him less and less. Its inflationary policies often threaten and sometimes bankrupt him. He objects, and points out what has happened, but most people fail to see the connection between the inflation and their increased costs; instead of blaming the government for expanding the money supply they blame *him* for charging more for his product.

Even if he sees the government as the culprit, what can he do? Most people want the subsidies and handouts that inflation makes possible. They don't care who has to put more cookies into the cookie-jar as long as they can keep getting *their* cookies out. And so the expenditures of government keep rising — covered partly by taxes, partly by borrowing (to be paid for by one's decendants), and partly by expanding the money supply (inflation).

The businessman sees all this happening — but what can he do about it?

4. A law is passed placing a ceiling on the profits he is permitted to earn. The businessman greatly resents this, and believes that it is unjust. Nobody helped him when he started his business from scratch, or when he put years of planning and effort into it, and used all his savings to start it. If he had been unsuccessful, if he had made even one major misstep, he would have gone bankrupt. That's the chance he willingly took. But because he planned carefully and worked hard and gave the enterprise his all, now that he is successful others want to take the fruits of his labor away from him. Yet if he complies with the law, he can't expand his business, and he will have to lay off some of his employees.

Those who didn't succeed as he did now call him an exploiter. He resents this even more. True, he didn't start the business to become a public benefactor. "Selling merchandise at rock-bottom prices is simply the best way he knows to become rich. However, in pursuit of riches he drives hard bargains from wholesalers for the ultimate benefit of his customers, for whom he provides low-cost, quality merchandise, while providing employment for over 75 people. So with hard work and by pursuing his own self-interest, he does more to reduce poverty than all the politicians with their slogans, promises, and plans."[6]

And now that he has won the struggle in which no one helped him, others want to take away his profit. In the Soviet Union, the government can take everything away, including one's factory or store; in the United States, the government wants to take only part of it, leaving just enough for the manufacturer to keep producing (at less profit, or none) so that he can pay more taxes next year. But the businessman doesn't believe that they deserve his taxes. What is he to do?

When the businessman has succeeded in producing something he may be able to sell, he can't force anyone to buy his product. All he can do is start a factory, hire workers, produce the product as cheaply and efficiently as he can, and then hope there will be enough people willing to buy it so that he can break even and hopefully turn a profit. When he does make profits, most of these are turned right back into the business so that he can expand it, hire more workers, and have more products available for consumers to buy. Yet many consider him an exploiter. Don't they know that having the products they want in the great profusion available to them now, depends on people like him being able to keep their business going, and expanding?

He knows that the government has no source of income except what it collects in taxes. If the government promises something to A, it can get it only by taking it away from B. If it promises A something for nothing, it can fulfill its promises only by giving B nothing for something. The government doesn't create wealth, it only transfers it from one person (who has earned it) to others (some innocent some not), who haven't. Only people in the business community, such as our businessman, *create* wealth— actually increase it by taking things from the earth and transforming them for people's use. And in so doing, those in the *business* community profit, *consumers* have new products, and *workers* have jobs. What is so wrong about this, one may ask, and what should one do when one is treated so unfairly by the laws of one's society?

Hostility to business, reinforced by the press and TV drama, continues to grow, and the restrictions on the businessman's activity continue to proliferate. The businessman votes against such restrictions on his ability to function, but he is in the minority and is regularly outvoted at the polls. He foresees his and other enterprises going out of business if the trend continues. He wants to keep doing what he does best, producing something people want, and hiring more employees to do it; he asks only that others leave him alone. Left alone, he can help to raise everyone's standard of living by providing new products and employing more people. But they penalize him to the degree to which he is successful (the more money he makes, the more he is taxed and regulated). He doesn't want to hand over his earnings to anyone, not to his neighbor, nor to the government that regulates and harasses him. Yet the government demands that he do so, and will punish him if he doesn't.

5.   There is a different kind of moral choice that many businessmen in America face today. Should they sell agricultural and manufactured goods to dictatorships that deny their people even the most elementary human rights—nations that torture and imprison innocent people and send political dissidents to labor camps and "re-education centers" from which they seldom emerge alive? Aren't businessmen helping those dictatorships by trading with them?

A businessman might argue: There isn't much we can do about conditions in other nations, however deplorable these may be. We can't really do anything to help the victims of these tyrannical governments, at least not without risking war. So we might as well trade.

Still, is it right to give support to these regimes by trading with them? Trade, of course, means not only sending them goods but getting goods back from them in return. We get gold from the Soviet Union, mined under the most brutal conditions with slave labor; we import articles of furniture made in death-camps where the inmates are dying of overwork and malnutrition. And sometimes we don't get anything at all in return: we extend long-term loans that are never repaid. Businessmen themselves are repaid through the International Monetary Fund (IMF), which relies on the taxpayers of various nations for its income, especially the United States. Thus, businessmen and other American taxpayers are helping to provide the payment for the goods sold.

The businessman, however, could argue: If we don't sell our agricultural products to the Soviet Union, other nations will do so. They will then reap the benefit, and American farmers will be left with extra grain, which they can't sell. Why should we suffer if our moral heroism does us no good? Of course, if *all* nations refused to sell to these dictatorships, the people would starve, and perhaps through revolution, the political system would change for the better; but there is no present hope of that, so we may as well profit.

American businessmen compete with one another to sell products to the Soviet Union; but does this not have the same effect as our selling scrap metal to Japan in 1938, which came back to us in the form of bombs and bullets in World War II? An American ball-bearing plant sold its entire stock to the Soviet Union, thereby making profits (thanks to the IMF); but the effect of this sale was to make Soviet missiles against us more accurate. American businessmen built the huge Kama River truck plant near Moscow, but the design of these trucks was quickly adapted for tanks, which killed American servicemen in Vietnam.[7] Should businessmen profit at the expense of human lives? Besides, what is gained by sending our enemies military equipment and then spending billions of dollars protecting ourselves against the armed antagonist we have helped create?

The Russian dissident Aleksandr Solzhenitsyn said to the AFL-CIO: "It is necessary only that the West stop making concessions . . . Our whole slave system depends on your economic assistance. It is American trade that allows the Soviet economy to concentrate its resources on armaments and preparations for war. Remove that trade, and the Soviet economy would be obliged to feed and clothe and house the Russian people, something our socialist economy has never been able to do. Let the socialists among you allow this socialist economy to prove the superiority that its ideology claims. Stop sending them goods. Let them stand on their own feet, and then see what happens."[8]

In general, American businessmen believe in free trade; we'll sell you what we produce best, and you sell us what you produce best. But no business can be conducted with Russian businessmen, for there are none: no private businesses are permitted to exist in the USSR; all trade must be conducted with the Soviet *government*. And considering what that government does to its people, the moral thing to do would seem to be nothing: no aid, no trade. We may not be able to stop the slaughter of innocents, but at least we should not aid and abet it. Profits are a necessary incentive and an integral part of the free enterprise system, but they should not be made at the cost of human lives.

But if one American businessman took this position and refused to sell to the Soviet Union while *other* businessmen still kept on trading, what good would it do him? He might go down heroically into bankruptcy, but what would he achieve? To be effective, *most* businessmen would have to join in a boycott. Indeed, it is probable that such a boycott could be maintained only if there was a law: a prohibition against anyone giving the Soviets any aid or trade. Many American businessmen have decided that such a law would be desirable, and many dock-workers have refused to load shipments bound for the Soviet Union. They have taken a moral stand, unrelated to what the law requires or prohibits.

Thus far, we have considered only the honest businessman—one who wants to make a profit honestly. Unfortunately, a growing portion of the business community belongs in a different category, and most Americans fail to see the difference between them. The businessman in the second category doesn't mind selling to the Soviet Union or any other dictatorship, even though doing so helps to keep those dictatorships in power and enables them to continue to enslave vast populations. He also agitates for federal subsidies, a form of legalized theft, which are paid for by every taxpayer in the land. This places those who don't receive subsidies at a great disadvantage, forcing them to help pay with their own taxes to sustain their dishonest (government-aided) competitors.

Much of "big business" today belongs in this second category. They don't want government merely to preserve "law and order." They want to use government for their own financial gain: if they can't or won't make it on their own, the taxpayer will keep them going. The big-time farmer who gets a hundred thousand dollars a year from the government for growing certain crops, or for *not* growing them, is an example. Not only do dishonest businessmen want subsidies for themselves from the federal government, they spend millions of dollars lobbying in Congress. They want to put their competitors out of business so that they themselves will have a monopoly on the market. They know that businessmen don't like most government regulations and don't like to fill out complex tax forms and spend many hours recording data and keeping detailed books for the government to supply it with mostly useless information. They don't like it, *but* they have on hand staffs of tax lawyers and accountants who will keep them afloat in spite of the taxes and regulations. New competitors can't afford to do this. Multiply the regulations, force businesses to spend 25% of their work-time filling out forms for the government, and they, who are already big, can survive, but newcomers can't. Established businesses don't mind heavy government spending on wasteful enterprises, which inevitably causes inflation, because they know that they, being already in the field, can survive the inflation—even use it to their own advantage—whereas the newcomer, who has a great idea but also has debts and hasn't yet had time to succeed, cannot survive.

None of this would be possible, of course, if government stayed out of the economic arena entirely and had no power to give away money to some at the expense of others. (Constitutionally, it is questionable whether the federal government does have this power.) But going to the government, hat in hand, has now become par for the course in the business community. The result is that business enterprises that were not able to anticipate the next year's consumer needs and desires, continue, and those that *would* have succeeded on their own but for the taxes, inflation, and regulations, go bankrupt; or, seeing no hope of succeeding under present conditions, discontinue their enterprises. As a consequence, their employees are added to the ranks of the unemployed, and the consumer is denied new products that, on a free market, would have been produced and that he would have been happy to buy.

The average American makes no distinction among businessmen and is inclined to be angry with them all. In so doing, he fails to see how he is harming the entire nation, including himself, by approving the high taxes and excessive regulations.

Moral Alternatives

Capitulation

All of the situations just described present a conflict between what the law *is* and what (at least in the businessman's opinion) the law ought or ought not to be. Government has made the laws, and can ruin a businessman if he fails to comply. At the same time, the businessman's sense of morality— including his beliefs about rights, justice, and fair play—strongly assures him that, in some cases at least, the law is unjust and requires of him acts that violate his sense of right and wrong.

Sometimes a businessman is simply helpless in the face of the armed might of government. Robert Hertzler, owner of the Sandia Die and Cartridge Company of Albuquerque for eighteen years, had never had an accident in his plant because, he said, "I have taken apart every machine in the place. I started this business with no help. I starved. I was shot at in Korea." But he had invented a patentable process to which he claimed the right to keep secret, and OSHA demanded pictures of it. "I don't give a damn about the Constitution," said the inspector, adding "You don't have any rights." "How do you figure that?" "You're in business, you have employees, and you have done business with the government."[9] When he still refused to open his premises to the inspectors, they said, "We'll get you with what we've already got."

Faced with such a situation, what can a businessman do? Sometimes he can evade the law without being found out: in such cases, he feels morally justified in doing so.

Sometimes, more devious devices are effective. A manufacturer engaged in extracting minerals out of sand and shale in Utah was levied a large fine by the EPA (Environmental Protection Agency) for allowing clouds of dust to rise into the air, which (they contended) contained some poisonous fumes. Though no poisonous fumes were discovered (nor indeed produced) and the whole operation took place more than fifty miles from any city, the EPA penalized him anyway. So he adopted a different strategy. "The only way you can continue to exist at all in dealing with these people," he told me, "is to realize that they can put you out of business at a moment's notice. So you have to flatter them: first, be friendly and cooperative; you can't lash out at them or they'll clobber you; you must at least give the appearance of friendly obeisance. Second, you have to pretend that their work is important—you must assuage their deep-seated doubts about the legitimacy of their jobs by reassuring them about the real services they are rendering their country. Third, you then have to assure them that you too wish to serve your country by cooperating with them. Once this is done, they will often be willing to 'compromise' to reduce the fines they should never have imposed in the first place, and even to have some of the charges against you removed, if you're lucky. If you do all that, they may still hobble your industry, and force you to spend a third of your employees' time in paperwork and other unnecessary busywork for submission to government committees who probably will never look at it, but they will, at least for the moment, continue to permit your business to exist, under [their] benevolent supervision."

Sometimes the businessman decides that the only thing he can do is knuckle under to their demands, pay the fines, and continue operating. "You can't afford to get involved—just save your own skin and do the best you can under the circumstances."

That is what the prospectors for natural gas did after the Supreme Court, in the 1954 *U.S. v. Phillips Petroleum Co.* case, decided that the government had the legal right to control the price of gas at the wellhead. They set it at a very low price; and considering the risks of drilling, with ten dry holes for every one that produces, drilling for natural gas was suddenly an unprofitable venture. Companies stopped drilling for natural gas sources because it wasn't worthwhile anymore. Investors looked for more promising places to invest their money. The production of natural gas declined sharply. Most of the producers simply went out of business. The public wanted *plentiful* gas at *low* prices. The low prices tended to make people waste gas, and the plenty was soon replaced by shortages when the amount of available gas declined. The producers, who alone could have saved the situation by finding new sources, were blamed for not supplying more. The predictable result, of course, was a shortage of an essential commodity.

On the other hand, the businessman may decide that he can't afford *not* to get involved. If he speaks up, his plant may be closed down; but on the other hand, he may tell himself, "You've said nothing so far, and you're already almost out in the street. If you continue to say nothing, you may end up crushing rocks for the government."[10]

Resistance

But how shall he resist? If he takes out newspaper ads defending his case against the government, most people will either ignore what he says or discount it, putting it down to "selfish greed." They already have him pegged as a "filthy profiteer," and righteously reiterate that he is an outlaw working against the authority of the state, that he is only trying to increase his profits at their expense. The antibusiness ethic being what it is today, most people will refuse to support him. So where is he to turn?

There is a long-established strategy that a person can use when he believes a law to be immoral: he can register his disapproval by an act of *civil disobedience*. Civil disobedience is a *public* act: the businessman does not try to keep his disobedience a secret; he displays it for the public to see, hoping that, in doing so, he will effect some change in the law. He doesn't want to destroy all law, he simply wants to change it; and an act of civil disobedience is intended to do this. Civil disobedience expresses disobedience to law within the limits of fidelity to law. In employing civil disobedience, one knowingly takes on responsibility for the consequences of one's act, including fines and possible prison sentences.

There are advantages to civil disobedience as a strategy: it is peaceful—no violence is attempted; it is optional—no one *has* to do it, and no one *has* to listen; it does, often, result in changes in the law (such changes may, not always, be improvements); most importantly, it calls the public's attention to the law as it is and to the manner in which persons involved are attempting to change it. As Mill constantly reminded us in *On Liberty* every idea takes on new life when it is publicly challenged and debated in the marketplace of ideas, and the public is, at the very least, better informed because of such actions.

But a businessman who attempts civil disobedience against the dicta of the regulatory agencies is in a particularly unenviable position. In the present climate of opinion, he cannot muster much public support. If a man is a conscientious objector to the draft, thousands will rally to support him; and in any case, the law already provides alternatives in his case: he can perform noncombat duties while still working for the military, and thus remain within the law. But no such option is open to the businessman. If he attempts a public act of conscientious objection, he will incur large fines and may go to jail, and most of those members of the public who hear of it will probably say "serves him right."

In the long run the only solution is for the *minds* of people to be changed by *education*. But education takes a long time, and the evils can proliferate beyond endurance. Moreover, the educational process in this country is largely in the hands of government (public schools), and so will not present antigovernment sentiments. Thus, any acts of civil disobedience by businessmen are more likely to worsen their situation vis-à-vis the government than to improve it: the government is likely to crack down on them all the more.

Revolution

Sometimes passive resistance will not suffice; no matter how peacefully you resist and try to make your grievances known, you will be fined till you are bankrupt or arrested repeatedly until you decide it isn't worthwhile to spend most of your life behind bars. In such circumstances, it is sometimes contended, you have no recourse other than to start an armed rebellion against the government that imposes these punishments.

Most of the time, the belief that revolution is the only solution is not justified by the facts. There is considerable reason to suppose that slavery would have been abolished even without the Civil War; the invention of agricultural machinery would soon have made slavery so expensive and uneconomical that the slaves would have been freed. Even the American Revolution, which was largely a revolt against British taxes, might have been unnecessary. If Americans had simply refused to pay those taxes, in time the British might well have decided that it was more economical for them to trade with America even without collecting taxes than to eliminate the trade entirely. But all these peaceful moves, of course, would have taken time, during which the injustices would have continued. Wasn't it necessary to have action *at once*?

Perhaps so; but quick and immediate action, rather than being patient and waiting for slow but peaceful change, carries with it a very high price for the following reasons:

1. Armed revolution involves the death of innocent persons—those

who would prefer to have no part of the conflict, those who oppose the conflict, those who think that slow but peaceful change is preferable. Who are we to decide that *their* lives are worth sacrificing just because *we* have decided that armed revolution is the best way? Are the lives of others ours to dispose of?

2. A revolution often brings down the entire social and political structure, the good along with the bad. How many revolutions are worth that price?

3. Most revolutions fail to achieve their announced goals. They begin with high ideals, but after a period of armed conflict during which there is torture and execution of suspects, the regime that follows is sometimes even more tyrannical than the one that proceeded it. Millions of people have died in the Bolshevik Revolution, but what followed was not anything the participants would have willingly died for. The peasants wanted to keep their land, but it was all confiscated by the new government and taken away from the former owners (who, admittedly, came by it in ways that are morally questionable and helped precipitate the revolution in the first place). Instead of "justice for all," what they got was a police state ruled by terror and characterized by the torture and executions of thousands — an average of six such executions per year under the czar and 40,000 per *month* under Stalin, a "hero of the revolution!" Accounts of the aftermath of the Bolshevik Revolution abound, but the most moving and morally compelling are those offered by Aleksandr Solzhenitsyn.[11]

Similar accounts could be given of the outcome of the violent revolutions in many other times and places. And so the question arises: even if conditions are bad, is armed revolution worth it? May it not be, as Shakespeare has said, "better [to] endure the terrors that there are than fly to others that ye know not of"?

Suppose we conclude that when people are living under the terrors of a police state — and even the petty tyrannies of government regulation and harassment can become terrifying to some members of a community — armed revolution against the tyranny is morally justified. Even given that people face the worst statist circumstances, morally speaking, the problem is that the very conditions that would justify revolution — omnipotent state with total police power over a disarmed population — are the very same conditions that would make it virtually *impossible for such a revolution to succeed.* Even if revolution *is* justified in these circumstances, how can it possibly be effective? Wouldn't it be brutally suppressed, with more thousands of lives lost, as has happened every time the inhabitants of a land conquered by the Soviet Union have tried to revolt against their oppressors? What good result would be achieved by an armed revolution that has no chance of success? By the time the people have a *right* to revolt, they usually no longer have the *power* to do so successfully.

The Dilemma

When the law itself becomes an instrument of injustice, or when the law is one thing and its enforcement is another, then from the *moral* point of view the situation is clear: the law — and its enforcement — should be changed.

But from the *legal* point of view, the situation is equally clear: as long as a law is still on the books, people can't be permitted to disobey whenever and wherever they feel like it. If this were permitted, anyone could simply break a law and be excused by the courts for doing so with the simple plea, "I don't approve of this law." Clearly, such violations of the law cannot be permitted.

Yet morality and the law are often on a collision course. One or the other must triumph. If a law can be peacefully changed, even if doing so takes considerable time, then the conflict between the two, which often tears a nation apart, can be eliminated and the wounds healed. This has often occurred in the history of the United States, and hopefully it will continue to occur in the future. But in totalitarian regimes, where a small group of men in power can have their way with a population armed with only fists and stones against the government's machine-guns, no such healing is possible. In such cases, only a revolt will change the system. But every such revolt, as we have seen, carries with it an enormous price of its own — not the least part of this price being that the very circumstances that justify the revolt are the ones that reduce to almost nothing its chances of success.

Law and Ethics: No Final Resolution

We have now covered some of the central issues surrounding the problem of the relationship between law, and morality or ethics. We have seen that for most ethical systems there is much more involved in figuring out what is morally right than considering what is legal. We saw that in business activities there is much that the law mishandles, and that government often compels citizens to do what, from a moral point of view, they should not be made to do. We also saw that sometimes the law permits what would most sensibly be regarded as morally objectionable. And finally we considered what options are possible when the law is unjust and tyrannical.

We have not tried to make a final determination of these issues, but have tried to encourage intelligent thinking on the topics involved. Perhaps one conclusion is warranted, however; namely, that the life of the professional in the business world can be both enhanced and undermined by a community's legal system. When one embarks on a business career, one is no less required to make sure that one keeps one's moral bearings straight than if one were to embark on a career in law, medicine, the military, or education.

Notes

1. Oliver Wendell Holmes Jr., *The Common Law* (Boston: Little, Brown & Co., 1881), p. 27.

2. Ibid., p. 108.

3. For many interesting examples of this, see Melvin Grayson and Thomas Shepard, *The Disaster Lobby* (Chicago: Follett Publishing Co., 1973).

4. The cases described here and many others are presented in Dan Smoot, *The Business End of Government* (Belmont, Mass.: Western Islands, 1973).

5. Ellen Frankel Paul, "On Three 'Inherent Powers of Government,' " *The Monist,* Vol. 66, No. 4 (October 1983), pp. 539-40. See also Tibor R. Machan and M. Bruce Johnson, eds., *Rights and Regulation* (Cambridge, Mass.: Ballinger Publishing Co., 1984) and Robert W. Poole, Jr., ed., *Instead of Regulation* (Boston: Lexington Books, 1982).

6. Irwin Shiff, *The Biggest Con* (Westport, Conn.: Arlington House, 1976), p. 133.

7. See Antony Sutton, *Western Technology and Soviet Economic Development* (Stanford, California: Hoover Institution Press, 3 volumes, 1966-72).

8. Aleksandr Solzhenitsyn, address of the A.F.L.-C.I.O., quoted in *The New York Times,* July 10, 1975. On the Soviet regime's treatment of its citizens, see A. Solzhenitsyn, *The Gulag Archipelago,* 3 Volumes (New York: Harper & Row Publishers); Robert Conquest, *The Great Terror* (New York: Viking Press, 1976) and *Kolyma: the Artic Death Camps* (New York: Viking Press, 1978). Of course, the Soviet example is simply the most drastic and morally obvious one. Similar moral problems may arise in connection with trading with the governments and sometimes even with firms of other nations, some of them examples of right-wing rather than left-wing dictatorships and collaborators.

9. Alan Stang, "Oshtapo," *American Opinion,* October 1974, pp. 83, 87.

10. Ibid., p. 87.

11. Aleksandr Solzhenitsyn, *The Gulag Archipelago,* Vol. 2, pp. 637, 646-67.

6

THE SOCIAL RESPONSIBILITY OF CORPORATIONS

FRED D. MILLER, JR., AND JOHN AHRENS

In recent decades, large corporations have come to play an increasingly important role in the economy of the United States. Corporations like AT&T, IBM, and General Motors, because they are able to pool the resources of millions of investors, exert enormous influence on their respective industries and affect the life and well-being of every American. It is thus no surprise that such corporations are the targets of a great deal of criticism. Many social and economic theorists argue that the modern corporation, because of its size and special legal status, cannot be treated simply as one of the kinds of organizations that individuals form for their private benefit. Instead, they contend, the modern corporation is a *public* institution, a creature of the state, so that it can and must be held to a higher *social responsibility* — that is, to more stringent standards of legal and moral responsibility — than the traditional business firm.

This chapter considers some of the major arguments for and against treating the corporation as a public rather than a private institution. Section I examines alternative theories of the structure and legal status of corporations. Section II reviews opposing theories of corporate social responsibility and their application to some of the more pressing public-policy issues of the day. Section III addresses the specific problem of the size and consequent political power of the modern corporation. Section IV explores the ethical responsibilities that a corporation may have beyond making profits for its stockholders. Finally, Section V considers whether the ideal of "economic democracy" could be most fully realized by transforming corporations into political entities or by preserving their traditional character.

I. The Modern Corporation: Private Property or Public Institution?

What is a corporation? At first glance, the answer to this question seems obvious: a corporation is simply one of the more complicated organizations individuals have developed to facilitate the pursuit of profit.[1] However, this obvious answer is not universally accepted. Some critics of the moderncorporation argue that it cannot be justified within the ideological framework of free-market capitalism. Some also argue that the modern corporation is really a public rather than a private organization and should be treated accordingly. These critics justify their claims by reference to legal and structural characteristics that seem to be unique to the modern corporation. These characteristics include the following: corporations are formed by means of "corporate charters" requiring legal sanction. In nearly all corporations with publicly owned stock, the owners (stockholders) are, for the most part, not the managers. The owners of a corporation are protected by the doctrine of "limited liability" from any loss in excess of their investments. (A stockholder of a chemical company, for example, cannot be held personally liable if the company causes harm by dumping hazardous wastes.) Corporations possess a great deal of economic power, in virtue of which they influence the lives of everyone in modern society. These features have prompted many critics of the corporation to argue that corporations are *"quasi-public" organizations* resembling political states or that they are *creatures of the law* established by acts of government and endowed with special legal privileges. Opposed to these theories is the doctrine that the corporation is essentially private, arising from individual contracts. These theories will be examined in turn.

The Corporation as a Quasi-Public Organization

One of the most conspicuous structural characteristics of modern corporations, especially the larger ones, is that most of the owners—the stockholders—have little or no input into the corporate decision-making process. Whether voluntarily or otherwise, most of the owners of modern corporations have turned over the responsibility for managing their property to professionals. And this characteristic of corporations disturbs even defenders of capitalism such as Irving Kristol. This separation of ownership and management, Kristol argues, indicates that "the large corporation has ceased being a species of private property, and is now a 'quasi-public' institution."[2] The problem now, in Kristol's view, is to preserve the corporation by redesigning it in ways that reflect the change in its nature.

Kristol's argument for interpreting the separation of ownership and management as a transition from private property to public institution is twofold: (1) the modern corporation deviates from the model of private property as it was understood by such early defenders of capitalism as Adam Smith.[3] In Smith's model, the free market involved myriads of businesspeople in competition to sell goods to myriads of consumers. Property was owned by individuals who decided directly and for themselves how it was to be used in their firms. The modern corporation, because it gives a small elite of professional managers the power "to make economic decisions affecting the lives of tens of thousands of citizens,"[4] is inconsistent with the liberal-democratic ideals on which this country's political and economic system is founded. Hence, the modern corporation is *not* private property and may not claim the protections and immunities normally granted to private property.

Both of these arguments have been criticized. The first argument rests upon a controversial interpretation of the nature of capitalism and, as one critic argues:

There is no justification for equating capitalism with a particular configuration of small firms run by their owners, and Adam Smith's preferences are not binding upon persons who prefer to create some other arrangement. The essence of capitalism is the inviolability of individual rights, including the right to use or invest wealth as one chooses and the right to associate with others for any purpose and under any mutually acceptable terms of association.[5]

In short, Kristol's appeal to authority is irrelevant; capitalism has evolved since the time of Adam Smith.

Kristol's second argument, based on the separation of ownership and management, may be criticized on the grounds that such a separation is objectionable only if it is involuntary on the part of stockholders. But it is obvious that stockholders make a voluntary and deliberate decision to entrust some of their resources to *professional* managers. And if stockholders find this arrangement unacceptable and the authority of management too onerous, they have only to sell their stock in order to regain control of their resources.[6] Therefore, the separation of ownership and management that characterizes the modern corporation is consistent with the ideals of liberal democracy. The authority of managers does not undermine individual autonomy and self-determination because it derives from a voluntary or consensual arrangement between owners and managers. And the freedom of stockholders to sell their stock if they are dissatisfied serves to discourage the arbitrary exercise of managerial authority.

Indeed, it might be argued that the modern corporation is, in fact, an economic analog to the only political arrangement designed to preserve liberal-democratic ideals, i.e., representative government. In the United States, at least, it is representative government that is supposed to preserve individual autonomy by giving each citizen an equal voice in government and to prevent arbitrary exercise of political authority by allowing citizens to review and replace their representatives. The stockholder in a modern corporation has at least this much control over managers, if not more. Potential stockholders can choose to invest in any of a vast array of different corporations with different management philosophies, or they can invest in none at all. And they can prevent or escape the arbitrary exercise of authority simply by selling their stock. Where do citizens have this much control over their political fate?

The Corporation as a Creature of the State

Some have argued that the special legal status of the corporation renders it a public rather than a private institution. Ralph Nader, an outspoken critic of the modern corporation, argues that corporations are and always have been creatures of the state. They are, he claims, dependent on the state for their very existence, because they are created by the government for the benefit of the public rather than for the private benefit of stockholders and managers. Hence, corporations may legitimately be held to higher standards of social responsibility than traditional business firms.

Why are corporations creatures of the state, even though they are owned by private citizens? Nader's answer seems to be that a corporation requires the government's permission—a government charter—in order to do business[7] and that there are features peculiar to the modern corporation that can only be granted by law.[8] Nader discusses a number of these special features, but the most important by far is *limited liability*. Corporate stockholders, unlike the owners of more traditional firms, are not liable to the extent of their total personal assets for the debts and torts (wrongful acts) of the corporation; rather, their liability is limited by law to their investment in the corporation. This is a substantial hedge against economic risk and a powerful incentive to invest in corporate stock. And it is a privilege that can only be granted by the state.

Nader's account of the corporation as a creature of the state has also been criticized on two main points. First, it is pointed out that what Nader calls a "corporate charter" is just the articles of incorporation, which do not constitute any sort of governmental authorization and do not bind the corporation to the service of public rather than private interests. The articles of incorporation contain the name, purpose, and intended duration of the business, the amount of start-up capital, the names of the incorporators, and other information of a similar nature. The state's role is to record this information, just as it records information concerning births, marriages, land sales, and so forth. In all these cases, filing the appropriate documents with the government gives legal validity to private contracts. But, as Robert Hessen argues, this does not make the corporation, any more than birth or marriage, a creature of the state:

On the contrary, procedural requirements apply to virtually all contracts. For example, to be legally valid, a marriage contract must follow specific procedural requirements: it must be performed by someone authorized by the state, it must be witnessed, and a signed certificate must be filed with the state. If these requirements make the state a party to a contract, then every marriage is a *ménage à trois*: bride, groom, and government. Quite literally, government plays a smaller role in the creation of a corporation than of a marriage. Yet who, for that reason, would describe marriage as a creature of the state or claim that a marriage certificate contains a promise to serve the public interest.[9]

According to Hessen, the state does not create corporations; it merely recognizes and records their creation.

It has also been objected against Nader's theory that features like limited liability for debts and torts do not have to be explained as special privileges granted by the state. Limited liability for debts needs no special explanation because it is not a privilege that is *guaranteed* to corporations. That is, a potential creditor is within his (legal) rights to refuse to extend credit to a corporation unless some or all of the stockholders assume personal liability for the debt. And limited liability for torts or wrongful acts does not need to be construed as any special and valuable privilege granted only to corporate stockholders. The strongest argument for treating limited liability as such is based on the doctrine of vicarious liability. According to this doctrine, individuals are (legally) responsible for damages or wrongful acts performed by their employees or agents. For example, if Jones, an employee of Smith, makes an illegal kickback to a public official to obtain special advantages for Smith's business firm, it follows by this doctrine that *Smith* is vicariously responsible for the illegal kickback. If the doctrine of vicarious liability were extended to corporate stockholders, then each stockholder would be held personally liable for the wrongful acts committed by the corporation or its agent (e.g., the illegal disposal of hazardous wastes). And, the argument goes, vicarious liability should extend to all owners, including all corporate stockholders. But limited liability provisions in the law shield stockholders from penalties for debts or torts of the corporation beyond the value of their stock. Hence, corporations enjoy a special privilege that is not granted to ordinary persons under the law.

This argument has been criticized on the ground that the first premise — that the doctrine of vicarious liability should extend to *all* stockholders — is false.

Vicarious liability should apply only to shareholders who play an active role in managing the enterprise or in selecting and supervising its employees and agents. The tort liability of inactive shareholders ought to be the same as that of limited partners, that is, limited to the amount invested. The same rationale applies to both because inactive shareholders and limited partners contribute capital but do not participate actively in management and control.[10]

On this account, therefore, limited liability is not a privileged status granted to corporate stockholders; it is simply a recognition of their limited responsibility.

The Corporation as Created by Contract

Not all contemporary theorists regard corporations as radically different from other forms of business organizations. Robert Hessen, for example, argues that corporations, just like other businesses, are created by contract and that the apparently unique features of corporations can be explained in terms of their contractual origins. Hessen's arguments for this view, which he calls the *inherence theory,* are really just extensions of the criticisms of the theories of the corporation discussed previously.

Once it is recognized that the so-called "corporate charter" is, in fact, merely the articles of incorporation, it is not difficult to see that the corporation is born of a contract. This is a contract between individuals who wish to pool some of their resources and, perhaps, delegate some of the responsibility for managing these resources. The same contract, quite obviously, accounts for the separation of ownership and management in the modern corporation. Hessen's justification of these arrangements is simple: so long as we recognize that they are the result of voluntary agreements, they need not be seen as either mysterious or illegitimate. Limited liability for debts is also the result of a contract; it is a contract between stockholders and creditors, and one that potential creditors are not obliged to make.[11]

The principle difficulty for Hessen's inherence theory is limited liability for torts, for it seems unlikely that the victims of corporate wrongful acts would voluntarily agree to an arrangement that protects the personal assets of stockholders from damage claims. However, Hessen argues, this arrangement is not always or even usually much of an advantage to stockholders or disadvantage to tort victims, especially when a large corporation is involved. Most large corporations have assets far in excess of the assets of any of their stockholders, and they carry substantial liability insurance. Hence, it is not clear that stockholders in large corporations need this protection for their personal assets or that tort victims would benefit to any great extent if stockholders were personally liable. Further, Hessen rejects the doctrine of vicarious liability discussed above and, hence, believes that the limited liability arrangement simply gives legal recognition to the fact that most corporate stockholders play no role whatsoever in the management of the corporation and thus are not personally responsible for corporate torts. Those who do take an active role in management can and should be held liable; but to make inactive stockholders personally liable for corporate torts would be to commit an injustice.[12]

Some critics of this theory object that it misses the point of the corporate social responsibility debate. Modern corporations are huge concentrations of economic power that exert enormous influence on the condition of modern society and the welfare of every human being. And, continue the

critics, the real concern of those who claim that the corporation is a public
institution is to bring these economic giants under greater public control.
Although there are attempts to find a justification for this view in the legal
tradition, the argument that has carried the most conviction has been the
social responsibility argument: the public's interests must be protected, and
the vast economic power of corporations must be harnessed for everyone's
benefit. Corporations must, in other words, be held to higher standards of
social responsibility than mere individuals. For even if the theory is correct
that corporations are private property originating in contracts, corporations
have *public effects* that are so great that they cannot be ignored.

II.   Theories of Corporate Social Responsibility

What are the social responsibilities of corporations? Even amongst those
who agree that corporations are public institutions, there is considerable
disagreement about the correct answer to this question. Some merely want
corporate management to be more sensitive to the social impact of their
decisions, others want to see more effective policing of abuses of corporate
power, and still others want to see corporations undertake extensive
programs for the melioration of social ills. Proposals for accomplishing
these goals range from more effective regulation and enforcement of
criminal statutes to direct public or governmental management of large (or
all) corporations. At the other end of the spectrum are those who argue that
the social responsibilities of corporations are essentially those described in
Adam Smith's theory of the "invisible hand" and that social ills must be
addressed by some means other than the "nationalization" of corporations.
In order to clarify the most important ethical issues in the social responsibility debate, this section will examine two diametrically opposed views of
what the social responsibilities of corporations are and how we can ensure
that corporate management undertakes these responsibilities.

Cases Calling for Corporate Social Responsibility

First, however, it is necessary to provide a context in terms of which
different theories of corporate social responsibility can be understood.
Numerous social ills are attributed in whole or in part to corporate activity,
but three sorts of cases will serve to indicate the importance of the corporate
social responsibility debate.
Plant Closings: As corporations have grown larger and larger, many
communities have become thoroughly dependent on one or a few companies for their tax base and for jobs. When a company decides to scale down

operations at a plant or close or relocate it, the economic consequences for the community can be catastrophic.

Product Safety: The modern marketplace offers a bewildering array of products designed to improve the quality of leisure, increase mobility, extend communication, relieve the day-to-day aches and pains of the body and spirit, enhance natural beauty, and so forth. Many of these products are the result of extremely complicated advances in science and technology, which the consumer is but little prepared to understand. And, as recent phenomena like thalidomide babies and the toxic effects associated with many cosmetics and feminine hygiene products indicate, the human costs that result from an error in judgment can be extremely high.

Deterioration of the Environment: Recent decades have witnessed rapid growth in the level of industrial activity and, consequently, rapid proliferation of new industrial processes and substances. Not all of these activities and processes and substances are benign; some produce significant and harmful changes in our natural environment.

Corporations, because they play such an important role in our economy, have undeniably contributed to the emergence of these and other problems, whether intentionally or otherwise.[13] And this is the impetus behind the corporate social responsibility debate and the variety of proposals designed to enlist the aid of corporations in attempts to solve these problems.

Corporate Democracy as a Vehicle for Social Responsibility

One approach to these problems is the corporate democracy theory. This approach is illustrated by the Corporate Democracy Act of 1980. This bill (which failed to gain passage) was introduced in Congress as H.R. 7010 and was actively supported by consumer activists like Ralph Nader and his associates. The bill, which would apply to all nonfinancial corporations with assets or annual sales of more than $250 million or more than 5,000 employees, includes the following significant provisions:

- A majority of the board members of corporations subject to the Act must be independent; i.e., they cannot have been officers or managers of the corporation for a period of five years prior to their election to the board and they cannot have been officers, directors, employees, or more than 1% equity owners of any organization providing significant service to the corporation for a period of three years prior to their election to the board.
- Among the committees of the board there must be a public policy committee, which will be responsible for policies concerning community relations, consumer protection, and environmental protection. A majority of the members of this committee must be independent directors.

- Corporations must give notice two years in advance of any plant closing or relocation that will significantly reduce employment in the area and must compensate local governments for the resultant decrease in tax revenues.

The intent of the Corporate Democracy Act was to reduce the control the managers and stockholders would have over corporate decisions and to bring corporations under substantial and direct public control. If this act had passed, corporations would have become essentially public institutions.[14]

An important objection that has been leveled against the corporate democracy approach is that it would substantially reduce the efficiency with which corporations can do business. Expertise in deciding policy for a business requires experience, but the Corporate Democracy Act effectively ensures that the majority of the directors of large corporations will lack the necessary experience. Further, the provision concerning plant closings and relocations would reduce management's ability to preserve the economic health of corporations by choosing the most advantageous sites for corporate activities. And this is certainly contrary to the interests of both stockholders and society as a whole. Efficiency is not the only virtue of economic institutions, but it is certainly one of their virtues and one which proposals like the Corporate Democracy Act seem certain to undermine.

Another objection turns on the ethical difficulties raised by this attempt and others like it to restrict the rights of property owners. The right to own property is a central principle of capitalism that is protected in the United States Constitution. And there is a long tradition of social and legal theory that views private property as an important shield against the arbitrary, capricious, and oppressive exercise of political power: if control of the resources people need to survive and prosper is decentralized, rather than concentrated in the hands of political authorities, it is more difficult for these political authorities to deprive people of their civil liberties.[15] Of course, one might argue that the gravity and urgency of the social problems discussed above outweigh the risks of placing substantial economic power in the hands of political authorities. But it seems reasonable that this drastic alteration in the economic system of the United States should only be undertaken as a last resort and after other ideas have failed. The existence of competing theories of corporate social responsibility suggests that we have not yet reached this impasse.

Profit Making Within the Rules
as Social Responsibility

A theory of corporate social responsibility, which lies at the opposite end of the spectrum from the corporate democracy theory, is proposed by Milton

Friedman. Like Hessen, Friedman believes that corporations are a species of private property and, consequently, that they have exactly the same social responsibility as other businesses in a capitalist economy:

In such an economy, there is one and only one social responsibility of business — to use its resources and engage in activities designed to increase its profits so long as it stays within the rules of the game, which is to say, engages in open and free competition, without deception or fraud. . . . It is the responsibility of the rest of us to establish a framework of law such that an individual in pursuing his own interest is, to quote Adam Smith again, "led by an invisible hand to promote an end which was no part of his intention."[16]

In short, the social responsibility of business is just what it has always been supposed to have been — to increase its profits within the framework of the law. And if we want to enlist the aid of business in solving social problems, the only legitimate way of doing so is to effectively police the fraudulent and deceptive practices that contribute to these problems and to frame our laws in such a way that businesses are able to profit by providing for social needs. This theory, defended by Friedman, is referred to as the *fundamentalist theory of social responsibility.*

In view of the seriousness of many of the problems facing contemporary society, this view may seem nothing more than a callous and shortsighted defense of private interests. But this appearance of callousness and short-sightedness fades on closer examination. For Friedman is not suggesting that we should ignore the economic power of corporations, or that we must resign ourselves to being unable to enlist this power in attempts to address social problems. He is, rather, suggesting that bringing corporations under more direct public control is neither a legitimate nor a particularly effective means of ensuring that their vast economic power is used for socially beneficial ends. We should instead adopt means that preserve the economic freedom that has served as a hedge against political oppression and that has contributed so much to the high standard of living enjoyed by so many Americans.[17]

Applying Friedman's theory to the social problems discussed above will help to clarify this point. What, for example, is the capitalist solution to the problem of unsafe products? The answer is really quite simple. The marketplace already provides unbiased information on the safety and quality of a broad range of goods and services in news reports and in publications like *Consumer Reports.* The fact that a consumer is not himself qualified to judge the claims of sellers does not mean that he must either accept these claims at face value or turn to the government for protection. If consumers feel a need for unbiased information, and surely they will if deceptive advertising or the marketing of unsafe or ineffective products is at all widespread, the market itself will satisfy this need. And if consumers are forewarned, unsafe or ineffective goods and services are no threat since consumers can avoid them. Hence, the market itself provides consumer protection. And Friedman would probably add that it provides it at a lower price than government can.

Plant closings and relocations pose a somewhat different problem. If the only responsibility of business is to increase its profits, then the responsible manager will close or relocate plants whenever he can improve the profitability of his operations by so doing. Thus, it would seem that only government intervention in the economic decision-making process can prevent the disruption of communities this causes. And this is probably true, but it is worth noting that government intervention is often the cause of this problem rather than the solution; and even when it is not the cause, it is not always a *desirable* solution. When a company decides to close or relocate a plant because the goods it produces are no longer saleable, or because the source of raw materials has shifted, or some similar reason, it is hard to condemn the decision. While the change may produce temporary disruptions in a particular community, it makes for more efficient use of resources and thus benefits society as a whole; it is, in other words, the socially responsible thing to do. Quite often, however, the decision to relocate operations is a result of the fact that some local governments offer lower tax rates or free services, or have pursued policies that reduce labor costs (e.g., antiunion policies). If government did not have the power to offer these incentives, i.e., to exploit some members of the community for the benefit of others, many plant closings and relocations simply would not occur. In cases such as these, the solution is not less economic freedom but more.

And the same is true of the environmental problems that threaten to destroy us all. Air pollution, water pollution, and the depletion of other resources that are not readily replaceable, have reached crisis proportions because these resources are, for the most part, public rather than private property. They are owned by government rather than by individuals; and since government is supposed to represent the interests of all people, it must give the interests of those who would pollute and pillage equal consideration with the interests of those who would nurture and preserve. Unfortunately, the activities of the former quite often render the demands of the latter pointless. If these resources were owned by individuals, the owners would have a strong economic incentive to preserve their property so it would be adaptable to a variety of uses and retain its value over time. Again, the solution is not less economic freedom, but more.[18]

Friedman's fundamentalist theory has, not surprisingly, been sharply attacked by most critics of the corporation. Two sorts of criticisms are especially worth noting here. First, Friedman's theory of corporate social responsibility presupposes a very sanguine view of the way in which a capitalist economy would function in the absence of government controls, and some critics object that his view is too optimistic. For even if it is true that unfettered capitalism would constitute the best treatment for social ills, one might question whether or not unfettered capitalism is attainable. Economic power can be used to acquire political power, especially in a democracy like the United States, in which public opinion is determined primarily by the media and by respect for the views of "experts." According to the critics, corporations will use their vast resources to ensure that legislation and public policy favor their interests over the interests of society and that they are never subjected to the rigors of competitive capitalism. It is evident from this objection that an understanding of corporate social responsibility requires a consideration of the political power of corporations, which is discussed in Section III.

Secondly, Friedman's theory has been criticized on the ground that it does not take into account many important ethical dimensions of the decisions that corporate managers make. In defining social responsibility, he seems to hold that managers should consider only two factors as morally relevant: honoring their commitment to the stockholders to maximize the profits of the corporation and following "the rules of the game." According to his interpretation, the rules of the game require that one "engage in open and full competition, without deception or fraud." Friedman's critics ask why these "rules" are so important and why other values should not also be given equal weight, e.g., supporting the local community even when this requires losses. Friedman's interpretation of "the rules of the game" is bound to seem arbitrary unless it is supported with an explicit, defensible ethical theory. Moreover, critics also characterize his fundamentalist theory as suffering from a type of ethical "tunnel vision." They argue that there are other moral goals besides the pursuit of profits, that these other goals are more often than not in conflict with profit-maximizing, and that when this happens, profits should take the back seat. In view of such objections, it will be necessary in Section IV to examine the *moral* dimensions of social responsibility.

III.   The Political Dimension of Social Responsibility

The economic power of corporations can be translated into political power in a variety of ways, and many of the more effective ways are completely legal and aboveboard. Former Senator Fred Harris has called for extensive revision of the laws governing campaign financing and corporate income tax deductions. He cites examples of business practices that influence politicians such as contributions to campaigns and political action committees (PACs), intensive lobbying, political advertising, and giving jobs to former government officials. Corporations are able to influence judicial decisions, legislation, and regulatory policy because they have the where-withal to sway public opinion and to ensure that their interests are effectively represented before Congress and the government's regulatory agencies. And one need not resort to charges of collusion or bribery to explain the disproportionate influence of corporations. Our political system provides numerous legal avenues to power and influence for those with sufficient wealth.[19]

Harris and other critics who make similar claims are no doubt correct, but one must be cautious in condemning the disproportionate political power of corporations and even more cautious in prescribing a remedy that includes federal chartering of corporations and more vigorous antitrust enforcement to break up large corporations. If government officials have been lax thus far in designing and enforcing regulations to protect the public's interests, is the situation likely to be improved by giving them the additional power to decide which corporations shall exist and how large they shall be?

Even if there were legislative means to prevent corporations from exercising political power, some would argue that we should not use it. For the apparently disproportionate political power of corporations seems less intimidating if we remember that large corporations are owned by thou-sands or even millions of stockholders. When the lobbyists of a large corporation represent corporate interests before government officials, it is the interests of all these stockholders that are really at stake. Moreover, it would be impossible to restrict corporate support for political advertising, PACs, and lobbies without violating the civil liberties of the owners and managers of corporations.

If the political power of corporations still seems threatening, we should consider whether or not there are alternatives to further politicizing the corporation by annexing it to the state. One alternative is suggested by Milton Friedman's theory of corporate social responsibility: we should strip government the functions that allow officials to exercise their power on behalf of corporations rather than "the public." For many of the political activities of corporations are directed at gaining special advantages through existing or proposed legislation: for example, protection from foreign competition through tariffs or "domestic content" legislation, special subsidies, price supports, low-interest or no-interest loans (as in the Chrysler bailout), government enforced monopolies (as in the case of utilities and local cablevision companies), special tax breaks (such as depletion allowances), and government contracts. As government has come to control the economy to an increasing extent, corporations have felt compelled to resort to political tactics rather than traditional economic competition. For example, corporations frequently use antitrust suits to defeat or destroy their competitors. It seems inevitable that as long as this arsenal of political weapons exists, corporations will use them, especially while the same weapons are available to other corporations, to organized labor, and to various groups dedicated to bringing corporations under total governmental control. According to Friedman, the solution to this is disarmament: curbing the governmental powers that the contending interest groups are seeking to use to their own advantage. There is, as we said earlier, no guarantee that this can be accomplished. But neither is there any guarantee that further politicizing the corporation will produce any beneficial effect. And, as Friedman points out, it is not only corporations who have "social responsibilities"; it is also the responsibility of each individual to ensure that there is a framework of laws and political institutions that brings private and "public" interests into harmony.[20] Perhaps, in the present context, the way to carry out that responsibility is not through any positive exercise of political power, but rather through the refusal to give any further economic power to political officials.

IV.   The Ethical Dimension of Social Responsibility

Closer examination of Milton Friedman's fundamentalist view of corporate social responsibility also indicates that ethical principles need to be taken into account. His view is that, in a capitalist economy, "there is one and only one social responsibility of business — to use its resources and engage in activities designed to increase its profits so long as it stays within the rules of the game, which is to say, engages in open and free competition, without deception or fraud." The managers of a corporation should use available assets to make investments that are expected to maximize the shareholder's profits rather than to engage in charitable contributions or follow "enlightened" but nonprofitable business practices. On the other hand, the managers should not attempt to make a profit by engaging in deception, fraud, or coercion against competitors. Although this view may have a certain pragmatic appeal to businesspeople, Friedman unfortunately does not support it with any explicit ethical arguments. Consequently, it is not clear why one should accept *his* view of social responsibility, rather than an opposite view: for example, "The social responsibility of a corporation is to make a profit — no ifs, ands, or buts about 'the rules of the game' " (the pure profit-making view), or "The social responsibility of a corporation is to serve the community by providing employment opportunities for all, improving the environment, promoting justice worldwide . . . even if it costs the shareholders money" (the community service view).

Respect for Rights

An ethical theory can provide a basis for defending one view of corporate social responsibility against others. One such ethical theory, which has been extremely important in the United States, is the theory of individual human rights. On this theory, individuals are free to pursue their own goals (provided that they do not prevent others from pursuing their goals), and other people have the duty not to interfere in this pursuit. Since the most flagrant form of interference involves the use of force or coercion, the theory of individual rights requires that individuals abstain from the use of force except in the defense of rights against violations by others. Threats of force against others also prevent them from pursuing their goals, so threats are also violations of rights. Individual rights include the right to produce and own property — so thefts or invasions of property are also infringements of rights. When individuals enter into voluntary contracts with each other, each person has a duty to keep the agreement. To take property from another by means of a false promise is to steal that person's property. Thus, fraud is a violation of the rights of others. Individual rights have a basically *negative* character. If Jones has the right to "life, liberty and the pursuit of happiness," this means that Smith has the duty not to interfere with Jones's exercise of this right. It does not mean that Smith has the duty to provide Jones with positive benefits. Smith can justifiably be forced to provide Jones with a positive benefit only if Smith has voluntarily assumed an obligation towards Jones, e.g., by signing a contract. If Smith has not voluntarily assumed an obligation but is forced to serve Jones's purposes anyway, then Smith is nothing but a slave whose rights are being violated.

This theory of individual rights provides support for Friedman's view as opposed to the pure profit-making view or the community service view.[21] For on this theory the individuals in a corporation have the duty to respect the rights of other individuals. Hence, they may not use force against workers or fraud against consumers in order to make greater profits, for this would be to violate the rights of the workers or consumers. Nor may they use force or coercion to drive out their competitors in order to increase profits, for this would again involve violating the competitors' rights. Thus, the theory of individual rights cannot support the pure profit-making view of social responsibility. Nor can it support the community service view. For managers have taken the stockholders' money with the understanding that it will be invested to make a profit and thereby benefit the stockholders. If the managers were to use the money for another purpose, they would be failing in their contractual obligations to the stockholders and thus be violating their rights. This is obvious if managers divert corporate funds for selfish purposes. But even if managers have unselfish motives, for example, to help the community, they will be in the same moral position as a person who forced Smith to serve Jones without his consent and thereby treated Smith as a slave. In general, then, if corporate social responsibility is understood as the theory that a corporation should respect individual human rights, it leads to a view like Friedman's rather than to the pure profit-making view or the community service view.[22]

Morals versus Profits?

The discussion of the ethical dimension of corporate social responsibility has, so far, been in terms of the respective duties and rights of managers, shareholders, consumers, workers, and competitors. Another ethical issue concerns whether or not profit-maximization is the only goal that should concern corporations and their owners. Should they be concerned about other values? Often this is presented as an "either-or" issue. Either the basic concern is with economic values such as productivity or efficiency, in which case corporations should concentrate on making profits and steer clear of social involvements, or else "social and human values" are the primary concern and business should assume greater social commitments even at the expense of profits.

But the argument that there is a dichotomy between morals and profits rests on a crucial assumption: that it is obvious to business managers which course of action out of many alternatives will lead to the greatest profits or smallest losses. For on this assumption, the obligation to maximize profits will severely limit the courses of action open to responsible managers. Managers will have very little flexibility in carrying out their primary directive to maximize profits. They will, in effect, function like profit-maximizing robots. But it is far from obvious that this assumption is true: in the real world it is not so simple for managers to determine which course of action is profit maximizing.[23]

For the question of what will enhance a corporation's profitability is ambiguous, and, consequently, so is Friedman's theory that the manager's social responsibility requires maximizing the profits of the corporation. One ambiguity concerns whether decisions are made with a view to *long-run* or to *short-run* profitability.

Friedman's theory does not specify which of these two strategies of "maximizing profits" should be followed, and it could be argued that it should not do so. For just as individual people have strikingly different views about the relative importance for them of benefits they will enjoy, or costs they must bear one year, three years, or ten years in the future, so also the managers of different corporations have different attitudes toward the future. It could be argued that in a free market, investors should be free to seek out the corporations with an attitude on profitability with which the investors feel secure. For consumers and investors have the right to decide for themselves just how long- or short-run their thinking will be under varying circumstances. Moreover, different investors and managers may well elect different strategies for return on equity because of different circumstances, abilities, and knowledge.

What many people would call "socially responsible" behavior on the part of business may turn out to be long-run profit seeking as well. For example, William C. Norris, founder of the Control Data Corporation, holds that "social problems provide profit-making opportunities." Norris developed a strategy of investing corporate resources in "inner city" areas to produce learning centers. These centers, containing Control Data products, are meant to develop entrepreneurial skills in disadvantaged populations, thereby creating future customers for Control Data. Such a strategy might require ten years or more to pay off. But it nevertheless illustrates the wide range of options open to "profit seekers" in the free market.

A further ambiguity in the idea of profitability is whether the factors contributing to profits are to be exclusively quantitative. Qualitative factors such as image, public relations, good will, and popular opinion can have an impact on profitability that may be indirect and hard to quantify, but are nonetheless important. Hence, one should not assume that certain types of corporate behavior are invariably inimical to profitability. Friedman, for example, mentions charitable contributions to universities as profit-reducing. This is to overlook the possibility that such philanthropy may enhance qualitative factors of the community, which are in turn favorable to corporate profitability. The Ford Motor Company was mistakenly criticized for ignoring profitability in 1914 when it reduced the workday to eight hours and raised wages to $5 a day.

The dichotomy between profits and morality may also be criticized on the grounds that it makes an overly simplistic assumption about how two values can be related: it assumes that either one of the values is a mere means to achieving the other (e.g., going to the dentist for the sake of keeping one's teeth healthy), or that the two values are in conflict with each other. But as Aristotle observed in his *Nicomachean Ethics,* a person can value a thing for its own sake and at the same time value it as a means to a further end. For example, you may decide to have a good vacation. You also value friendships for their own sake. Given these values, you plan your vacation to include frequent visits with friends. In such a case, you are both valuing your visits with friends for their own sakes and valuing them as a means to having a good vacation. It would be quite unfair for someone to criticize you for "just using" your friends as a means. You could sincerely protest that you do value their friendship for its own sake. The same kind of reasoning can and does occur when managers make corporate decisions.

Consider a case in which the manager of a corporation is trying to deal with the problem of alcoholism among his employees. The manager might be committed both to maximizing the profits of the stockholders and to treating the employees fairly and humanely. In the course of considering whether the company should finance a rehabilitation program for employees with an alcohol problem, he finds that it would be no more expensive to introduce such a program than to fire the employees and retrain new ones. He may also have reason to think that such a program would enhance the prospect for better employees in the future. The manager may introduce the rehabilitation program on the grounds that it is morally correct in terms of both profitability and the welfare of his workers. The manager in such a case clearly is not concerned only about profits. But what if the manager discovers that the company cannot afford such a program given its marginal market position? He might then conclude that he has no choice but to fire or lay off employees with a drinking problem. But even in this case the manager can be concerned not only with profits but also with the well-being of his employees.

Three Principles of Social Responsibility

Douglas Den Uyl, a professor of business ethics, has formulated three principles that define the ethical dimensions of social responsibility:

(1) *The principle of respect for individual rights.* This is the principle that managers should respect the rights of their shareholders and of other persons with whom they deal: consumers, workers, competitors. By the same token, government and the critics of corporations should respect the rights of managers and owners of the corporations.

(2) *The principle of responsible recommendation.* This principle recognizes the central place of profitability in the development and, indeed, the survival of the corporation. Shareholders invest their money in a corporation with a view to making a profit, and managers have an obligation to them. It is not responsible to recommend policies to corporations that would prevent managers from meeting this obligation.

(3) *The principle of moral consideration.* This principle states that because managers generally have a degree of flexibility in pursuing the overall goals of the corporation, they should be open to the moral dimension in making decisions. They should take into account the interests of others and how their decisions are affecting others.

To see how Den Uyl's principles would be applied, suppose that the managers of a corporation decide that because of a drop in demand, it is necessary to close a plant on which a small community is heavily dependent for employment. This could qualify as a "socially responsible" action on the three principles, provided that the corporation fulfilled all of its contractual obligations to workers and members of the community as well as investors (principle 1), it determined that closing the plant was necessary to maintain the corporation's profitability (principle 2), and the managers took into account the interests of the local community and sought out alternatives (consistent with principles 1 and 2), which would minimize the adverse impact of the plant closing (principle 3).

Organizations critical of American corporations, such as the Interfaith Council on Corporate Responsibility, frequently submit proxy resolutions at shareholder meetings that are intended to make the corporation more "responsible." A typical example is a proxy resolution submitted to Caterpillar Tractor Company dealing with plant closings and layoffs:

Be it therefore resolved that the shareholders request the Board of Directors to adopt a written policy for permanent or indefinite plant closings and mass layoffs, affecting 100 employees or more, which would include: 1. Committing Caterpillar to provide financial, technical and other assistance in retraining workers who are being laid off permanently or indefinitely so that they may qualify for current and future job openings; 2. Providing workers with information about current and expected job openings in their region as well as vocational counseling; 3. Providing advance public notice of at least six months of a plant closing and at least four months of a mass layoff; 4. Giving dislocated workers first priority for jobs in other plants; 5. Placing new installations in or near plants which are closing or losing operations.[24]

Such a resolution would not be supported by any of Den Uyl's three principles of social responsibility. It most clearly violates principle 2, responsible recommendation. For although the group that made this proposal is concerned about the future employment of the workers laid off, it shows little or no concern for the financial viability or improvement of the corporation. For example, the fifth proposal, requiring Caterpillar to put new installations near plants that are closing or losing operations, is to demand that Caterpillar make itself vulnerable to economic forces that have already destroyed other companies. The framers of this resolution evidently intend to solve a "social problem" by transferring wealth from Caterpillar's shareholders to unemployed workers. Further, in closing a plant, the company would not violate the rights of the workers, since the employees do not have a right to those jobs beyond what the company contractually agreed to provide. So principle 1, respect for individual rights, does not support the resolution's proposals. Nor does it receive support from principle 3, which only implies that a responsible management would handle the plant closing humanely and take whatever steps it can to ease the transition. For this proxy resolution goes much further than this. In fact, it considers only the benefits that would be brought to particular localities. It does not consider other geographical areas that might benefit from new plants. Nor does it give indication of any concern for those who will bear the cost of implementing such a proposal. Hence, such resolutions themselves violate principle 3, since they fail to take fully into account how the interests of others would be affected if the resolutions were adopted.

V.   Conclusion: Corporations and Economic Democracy

The corporate social responsibility debate is largely the result of a rising tide of sentiment in favor of what has been called "economic democracy." The ideal of economic democracy is the analog of the ideal of political democracy. The latter is achieved by erecting political institutions that give each person an equal voice in government and thereby protect us from the arbitrary and oppressive exercise of political power. The former, we may presume, is to be achieved by giving each person an equal voice in important decisions concerning the disposition of society's resources, thereby protecting us from the arbitrary and harmful exercise of economic power. And most proposals for accomplishing this include politicizing economic decisions and bringing corporations (and perhaps other businesses as well) under the direct control of the political process.

But perhaps the evolution of the modern corporation as a *private* economic institution is an even more significant step in the direction of economic democracy. It is possible for private corporations to operate in such a way that they do not usurp political power and for them to pursue the goal of profitability in an ethically responsible manner. It is true, of course, that not every citizen, nor even every stockholder, has an equal voice in the economic decisions that affect his welfare; this will probably never be achieved, and some of the theories we have discussed suggest that it should not be. But the modern corporation, operating in an environment of economic freedom, gives each of us the opportunity to use our resources in a responsible way to influence economic decisions and to protect ourselves from their consequences. And this, after all, is the point of economic democracy.

Notes

1. Of course, not all corporations and perhaps not even most are created for the purpose of making profits in the narrow economic sense. There are numerous so-called "nonprofit" corporations that are devoted to charitable, artistic, and other purposes. However, we will restrict our remarks to the former, since it has been the subject of virtually all the criticism directed at the modern corporation.

2. Irving Kristol, "On Corporate Capitalism in America," *The Public Interest,* no. 41 (Fall, 1975), p. 138.

3. Ibid., p. 125.

4. Ibid., p. 128.

5. Robert Hessen, "A New Concept of Corporations," *The Hastings Law Journal,* vol. 30 (May, 1979), pp. 1342–43.

6. Ibid., pp. 1344–49.

7. Ralph Nader, "The Case for Federal Chartering," in *Corporate Power in America,* Ralph Nader and Mark Green, eds. (New York: Grossman Publishers, 1973), pp. 81–84.

8. Ralph Nader, Mark Green, and Joel Seligman, *Taming the Giant Corporation* (New York: W. W. Norton, 1976), pp. 33–61.

9. Hessen, op. cit., p. 1337.

10. Ibid., pp. 1333–34.

11. Hessen provides a detailed account of these and other features of the modern corporation in his *In Defense of the Corporation* (Stanford, Cal.: Hoover Institution Press, 1979), esp. chapters 1–4.

12. Ibid., pp. 18–22.

13. A more detailed and substantially more vituperative discussion of corporate contributions to contemporary social ills is provided by Ralph Nader, op. cit., pp. 15–32.

14. For a complete text of the Corporate Democracy Act, as well as texts of some of the testimony given to Congress in support of something like this type of legislation, see *Protection of Shareholders Rights Act of 1980,* U.S. Government Printing Office, Nov. 19, 1980 [y 4.B 22/3:P 94/8].

15. For an extended discussion of the relationship between economic liberty and political liberty, see F. A. Hayek, *The Road to Serfdom* (Chicago: University of Chicago Press, 1944).

16. Milton Friedman, *Capitalism and Freedom* (Chicago: University of Chicago Press, 1962), p. 133.

17. Ibid., pp. 133–36.

18. For a more detailed discussion of the relationships between economic freedom and environmental issues, see John Ahrens, *Preparing for the Future* (Bowling Green, Ohio: The Social Philosophy and Policy Center, 1983), esp. chapter IV.

19. Fred R. Harris, "The Politics of Corporate Power," in Nader, op. cit., pp. 25–41.

20. See note 16.

21. For a more systematic and detailed presentation of the theory of individual rights, see Ayn Rand, *Capitalism: The Unknown Ideal* (New York: New American Library, 1967), and Robert Nozick, *Anarchy, State, and Utopia* (New York: Basic Books, 1974).

22. It should be noted that the theory of individual rights is part of the classic ideal of *libertarianism*. As has been noted earlier, this ideal has been an important intellectual tradition in the United States, but there are other classic ideals (including, most obviously, Marxism, socialism, and facism) that would reject both individual rights and Friedman's view.

23. This section owes a good deal to the analysis in Douglas Den Uyl, *The New Crusaders* (Bowling Green, Ohio: The Social Philosophy and Policy Center, 1984).

24. Den Uyl, op. cit., p. 48.

7

GOVERNMENT REGULATION OF BUSINESS

TIBOR R. MACHAN

Introduction

The central concern of business ethics is how someone engaged in business should guide his or her conduct. This question covers everyday commercial activities we all carry out, as well as the specialized endeavors of professionals such as advertisers, marketing executives, personnel managers, and others.

But once answers have been secured to the questions about the dos and don'ts of business conduct, another important question arises. Should public policy be established to enforce compliance with these answers? Suppose it is found that it is morally proper for businesses engaged in hiring and promotion to give special treatment to members of groups that previously suffered injustice. Should it be left to the good will or the conscience of members of the business community to act on this ethical imperative? Or should the government *enforce* compliance? Suppose, again, that operators of mines should indeed provide a given level of safety to their employees and not simply rely on the decision of the employees to work in the face of grave risks. Is there is a moral obligation to provide such protection on the job? Should it be left to management to provide it? Or should government regulate the mining industry by requiring management to implement this ethical directive?

In this chapter, we will consider arguments for government regulation of commerce and will examine various responses to those arguments. Our first task is clarify what government regulations of business actually entails.

The work on this essay was partially supported by the Earhart and the Reason Foundations. I am grateful to those organizations.

What is Business Reguiation?

In partially free market systems such as those of some Western democracies, private individuals and companies, not governments, conduct most business. Trade is not conducted at government direction and it is a crime to disrupt commerce. Many exceptions exist — e.g., the U.S. Postal Service or Swiss Railway System are not firms that do their business on what is usually called a free-market basis because a considerable portion of their revenue comes from taxes. Still, production and distribution of most goods and services is largely in private hands. Toys, movies, vacation packages, insurance, furniture, farm produce, television sets, buildings, plumbing, lamps, and many other consumer goods are all provided by private industry, although even here subsidies from government can render the industry something other than a free market phenomenon. Still, market exchange tends to dominate the commerce of many Western societies.

Whenever city, county, state, or federal governments set enforceable standards by which those goods and services must be traded — or transported, marketed, sold, financed, bequeathed, or otherwise produced and disposed of — that is called government regulation of business. These standards do not include the basic criminal law that prohibits the violation of basic rights or contracts. Such standards apply to everyone in society and prohibit certain acts — murder, rape, embezzlement, robbery, burglary, kidnaping, assault, theft, and other acts defined as crimes. Government regulation involves setting standards for conduct that governments do not prohibit — e.g., manufacturing toys or trading securities. When governments own and thus either operate or lease property — land, roads, lakes, rivers, broadcast frequencies — that is not regulation but management.

There are some overlaps, of course. The government owns the roads and makes rules for using them, but this can spill over into regulating other behavior as well (e.g., the use of seat belts, air bags or motorcycle helmets).

In most government regulation of business, some federal, state, or municipal agencies — e.g., the Federal Trade Commission (FTC), Securities and Exchange Commission (SEC), Occupational Health and Safety Administration (OSHA), National Labor Relations Board (NLRB) — determine how production and trade within their range of jurisdiction must be conducted. Toys must not be dangerous, pajamas must not be flammable, securities must not be traded on insider information, labor organizers may not be barred from the workplace. The point is not just that persons in the various types of businesses *ought not to do* these things. That would be a concern of business ethics. The point is that government regulation *legally requires that people behave in certain ways* in the conduct of their professional tasks. (For example, the Ivan Boesky insider-trading case, in early 1987, concerned neither Boesky's immoral conduct, nor the violation of his fiduciary contractual responsibilities. Boesky violated the SEC's regulation that requires all securities' trading to be conducted on public information about what firms are about to do. He was fined and also coerced into revealing the names of others he knew to have carried on in a similar fashion. So we can summarize our characterization of government regulation as follows:

Government regulation of business is the setting of legally enforceable standards for carrying out what are regarded to be legitimate business activities.

Of course, there is a good deal more to government regulation *per se* than setting enforceable standards for business activities. Many noncommercial activities are also regulated — e.g., education, science, medicine, sex, child-rearing, sports, and even speech that is not protected by the First Amendment or some similar restriction on government power. Recently, the Supreme Court upheld the right of the state government of Georgia to regulate sexual conduct by excluding sodomy. That is government regulation that has little to do with business or economics. There have been cases where commercial speech has been curbed: the Supreme Court ruled that a Puerto Rican law banning the advertisement of gambling (which is legal there) had no First Amendment protection. Some states and municipalities regulate entertainment or even the press when it engages in the obscene treatment of certain subjects. And many more governmentally regulated noncommercial activities could be cited.

Government regulation of business is then just a fraction of the total scope of regulation carried out by the various levels of government throughout a society. Nevertheless, there are some fairly distinct sets of arguments that have been advanced in support of government regulation of commerce, and it will be a useful task to examine them.

Creature of the State

In feudal societies, with a firm class structure and inherited political power, corporate commerce had been established by the crown, the monarchy. Nations were governed with the maintenance of economic power as the main objective. Commerce could, of course, increase such power. We should recall that when Adam Smith wrote his revolutionary book on political economy and attacked the feudal or mercantilist system, he called this book *An Inquiry in to the Nature and Causes of the Wealth of Nations*. Despite its advocacy of free trade, the ostensible purpose of the work was to inform readers about increasing a nation's wealth.

Before Smith published his views, the most prevalent view was that nations are wealthy if they are well managed. It was in this milieu that corporate commerce began and grew through the mandated formation of joint stock companies, the early equivalents of shareholder-owned companies. It has been argued that since the creator of something takes responsibility for what the creation causes — as parents take responsibility for the conduct of their children — the state has both the authority and the responsibility to supervise, guide, and regulate corporate commerce.

This, in essence, is the "creature of the state" argument for government regulation. Its main proponent is the consumer advocate Ralph Nader: "In order to exist it [a corporation] must obtain a charter. A corporate charter is in effect an agreement whereby a government gives the corporate entity existence and that entity, in return, agrees to serve the public interest."[1] Corporations are, therefore, merely an extension of government. Governments have the duty as well as the authority to make sure that corporations behave properly, i.e., in the public interest. From a moral point of view, this doctrine is based on the idea that when something has been created by another, this "other" has the responsibility over the creature's conduct. Government regulation is, then, simply the exercise of government's proper responsibility.

Now this idea about the relationship between state and corporations seems to be foreign in the American context of politics. But simply because this relationship is unusual does not mean that few people support it. Indeed, many notable legal minds have subscribed to the "creature of the state" doctrine concerning the nature of corporations. This appears to be in disagreement with the intent of the 14th Amendment to the Constitution, which rejects the federal government's authority to interfere with freedom of contract. That freedom would seem to be the foundation of economic association, meaning, the freedom of the corporation as a morally legitimate and legally protected institution in a free society.

Market Failure and Regulation

Economists talk about market failures and refer to them as occasional inefficiencies in free markets. For example, some argue that the supply of electricity or telephone services to a given community would be inefficiently supplied if several firms were to compete among themselves.[2] There is a market failure in any community where what are called "public utilities" compete with each other. Government should intervene, the argument is made, so as to remedy the situation by establishing a legal monopoly in, for example, electrical power generation and distribution. This will restore the efficiency that markets themselves usually produce but now and then make difficult to obtain.

The concept of a market failure has, however, been expanded to mean something different. It has come to be used to refer to the failure of a free market to produce some goods or services at a cost deemed to be reasonable or desirable. For example, it is often argued that some markets fail to produce affordable education, housing, libraries, symphony orchestra performances, beaches, parks, zoos, or equality of opportunity, job security, or safety. The political process, as the main alternative approach toward the achievement of various goods and services, can remedy market failures by political action. If the free market does not produce the education people want, or education at a given price, the political process can be utilized to remedy this market failure. And if it does not produce goods and services we should have or in a way they should be produced, government should interfere and regulate the market to remedy this failure.

Underlying this argument for government intervention in the market place, we find a slightly revised version of the economist's idea of market failures. For the economist, there is only one norm. This norm is economic efficiency — producing and distributing what is in demand at the lowest possible cost. The expanded idea of market failure accepts that what is demanded should be produced efficiently. But it denies that goods and services in demand on the market are all that should be produced. The addition is made that the political process should also be used to register demand and should be utilized in order to spell out the conditions under which such demand must be satisfied.

Both of these ideas are, to some extent, indebted to the institution of democracy or to the belief in public participation in social decision-making processes. If people demand some good or service, it should be supplied by the market. Without obstacles, the good or service *will* be supplied efficiently. And if people demand some good or service via political intervention, it should be supplied by either the market or by a combination of market and the political process, whichever does the best job.

The underlying idea here is that any demand of a substantial number of people — e.g., the majority of the voters — should be satisfied. This may require government intervention in economic affairs. Such practices as the regulation of advertising, the implementation of affirmative action programs, the setting and enforcement of standards for safety on the workplace — all these and similar ones, usually referred to as government regulation of business — are morally and politically legitimate because the people demand them.

Human Rights and Regulation

Within the political tradition to which the United States owes its greatest debt, namely, that of a constitutional democracy or republic, the doctrine of human rights has a very important place. It is a central tenet of this tradition that individuals possess certain basic rights and that government is instituted among members of human communities so as to give these rights protection from potential domestic and foreign invaders. In this framework, the government has as its main business the protection of individual rights.

There are, of course, various theories concerning just what rights individuals do have. In recent years, the most prominent rights position has been one according to which individuals have basic rights that require governments to regulate commerce. For example, the United Nations Charter of Human Rights identifies the right to employment as a basic human right. Thus, when in the course of commerce individuals are faced with employment problems, for instance, the loss of their jobs, it is the role of the government, in part, to make certain that an individual's right to employment is protected as vigorously as possible. What counts is that the person is a human being, a member of the human community.

Several other basic rights have been designated as those that government has the responsibility to protect. They include the right to education, the right to safety on the job, the right of consumers to know the products they purchase and to be treated fairly in the marketplace (e.g., not to be discriminated against unjustly). If indeed these rights do exist — if individuals in the marketplace possess these rights — then governments should give them adequate protection. One of the ways these rights can be protected is by government regulation.

For example, if individuals have the right to safe working conditions, then government would have the authority to make periodic inspections of the workplaces where individuals are likely to be doing their work. Governments should also provide remedies wherever safety measures deemed appropriate by the best available experts are not in force. Indeed, such U.S. government regulatory agencies as the Occupational Health and Safety Administration are given intellectual and moral support precisely on the ground that their existence and operations are required for the sake of protecting the rights of workers.

Do individuals have the rights generally held to be protected by way of government regulations? Two arguments have been advanced to show that they do. First, utilitarian ethics, as outlined in the Introduction (and political theory), would provide strong support for the existence of these rights. Second, the general approach to ethics and politics called intuitionism — meaning trusting your first impressions as to what is right and wrong — would also give backing to the rights argument supporting government regulation.

Utilitarianism holds that the prime goal of human conduct is the greatest happiness of the greatest number (usually only of human beings, but for some utilitarians also of all sentient beings). In turn, social, political, and legal institutions should be devised to further this goal. Many utilitarians believe that the greatest happiness of the greatest number of people will best be achieved if a society has a legal system that protects the right to individual liberty. Many of them also hold, however, that other rights must also be given protection to achieve this goal. When the protection of the right to liberty does not serve as an adequate means for the promotion of the general welfare — which is another way to talk of the greatest happiness of the greatest number — then other general rules must be identified and government must enforce them so as to serve that goal. And many utilitarians believe that aside from the protection of individual liberty — and thus of a relatively unregulated marketplace — government should also protect the right to employment, a minimum wage, safety in the workplace, social security, environmental health, medical care, and so forth. It is only if these rights are given adequate protection that the greatest happiness of the greatest number will be pursued most efficiently.

According to utilitarianism then, the rights individuals have depend upon what institutions, legal principles, and governmental policies will most effectively contribute to the general welfare. Government regulation is, in turn, defended by utilitarians on grounds that it can most effectively protect the rights identified by way of utilitarianism.

The intuitionist defense of government regulation is based on this view: by way of our considered moral judgments, we can attest to the importance of certain values in social life, among which liberty and welfare are foremost. Intuitionism holds what is morally right and wrong is not known by way of elaborate theories or arguments. Rather we have a sense of right and wrong and relying on this sense is the best means to obtain moral and political understanding. For example, we all "know" — in our bones or guts, as it were — that depriving someone of his or her personal liberty is evil. To assault another, to rob him of what is his, is wrong. We don't need a philosophical theory to discover this — we know it intuitively. We also know, intuitively, that leaving an unfortunate individual helpless is morally wrong. Generally speaking, then, we know that both the liberty and the welfare of human beings are morally important and that a decent society will provide institutional means for the securement of both individual liberty and welfare.

Criminal law tends to take care of individual liberty. One's life, freedom of action, and property are protected by criminal law. Regulatory law, including the rules and regulations laid down by such bodies as the Food and Drug Administration, the Department of Education, the Environmental Protection Agency, the Federal Trade Commission, and the Securities and Exchange Commission, look after the general welfare, usually by government regulation.

Both utilitarianism and intuitionism are ethical perspectives that give intellectual support to the value of individual liberty and to the value of human welfare or happiness. That is why they are given as defenses of a system of government regulation, not a system of socialization or nationalization. Both of them stress the crucial significance of individual liberty and thus uphold the idea that commerce and free trade are ethical or moral to a certain extent. Socialists reject the basic value of the sort of individual liberty that both utilitarianism and intuitionism embrace, namely, the value of the individual's liberty from the intrusion of other people, including governments (who claim to act for society). On the other hand, libertarians uphold individual liberty as the dominant and overriding principle for governments to protect, so they do not accept the moral legitimacy of government regulation (e.g., inspection of the workplace, collection for social security). Government regulation of business, however, is giving such rules and directives to those doing something legitimate, namely conducting business. The activities themselves are regarded as morally legitimate, and the regulation is seen as morally proper. Neither socialists nor libertarians accept this.

This then is the defense of government regulation based on human rights. According to either utilitarianism or intuitionism, all persons are taken to have rights to welfare, fair treatment, and safety on the job, the securement of which requires that government regulate economic affairs.

Such views may, of course, be used to give intellectual support to government regulation of other than business activities. Sometimes people are deemed to have a right to cultural progress, a healthy moral climate in which case government *social* regulation — as distinct from economic regulation — is being promulgated. Such regulation may bear on the sale of pornography, the promotion of decency, or the stemming of drug use. So government regulation may be defended for other than economic reasons. The main thrust of the rights defense, as well as others covered in this chapter, bears on economic regulation.

Judicial Inefficiency

When the courts are unable to resolve disputes in line with standard legal doctrine, we are experiencing judicial inefficiency. It is argued that much of what government regulation tries to attain could be handled by way of the courts. The law of torts, or negligence, or liability might be able to handle what is now dealt with by way of government regulation. When working conditions are regulated, the objective is to save workers from unnecessary hazards and hardship. Workers might be able to achieve this objective by way of bargaining or lawsuits charging employers with negligence.

There are, however, some forms of commercial activities that cannot be handled this way. When factories pollute the atmosphere or water basins of their areas, they are not violating anyone's property rights. So they cannot be sued for damages, which would then set a precedent against such pollution. Instead, they produce what economists call "uninternalizable negative externalities". This means that they cause harm to others in a way in which they cannot be directly identified as the cause of the harm, nor can the victims be directly identified. When cars or factories pollute air, unidentifiable others are harmed. It cannot be determined whether this or that polluting activity produced such harm. This is the substance of judicial inefficiency. And it is at this point that even strong supporters of an unregulated economy defend government regulation.

Because of this, government regulation is thought to be necessary. Instead of leaving matters to litigation between various particular individuals who can be clearly identified as "plaintiff" and "defendant" in a courtroom, these advocates believe that government should regulate how much pollution should be allowed and by whom. The usual approach recommended is general cost-benefit analysis, although sometimes other methods may be used – e.g., the establishment of priorities by way of the political process.

A good deal of public policy results, in our very own time and in most Western societies, from the decisions of government regulators at various levels of the body politic. State, county, municipal, and federal regulators are often asked to decide the optimum (or acceptable or tolerable or proper) pollution levels of air or water. Based on the various means available in different political systems as to how cost-benefit determinations are to be made, regulators proceed to issue permits and restrictions. They determine how much pollution will be tolerated. This, roughly, is how levels of pollution in Lake Erie, Los Angeles, and the lakes of the state of Washington are established.

Just what conclusions should be reached from such a decision-making process is left open. The proponents of this view believe that the various manufacturing or transportation activities that pollute are desirable, therefore, what regulation should do is to determine the levels of pollution that can be tolerated within various communities. Based on various factors, including the priorities expressed by the population (by way of the political process), government regulation is different in political jurisdictions. Given the overall value attached to pollution-producing activities, the burdens of pollution need to be distributed fairly. And what will be fair is exactly the responsibility of the regulators to determine, with the aid of the legislature and the courts.

The underlying ethical framework of the judicial inefficiency defense of government regulation is complex. There are both utilitarian elements, meaning a concern for the greatest satisfaction of the greatest number of people, and libertarian elements, meaning a concern for individual rights, present in that argument. We will see more precisely just why this is the case when we discuss a prominent reply to this argument.

Response to Arguments for Regulation

We are discussing government regulation of business, not merely regulation of business. Other kinds of regulation are possible; for instance, in many drive-in banks, no one is allowed to approach windows on foot. One might think this is a clear case of government regulation. It does not involve the prohibition of banking, merely the direction of its clients by way of certain rules or regulations. Yet, the prohibition against walking to drive-in windows is regulated by insurance companies. This is not government regulation, yet it *is* regulation of commerce.

Generally speaking, those who dispute the advisability or morality of government regulation do not necessarily oppose all forms of regulation — quite the contrary. They maintain that alternatives to government regulation exist that would avoid the pitfalls and achieve the appropriate goals of that system, at least as efficiently as government regulation does, if not more so.[3]

This is important to realize. Many of the *goals* said to motivate government regulation — at least goals having to do with widely accepted social values such as job safety, social security, product safety — are undisputed by opponents. Proponents and opponents of government regulation tend, in the main, to be at odds on the more subtle issue of which values are more important than others, not on whether what is at issue are values at all. Even those who oppose government regulation on grounds of the alleged inefficiency of this institution — its extensive economic cost, its engendering of enormous bureaucracies, and the like — will ultimately involve themselves in a dispute about which values have priority. When they declare government regulation of business inefficient, economists may have to commit themselves to the virtue of thrift or frugality, as against extravagance and waste. Indeed, some economists hold that that is the only normative aspect of their science.

Let us look now at the more specialized rebuttals to four of the arguments for government regulation. For the affirmative side, the rebuttals will only be outlined and the debate will not be fully resolved here. But touching on certain affirmative and negative views about government regulation should provide a start to the topic's relationship to values.

1. *"Creature of the state," by accident!* It need not follow that modern corporations are necessarily "creatures of the state" merely because their predecessors, joint stock companies from the 11th through the 19th centuries, were established during a historical period of strong feudal and mercantilist influence. According to Ralph Nader, "The charter (by which corporations are established in various government jurisdictions) is basically a contract between the corporation and the state acting as representative of the people. As a legal entity, the corporation is given many

privileges, such as limited liability, by its charter."[4] However, responds Robert Hessen, "the theory has no basis in fact."

A corporation is created by a voluntary contractual agreement between individuals seeking to promote their financial self-interest. The articles of incorporation (or charter) are a contract solely between the individual founders; the state is not a party to it. The articles contain purely factual information, such as the name and purpose of the business, its intended duration, the number of shares to be issued, and so on. The state does not give life or birth to the corporation. Just as the registrar of deeds records every sale of land, and the county clerk records the birth of every baby, so the commissioner of corporations records the formation of every corporation— nothing more.[5]

As to special privileges, such as limited liability, some are a matter of the stated condition of doing business with corporations. Those who wish to do business with the corporation are free to accept or reject some of these. But some are indeed special legal privileges achieved by corporations, similar to those achieved by unions or churches or educational institutions, mainly as a result of political lobbying. This may be objectionable, but has no bearing on the essential nature of corporations or on corporate commerce. Such privilege can be attributed to the practices of a government that refuses to stay out of people's economic affairs (as it stays out, at least largely, of people's religious affairs).

This, at least, is the central response to the view that government is not only authorized but also ought, responsibly, to regulate corporate commerce. Let it be granted that a basic change of the relationship between citizens and government occurred in the eighteenth century when a system of constitutional democracy, such as the American one, had been established. If it was a wise and morally justified change, then it ought also to effect the relationship between commerce and the state. In a society in which the state is sovereign, commerce would, of course, be a matter of state, and indeed historically it has been. So the joint stock companies of the past could be expected to be creatures of various feudal states. Other human institutions, at that time, were also under the primary control of governments.

But then as far as ultimate sovereignty is concerned, a shift occurred from state to citizen. Governments became servants of the citizenry and the latter stopped being the mere subjects of the state. Various human institutions gradually came under the control of private citizens, even as governments continued to be retained as administrators of law and, presumably, justice. So with commerce. Private citizens could now embark upon their own economic endeavors, some of which of course would resemble closely enough what previously had been done by states.

Accordingly, government has no authority to regulate commerce on the morally objectionable grounds that it has created one of the paramount institutions of commerce, namely, the corporation. The response to the "creature of the state" argument, then, acknowledges the historical fact that is raised as the foundation of that argument. However, it declares that historical fact irrelevant, given the (presumably suitable, proper) reconsideration of the relationship of citizen to the state along constitutional democratic lines.

2. *Market failure, political failure.* Markets are often inefficient or even misguided. Does this warrant the introduction of government intervention to remedy matters? There are those who deny this, noting the propensity of government to remedy things that go seriously astray. In short, government response to market failures, conceived either narrowly or broadly (as either inefficiencies or inadequacies of markets), will almost certainly result in political failures.

All of this isn't even supposed to involve the more serious political failures associated with attempts by government to remedy the alleged inadequacies of the market. It is held that these inadequacies can include such matters as the market indulgence in junk food, disco bars, or pop records, as against nutritious food, art museums, and symphonic orchestras. In addition, the market tolerates production of marketing appeals, which can be poor and tasteless, simply because some consumers are willing to pay for them and demand, from ignorance or neglect, nothing better, or so the critics would maintain.

But, the critics of political efforts to reform society and remedy such market failures are pessimistic. They say it is hopeless to expect the desired result from government intervention and regulations, as a matter of political logic. Even where remedies appear to be forthcoming — say, in the creation of the public library system, the regulation of toy manufacturing, or the requirement of truth in labelling — the cost to be paid for such attempts is so great that ultimately more harm than good is done. Everything that counts against government being able to make markets more efficient counts also against government being able, in general, to make markets more decent, equitable, safe, tasteful, honorable, and otherwise virtuous. The very factors said to lead to certain deficiencies of markets — pointed out by such critics of the free market as John Kenneth Galbraith and Ralph Nader — will assert themselves within the political arena, especially in a relatively free, democratic society where no elite class or kind dictator can command good behavior from producers.

Let us take the case of market inefficiencies. Yes, on first sight it does appear that if the market is left entirely free and unregulated by the state, some duplications, as in the production of electricity, telephone service, water supply, and other public goods, will emerge. This does seem to be a market failure. Markets are supposed to be the means for attaining the most efficient distribution of goods and services within a given community. But perhaps such duplication should not be taken to be inefficient, nor need any remedy by government amount to more than an exacerbation of problems.

First, it may be a fortuitous thing within a given market to have some types of service lines duplicated. In a free society, the right to strike exists. When public utilities experience a strike, this can lead to severe problems. To avoid such problems, one solution would be to accept duplications in the form of inefficient competition. Alternative remedies for such labor stoppage would go squarely against the principles of a free society — e.g. by prohibiting of strikes, or injunctions.

Second, the political failures accompanying efforts to remedy market failures via government intervention and regulation are numerous. Strikes against public service industries qualify as one such political failure. Such political failures would also include the capturing of the regulatory process by industry experts; the influence of vested interest (on public service corporation pricing practices, industrial policy, labor negotiations); technological innovation lag, and the whole array of potential abuses of political power that goes hand in hand with the political administration of human affairs.

Some critics back up their position with historical and empirical studies, others with conceptual analysis. In either case, the basic point against the market failure argument supporting government regulation is that what propensity markets have for shortcomings, the political arena not only matches but increases this severalfold. Whatever would make it possible for human beings who interact on a voluntary basis — to mismanage their lives whether they be rich, poor, black, white, men or women, natives or naturalized citizens — the likelihood of doing so by means of the introduction of politics (beyond the scope of the ordinary criminal law that merely protects basic rights to life, liberty, and property) is going to be greater. Politics, after all, involves some people gaining special *powers* over others in how life is to be conducted, concerning what is more and less valuable, or whose goals are more worthwhile or important. It is not, as many critics of government regulation claim, that no such value judgments are valid, that everything is a matter of subjective opinion, so that government could not judge in such matters. Rather, effectuating the conduct, institutions, practices, and habits that conform to standards of worthwhileness and the like by political means is less probable than by means of a free market.

3. *Human rights versus natural rights.* The question here is which theory of rights is correct. That is not easily determined. Those who defend government regulation from a basis of human rights theory subscribe to a view of what rights persons have, which is different from the view of individual rights opponents of government regulation invoke. It is important, however, to point out that opponents of government regulation invoking human rights theory tend to embrace a rather traditional natural rights viewpoint and do not usually — though there are exceptions — embrace utilitarianism and intuitionism.

The natural rights viewpoint argues that, yes, there are basic human rights. These can be identified by reference to the universal moral nature of human beings. What this requires is that a society uphold, first and foremost, the principle of individual rights to life, liberty, and property and leave the securement of other values to nonpolitical means.

Essentially, the argument holds, everyone has the task, within or outside society, to advance his or her life, to make of himself or herself a good human being. The primary means available to all persons to accomplish the good life is the use of one's own mind and abilities, in other words, autonomous self-initiated, rational conduct. The main preventable danger to such conduct in society is the activity of criminals. Without them, it becomes a matter of one's own responsibility to succeed or fail at living the good life (within his or her own context of possibilities).

True, it is desirable to have the assistance, support, or cooperation of others in this worthy pursuit; coercion, the most severe social injury that a person can suffer, is far worse than the absence of help or support. This is a general social policy judgment. It concerns what is the primary value to uphold within a human community as a principle of human interaction. It does not preclude the possibility that for individuals, in their own lives, other values may take precedence. They may be in a position in which they should strive to secure such values instead of individual liberty. The point is that, as members of a human community, their highest value is individual liberty, what their political representatives are required to protect over all else.

Evidently, this proposition depends on a number of assumptions in arguments that have to be advanced. These arguments cannot be fully developed here. It may be useful to mention, however, that the natural rights viewpoint rests on the premise that everyone (under normal circumstances where he or she is not crucially incapacitated — in which case special exemptions would apply) has the basic choice to apply himself or herself to living, regardless of the complexity of one's society, and for everyone it is his or her moral responsibility to carry out this task well. This assumption rests on a conception of what human beings and human life most importantly amount to, that is, on one's conception of the nature of human existence. Such a conception assumes free will — that individuals, as adults, are their own governors and are owed respect as such, even though they might misgovern their own lives or fail to treat others with kindness, generosity, or respect — so long as they do not violate others' rights to equal moral independence. Moral independence applies not only to the beliefs one has but also to the actions one takes, including those actions that are essentially productive, namely commercial or economic actions. That is where the idea of the right to private property as an essential personal, individual right, emerges. That right, in turn, gives rise in a large human community, to the institution of the free, unregulated market place, blocking the implementation of government regulations that aim to secure the so-called human rights, spoken of by advocates of government regulation.

For now, the debate cannot be fully resolved. Who is right depends on which theory, if either, is correct. Both invoke a respected tradition, especially in Western liberal democracies. And one who considers the merits of government regulation of business must take into account the arguments for these two positions before making a decision pro or con.

4.   *Quarantine is judicially efficient.* Put plainly, there is no problem of judicial inefficiency. Anyone who imposes unjustified harm upon others — even in the course of carrying out benign tasks, such as the production of steel or travel via a polluting vehicle — is in violation of standards of decent human community life. Such a person or company should be stopped or punished. Government regulation of such pollution *is*, however, judicially "inefficient." It imposes unjustified harm on many members of a community. The utilitarian attempt to justify such government regulation is countered by a natural rights argument that defends the right of autonomy and freedom of choice.

What does the judicial efficiency argument supporting government regulation accomplish? It maintains that since it is impossible to do some things without unjustly hurting people, the degree and scope of the unjust infliction or injury should be regulated by government. But has it been established that any unjust infliction of injuries is morally defensible? Utilitarianism avoids this problem by treating as justified any infliction of injury that produces or accompanies the production of greater overall benefit.

In the last analysis, however, all this rests on the belief that helping many can excuse hurting a few. But this is not accepted as an adequate moral ground by those who deny that individuals should be made to suffer unwanted, unearned harm so that some others may enjoy benefits. Utilitarian trade-offs seem reasonable because one usually thinks of the groups involved in the distribution of the costs and benefits as willing participants. For example, consider military operations in the voluntary defense of one's society. Those involved are aware of the fact that they may be subject to decisions resulting from cost-benefit calculations applying to the whole group, given its agreed-upon overriding goals.

The argument based on the alleged judicial inefficiency can be countered by claiming that human communities and their participants ought not be regarded in the same light as voluntary or quasi-voluntary groups (or teams) may be. Many members of communities of course experience air or water pollution. Some of them have not consented, either explicitly or tacitly to be part of the process of cost-benefit distribution. They shouldn't be subject to others' determination as to whose respiratory well-being may be sacrificed so as to obtain the benefits of, say, steel production or car transportation.

No one would maintain that if potential rapists were to obtain immense sexual gratification from the assault of rape, and their victims might only suffer minor psychological or physical injury in the process, rape should be regulated by government.[6] No one need deny that sexual gratification is desirable in order to deny the rapist his benefits at his victim's expense. The strong intuitive base of this example should suffice to counter the intuitive strength of the utilitarian's case.

For example, it might be objected that with the approach modelled on quarantine, we must bar cars outright. Taken literally, the quarantine path would require that all presently known ways of generating electricity be banned, since all have some forms of remote statistically occurring health consequences. In light of this, there may well be a case for some sort of governmental trade-off-enforcing here, as much as we would like to avoid it.

Yet, of course, all this argument says is that there should never have been allowed any pollution in the sense of imposing uninternalizable negative externalities on innocent third parties. Now that we have had it for many decades, there is a different question, namely, how to stop the practice. That is like arguing that there should never have been any slavery in the first place, but now that we have had it for many decades, how do we abolish it? While that is an important matter, the issue here isn't concerned with such public policy matters, only with whether this or that public policy is just. It may well turn out that abolition must proceed slowly, with care that justice be preserved in the process.

Yet it might be noted, as an aside, that had there been a policy of quarantine in the first place, had such indiscriminate pollution been disallowed or prohibited from the beginning, cars might have been built differently; transportation might have developed differently; and indeed many of the environmental problems that now plague us might not have occurred at all. Adjustments would have been simpler to make at an earlier stage. Instead of a very cheap car and the accompanying highway system, cars might have turned out to cost more from the start and the highway system that developed might have been more modest, with corresponding expansion in research toward other forms of transportation. Once, of course, the wrong actions are taken and practices and institutions are developed from them (as if these actions were acceptable) matters become more difficult to set right. But that is not a reason for not making every effort to remedy past wrongs.

It might also be noted that not all emission of possibly harmful wastes are harmful in low dosages. There are levels that are tolerable by all persons, and waste emissions from coal or nuclear power would not involve pollution up to a certain point. That is perhaps analogous to why no quarantine is instituted when people have colds or some other contagious condition that is barely harmful and certainly is not incapacitating. The "reasonable man" doctrine, which courts employ, can be made applicable to risks that normal living imposes on people. So "judgment calls" apply here, but they do not invite government regulation, merely the application of the rule of law to the conduct of producers who are suspected of spreading indiscriminate harm within the community. When this harm becomes rights-violating, it must be prohibited.

So, in the end, the argument for government regulation based on judicial inefficiency is countered by the doctrine that members of society have natural rights to be free from having their lives, liberty, and property interfered with by others. Imposing upon them the (inevitably) injurious side-effects of otherwise benign (productive, entertaining, religious, and any other) activities that others may wish to engage in is unjust. When such injustice has been tolerated for many years, judicial means must be found for remedying matters. In other areas, we have found such methods already — land reform, repatriation, compensation, restoration — are examples that come to mind. And exactly how such remedy should proceed is not itself at issue; obviously one would not wish to remedy past wrongs in ways that would engender greater wrongs in the present. But, as noted above, that is a matter of public policy, judicial process, and similar technicalities that any society faces when it wishes to conform to the requirements of justice.

Conclusion

Any further exploration of arguments surrounding government regulation would require detailing what those taking the various sides have advanced. (The bibliography contains the writings of the original protagonists and antagonists.) We, of course, have not touched on what purports to be entirely nonmoral arguments for and against government regulation. It is likely that so long as we are discussing whether to maintain or abolish or even reform human institutions, the points raised will make some, ever so indirect, reference to matters of morality. (Thus when economists defend or attack something on grounds that efficiency is promoted or thwarted, respectively, they hold that the production and distribution of wealth — i.e., what people value — is itself important, so that doing it efficiently should matter to us.)

What we have done here is provide outlines of four arguments and four rebuttals. The selection is based on what has been the most widely and systematically considered normative aspects of government regulation. We have also focused on the debates that have ensued in the United States, although my experience has been that similar viewpoints emerge in the context of discussing other countries.

None of what has been said above touches on whether the values of individual human liberty and well-being are themselves perhaps not very significant, after all. Within some systems, it is not human beings as they are today but as they assuredly must eventually turn out to be that matters. Politics in those systems should be a field with a concern for the well-being of this yet-to-emerge "human race." But such philosophies, e.g., Marxism, do not address themselves to problems in connection with which the topic and institution of government regulation of business arise. Non-Marxist socialism or communism, too, deals with communities that reject the principle of the right to private property, especially in the major means of production. What they are after is not government regulation but the wholesale socialization of the community's productive processes.

The issue here has been a relatively narrow one, therefore. Should commerce, as some maintain of religion or the arts, be left to individuals as a matter of their own choices — alone or cooperatively, competitively, or corporately — with law merely providing protection and remedy against the violation of individual rights to life, liberty, and property? Or should the government embark upon the supervisory project of market regulation? Should government make sure that, beyond respecting the libertarian or negative rights of all parties, commerce also concern itself with various ideals, a broad conception of human rights, or the general promotion of the overall welfare of the society? It is to achieve these latter objectives that government regulation of business has been promoted.

Notes

1. Ralph Nader and Mark J. Green, "The Case for Federal Charters," *Nation,* February 5, 1973, p. 173. For a fuller exposition of the views of Nader, see Ralph Nader and Mark J. Green, eds., *Corporate Power in America* (New York: Grossman Publishers, 1973).

2. John Stuart Mill, *The Principles of Political Economy* (Toronto, Ontario: University of Toronto Press, 1965).

3. Robert W. Poole, Jr., ed., *Instead of Regulation* (Lexington, Massachusetts: Lexington Books, 1981) and Michael S. Baram, *Alternatives to Regulation* (Lexington, Mass.: Lexington Books, 1981).

4. Ralph Nader, "Chartering Corporations," *The New Republic,* March 11, 1972, p. 9.

5. Robert Hessen, "Creatures of the State? The Case Against Federal Chartering of Corporations," *Barron's,* May 24, 1976, p. 5. For a fuller exposition of this view, see Robert Hessen, *In Defense of the Corporation* (Stanford, Calif.: Hoover Press, 1979).

6. This analogy has been presented by Steve Kelman who objects to cost-benefit analysis, although not to government regulation, quite the contrary. See Steve Kelman, "Paternalism and Regulation," in T. R. Machan and M. Bruce Johnson, eds., *Rights and Regulation* (Cambridge, Mass.: Ballinger Pub. Co., 1983).

References

Kenneth J. Arrow. 1981. "Two Cheers for Government Regulation." *Harper's* (March).

Michael S. Barnam. 1981. *Alternatives to Regulation*. Lexington, Mass.: Lexington Books.

Jonathan R. T. Hughes. 1977. *The Governmental Habit*. New York: Basic Books.

Louis M.Kohlmeier, Jr. 1969. *The Regulators*. New York: Harper and Row.

Tibor R. Machan and M. Bruce Johnson, eds., 1983. *Rights and Regulation*. Cambridge, Mass.: Ballinger Pub. Co.

Barry M. Mitnick. 1972. *The Political Economy of Regulation*. New York: Columbia University Press.

Robert W. Poole, Jr., ed. 1981. *Instead of Regulation*. Lexington, Mass.: Lexington Books.

8

BUSINESS ABROAD

ELLEN FRANKEL PAUL

Introduction

An area of commerce that poses ethical as well as public policy challenges
is foreign trade. With the phenomenal rise of multinational commerce,
people in the business world need to think clearly about proper conduct and
sound public policy in foreign trade.

Should corporate executives sanction payoffs to government officials of
foreign countries in order to secure contracts to sell or purchase goods
within those countries? Is it permissible for United States corporations to
engage in business activities within countries that practice racial discrimination and deprive blacks of basic human rights as a matter of governmental policy?

Questions like these have dominated the public media and its treatment
of international business, particularly in the post-Watergate era, for
Watergate brought to public awareness the fact that multinational corporations often acted in ways that did not conform to our intuition about how
moral individuals ought to act. When it was revealed that corporations
often kept slush funds to make contributions of a dubious nature to
domestic politicians, and that corporations also engaged in activities that
smacked of bribery of foreign officials, big business suffered a tremendous
loss in public esteem.

But how are we to determine whether such seemingly dubious business
activities are actually unjustifiable from a moral point of view? Given that
we live in a world in which moral codes conflict, how ought these issues to
be decided? After all, we are not simply engaged in an idle, albeit
interesting, academic discussion, but rather in an enterprise with direct
implications for public policy. While virtually all moral systems developed
in our Western tradition have condemned such activities as murder, theft,
bribery, or lying, they have done so from different foundational principles,
and sometimes these principles have led their practitioners to differ about

180

the classification of the same sorts of activities. For example, some moral theorists might claim that stealing another person's property is always to be categorized as theft and condemned, while another theorist, operating from different principles, might declare that if a person were starving and another had an abundance of goods, then the destitute man would be justified in stealing from the rich man, while still a third moralist might claim that private property is illegitimate by its very nature, and therefore everyone should receive from society what he needs.

It might be helpful in examining these troublesome issues relating to international business to pause for a moment to examine several ethical systems that have shaped the thinking of moralists in the Western tradition, especially during the last three centuries. Three systems appear to have dominated the field of ethics during this period: (1) utilitarianism, (2) natural rights theory, and (3) Kantianism.

Utilitarianism is an ethical system devised principally by Jeremy Bentham, a British moral philosopher who wrote in the late eighteenth and early nineteenth century. Although utilitarianism was modified by Bentham's illustrious successor, John Stuart Mill, to allow for more conformity to conventional ethical judgments, its essential character has remained constant to this day, and many contemporary philosophers and public policy analysts are still adherents of utilitarianism. In fact, the currently popular notion of cost/benefit analysis owes its inspiration to this doctrine. Utilitarianism is based on the perception that human beings are pain-avoiders and pleasure-seekers. More importantly, utilitarians conclude from this observation of how individuals actually behave that they *ought* to act in this way. Thus, if one wishes to behave morally and be a good utilitarian, one should seek to maximize one's pleasure and minimize one's pain. From this moral precept, utilitarians seek to generalize from the behavior of single individuals to how people ought to behave in society, and how their governments ought to legislate. The famous utilitarian maxim proclaims — act to achieve the greatest happiness for the greatest number. Therefore, when a government examines a proposal for, let us say, building a new hospital, it should consider the pleasure to be gained by the likely beneficiaries and balance that against the harm to be suffered by the projected losers. Also, the onerousness of any legislative action must be taken into account and the advantages and disadvantages of using public funds for a different purpose. It is easy to see how modern cost/benefit analysis developed from this approach to morality.

In contrast to utilitarianism, which tends to be very pragmatic because it weighs harms and benefits to reach its moral and policy perscriptions, natural rights theory is more abstract and theoretical. John Locke's *Second Treatise of Government* is the veritable bible of natural rights theory. Written in the late seventeenth century, again by an English author, it proclaimed the importance of individualism and the protection of individuals from governmental oppression in their pursuit of property and in their exercise of liberty. Locke went so far as to proclaim a novel thesis, that government exists for the protection of the property—and he meant by property, life, liberty, and estates—of individuals, and, indeed, that government is nothing more than a trustee established by the consent of individuals for the purpose of protecting their rights. Government, consequently, can be overthrown if it acts in ways that violate the rights of men.

Our third moral system was developed by a German philosopher, Immanuel Kant, in the late eighteenth century. Kant argued that to act morally an individual ought to conceive the principle upon which he acts as one upon which everyone should act. An example might help clarify his position. Let us imagine that you are thinking about murdering your rich uncle, who also happens to be a genuinely despicable character. But if we apply the principle embodied in this proposal—that everyone ought to eliminate rich people who also happen to be nasty—one can foresee some really horrendous consequences for the future welfare of society. Kant called this principle the "categorical imperative." Another element of Kantianism has remained influential—his precept that one ought to treat people as ends only and never simply as means to the pursuit of one's own ends. What this principle captures is the notion of the moral autonomy and importance of every living person, that is, the idea that people ought not be treated as tools to be used for another person's pleasure. If these Kantian ideas sound familiar, it is not surprising, for Kant acknowledged that what his moral principles amounted to was the Christian precept that one ought to treat others as one wished to be treated—the Golden Rule.

In what follows, we will examine two major issues of controversy regarding American business practices abroad: (1) the payment of allegedly illicit payments to foreign government officials, and (2) the practice of doing business in countries with objectionable social practices. It is my hope that the three ethical positions adumbrated above might prove helpful in refining our intuitive reactions to each of these practices.

Foreign Bribery

In December 1977, Congress passed the Foreign Corrupt Practices Act (FCPA) without a single dissenting vote. This remarkable unanimity was the result of a series of revelations of bribery engaged in by some of America's leading corporations in their business dealings around the world. It was revealed that officials of Lockheed, Gulf Oil, Northrop, and Boeing (among others) had made payments to officials of foreign governments in order to secure business for their firms. In an orgy of self-revelation, some 450 United States corporations revealed to the Securities and Exchange

Commission that they had made three hundred million dollars worth of under-the-table payoffs.

The FCPA made it a criminal offense for any United States corporation to make any payment to a foreign official or foreign political party or its official for the purpose of influencing that person to exercise his authority or connections to affect decisions of his government. In other words, United States corporations were prohibited from paying bribes to foreign officials to solicit their assistance in securing contracts. Companies caught violating the Act would be subject to a fine of up to one million dollars, while officers or directors of the offending companies could receive sentences of up to five years in jail and ten thousand dollars in fines. In addition, the Act called for detailed disclosure in the accounting records submitted by companies to the SEC in an attempt to eliminate double bookkeeping that could hide secret payments. This provision, too, carries criminal penalties. As of April 1983, twenty-six cases had been brought against companies by the SEC and another eight cases by the Justice Department, which shares enforcement powers with the SEC.

Despite the unanimous support that the FCPA garnered in Congress in 1977, it has provoked widespread objections in the business community. Since 1981, lobbying for amendments to the legislation has been intense, with business groups pressuring Congressmen to eliminate what they feel to be some of the more onerous elements of the Act. While their efforts had not met with success (as of 1984) as the result of some powerful opposition in the House, the Senate did pass amendments to the act in November 1981, but that effort failed to reach the House floor. These efforts at amending the FCPA have continued. The principal objectives of these proposed amendments is to remove the criminal penalties attached to the accounting disclosure requirements and to weaken the liability placed on corporate officers for payments made by third party intermediaries. This latter objective would be achieved by diluting the original language of the Act, which placed liability on officers if they had "reason to know" that payments might be made by intermediaries. This provision would be replaced by one that limited liability to instances in which the executive directed or authorized the payment "expressly or by a course of conduct." Representative Timothy Wirth (D., Colorado) the leading opponent of this reform in the House considers such language to be much too vague, and he condemns the effort at reform as an attempt to emasculate the Act and evade its intent.

Businessmen who favor modifications of FCPA and their Congressional allies—most conspicuously Senators John Chafee (R., Rhode Island) and John Heinz (R., Pennsylvania), and Representative Dan Mica (D., Florida)—view the matter quite differently. While no one goes so far as to endorse bribery or urge the outright repeal of FCPA, they do point to its tendency to undermine our exporting effort both by discouraging companies from actively pursuing foreign contracts because of uncertainty about when they might fall afoul of the vaguely defined prohibitions of FCPA, and by placing even the willing companies at a competitive disadvantage. If European companies, for example, can enter a country like Saudi Arabia and pay bribes disguised as "commissions" to members of the royal family, how, these critics ask, can American companies compete? Indeed, no other country has followed our lead, they point out, in prohibiting such payoffs so scrupulously, and this despite the fact that the United States, ever since the passage of the FCPA, has been working through diplomatic channels to achieve such an international agreement on the prohibition of these questionable practices. In West Germany, such payments are fully tax deductible; in Italy, a 1980 law established that payments to foreign officials to secure business are legal; and in France no law exists to curb foreign bribery.[1] In a Louis Harris poll conducted in the Fall of 1983 among corporate officials, 78% of the respondents agreed that the law makes it difficult to sell in countries in which bribery is a way of life and that U.S. exports are, therefore, hindered. About one-fifth of the respondents also felt that they had lost business as a result of the Act, a figure only slightly less than the 30% who claimed losses two years earlier in a General Accounting Office survey.[2] What the Harris Poll also indicated was a division of opinion about what ought to be done about some controversial elements of the FCPA, with opinion divided over the elimination of criminal penalties for violating the accounting provisions and the effort to ease executives' accountability for payments made by intermediaries.

While it is difficult to quantify a nonevent such as the loss of potential business, some evidence does exist that the U.S. export effort has been adversely affected by the Act. For example, the Emergency Committee for American Trade surveyed its 65 member-companies and they reported an estimated two billion dollars in lost business. This translates into 60,000 to 80,000 lost jobs in the United States, according to Commerce Department estimates.[3] Norman Pacun, vice-president and general counsel of Ingersoll-Rand, a company with over one billion dollars in foreign sales per year, testified before the Senate Banking Committee that while it is difficult to quantify such lost business, many experts have pointed to the negative impact of the FCPA in the OPEC countries in particular. As confirmation of this conjecture, he pointed to the much slower growth of our exports to OPEC countries than throughout the rest of the world after the passage of the Act.[4] And President Carter's task force on export promotion concluded that the FCPA constitutes the second most serious legal disincentive for U.S. exports, with only the tax code presenting a graver barrier.

Business critics, like Mr. Pacun, have also pointed to the fact that America's scrupulousness in policing its own corporations has not significantly ameliorated the problem of bribery around the world. While American companies have undeniably been curtailed from committing these "shady" acts, foreign companies have not been so constrained. Some critics even argue that if our objective is to greatly constrain such activities throughout the world, our unilateral attempt serves to hamper that effort rather than encourage it because other countries realize that by refusing to sign an international prohibition they can still reap the benefits of eliminating American competitors. Thus, the only true beneficiaries of the FCPA would be our foreign competitors, and we will have accomplished little or nothing for the cause of international morality.

Critics have also pointed to the deleterious foreign policy implications of the FCPA. Foreign governments, they maintain, are often offended by our "holier than thou" attitude and deeply resent our attempt to foist our values upon them. Curiously, in May 1981 a former State Department official who handled the attempts at negotiating an international agreement on the prohibition of bribery testified before the Senate Banking Committee that "it is hard to overestimate the potential damage to U.S. relations with another country if we find ourselves investigating and disclosing misconduct by the head of government or other senior officials of that country. It is likely that one day the policies of this Act and critical U.S. foreign policy interests will come into sharp conflict."[5] Little more than two years later former Japanese Prime Minister KaKuei Tanaka was found guilty of taking nearly two million dollars in bribes from Lockheed to get All Nippon Airlines to purchase a fleet of planes from Lockheed. When these payments were revealed in the 1970s, they weakened the Japanese government, and the aftereffects are still being felt.

In addition to these more weighty objections, opponents point to the vagueness of the Act's requirements, and their consequent inability to distinguish a permissible payment — so-called "grease" payments to minor officials such as customs agents to facilitate the entry of goods — from impermissible acts of bribery. Given that the Act excluded such trivial payments to minor governmental functionaries, the problem of where to draw the line is rife for differences of opinion. Thus, the ambiguity of the law has engendered much confusion. And finally, the detailed record-keeping and the lack of precise standards for the information required in these disclosures, has disturbed some businessmen and added to their accounting costs.

Those who favor the Act tend not to go into such great detail as their critics. For them, the Act's necessity is nearly self-evident, given the unacceptably immoral practices that many businesses perpetrated prior to its passage. While they might concede that some technical clarification to the wording of the Act would be acceptable, and even Representative Wirth has seemed more accommodating, they bitterly resent any attempts to dilute the criminal liability elements imposed on executives by the FCPA. Although some supporters deny that American businesses have suffered loss of trade as a result of the Act, most acknowledge that this might well be the case, yet they hold morality to be more imperative in this case than the marginal promotion of the U.S. export-import business.

Now that we have perused some of the arguments for and against the FCPA and its modifications, let us proceed as moralists to examine this Act. It is difficult, indeed, to discover a moral system that explicitly and unqualifiedly endorses bribery. But as Mark Pastin and Michael Hooker have pointed out in their article "Ethics and the Foreign Corrupt Practices Act,"[6] there may well be countervailing considerations of a moral nature that can modify a general prohibition against bribery in the types of cases covered by the FCPA. They examined the Act from two different moral positions, one utilitarian and the other, more or less Kantian. As they examined the law from a utilitarian moral perspective, they concluded that it might be preferable to have no law at all. In reaching this conclusion, they cited the Act's adverse effect on our balance of payments, the loss of business and jobs, the fact that American bribes have simply been replaced by bribes given by businesses from other developed countries, and the bureaucratic infighting between the SEC and the Justice Department. On a utilitarian, cost/benefit analysis, then, they found that the gains in heightened moral conduct by American businesses did not outweigh the losses from the other factors just mentioned. On another moral framework, which the authors called "rule assessment" a law is morally sound if and only if it accords with a code of correct ethical rules, they also found the FCPA wanting. For the rule against bribery is merely a *prima facie* rule (that is, one that can be overriden by a conflicting rule) not a categorical rule (one that can't be overriden), and in this case the rule against bribery can be overriden by corporate obligations to shareholders and workers to make a profit for the former and to retain the jobs of the latter. If a little bribery is necessary to keep these promises, then so be it. And besides, the authors argue, such payments are usually extorted by the foreign official from the American businessman, so he may not be involved in the evil of promoting deception, particularly when these practices accord with recognized local practices. Many of the business critics of FCPA, by the way, also make this point: that in many areas of the world such practices are accepted as standard business procedures.

Not surprisingly, Pastin and Hooker's position generated much controversy, as it seemed to place the moral onus more on the FCPA itself then on so-called corrupt business practices. Kenneth Alpern, in his "Moral Dimensions of the Foreign Corrupt Practices Act: Comments on Pastin and Hooker,"[7] took them to task. He concentrated his fire on their application of the "rule assessment" model, arguing that corporations are the agents of their individual shareholders and, as such, promise only to work to increase the value of their investments, but not by any means whatsoever. Thus, he sees no conflict between the moral rule against bribery and the promise of a corporation to its shareholders, merely a conflict between the antibribery injunction and the self-interest of the shareholders. And moral rules must always take precedence over self-interest, for that is the whole purpose of having moral rules. The FCPA, thus, is perfectly compatible with morality, according to Alpern.

We have seen how a utilitarian analysis might lead to the repeal of the FCPA, or at the very least its modification. For a utilitarian, the weight of its negative consequences is simply too great to bear when measured against its dubious benefits in promoting international morality. But what might a natural rights moralist make of this law? He might proceed to reason in this fashion. Corporations are simply the agents of individuals who pool their assets, they hope, to augment them through the production and sale of commodities or services that consumers desire to purchase. As an agent, the corporation is not entitled to commit any acts that would be immoral if committed by an individual. If it is immoral for you to bribe a purchasing agent for a large corporation in order to induce that man to buy your inferior product for his company's use at an inflated price, then it is wrong for a corporation to do the same thing. But why is it wrong for an individual to engage in such a practice? It is wrong because it deprives the shareholders of the bribed official's company of a portion of their assets because the official will not make the decision on the basis of the only relevant considerations — price and quality. The moral question seems to be decided against bribery when we are dealing with a case of trade between two privately-held companies.

However, the issue becomes somewhat clouded when we examine the kinds of cases addressed by the FCPA, that is, where a private U.S. company is having dealings with a Third World government for the construction of some public works project or for the purchase of some raw materials native to that country. One might argue that the government official in the Third World country is an agent, now, not of shareholders, but rather of the citizens of his country and, as such, the same argument ought to hold against bribing him. But things are not as simple as they might first appear. In most such countries, the governments are dictatorships or even Marxist regimes who in no sense can be analogized to our system of government, which is based on the theory that the government is the agent of the people. Rather, these governments have usurped authority, usually by force of arms. Such governments are more like thieves than representatives of the people, for they oppress their people, deprive them of their property, and claim the right to make business decisions for the whole country as though they owned it exclusively for themselves. In such a situation, what does morality dictate? It seems that two sets of circumstances need to be differentiated: (1) if the government is really thoroughly treacherous, even to the extent that it exterminates its own citizens, then we ought not deal with such murderers; or (2) if the government is less oppressive and marked by corruption more than outright villany, then we can either deal with it or not, and from a natural rights perspective, morality does not seem to favor one of the courses of action over the other.

A bit of explanation is in order. In the first case, if an American company proceeded to sell arms, computers, film, or whatever to that treacherous government, it would be abetting the persecution and slaughter of innocent people. Thus, to have traded with Idi Amin's bloodthirsty regime in Uganda by the use of bribes or not would be morally reprehensible. In the second type of case, for example, a decision of whether or not to do business with the Saudi princes who control their country's oil reserves—it seems more a matter of personal taste than a question of natural rights whether one should or should not conform to local customs and submit bribes in order to do business there. The American company would be entitled to its resources, having received them initially from shareholders and later through profits reaped from the sale of merchandise to willing customers, while the Saudi princes would not be entitled to their resources, having gotten them through conquest and by treating the resources found within their territory almost as the personal property of the royal family. If the American company determines that the most profitable use of its assets, the use most likely to produce the greatest profits, lies in consummating a deal with the princes, even when the bribe is factored in, then I see no reason in rights theory to deny them that pursuit. It should be purely a matter of corporate choice whether they wish to use their assets in that way, and chalk up the bribe or the extortion payment, whatever one wishes to call it, to a cost of doing business. Other companies, when faced with a similar circumstance, may find it too offensive to engage in that type of activity, and that is their privilege. Where natural rights theory leaves the option to the individual in this kind of ambiguous case (or "gray" area), utilitarian considerations of cost/benefit might be advantageously employed to reach a decision. But what is unambiguous is that on this moral foundation of natural rights, the FCPA appears as an unjustifiable intrusion upon individual and corporate decision-making.

Undoubtedly, a Kantian moralist would see things differently when applying a golden-rule standard. "If you do not wish to be subject to the temptations of corruption by others, then don't engage in bribery yourself"—so their categorical imperative might read. This moral absolutism is, however, difficult to justify when applied to business activities in a less than perfect world, and a world in which moral precepts and customs differ so greatly from country to country. While I do not wish to endorse moral relativism—the position that everyone and every culture is entitled to make up its own moral rules and we are incapable of judging which are better— I do see the adaptability of natural rights theory, here, as preferable to the absolutism of the Kantian position. It seems preferable in these murky situations to leave the decision to individuals and not have government dictate *the* one and only moral course.

South Africa: Morality and Moralizing

Since the early 1970s, various church groups and activists on university campuses have been urging the divestiture of American investments in South Africa. These church groups, most conspicuously the Interfaith Council on Corporate Responsibility, have introduced proxy resolutions to shareholders of corporations doing business there, resolutions which, if accepted, would mandate a corporation to relinquish its holdings. While these groups have been vociferous in promoting their cause, corporate shareholders have not seen fit to endorse their position. On university campuses however, the attempt has been somewhat more successful, with several universities' boards of trustees agreeing to sell their shares of stock in companies doing business in South Africa. In 1986, these groups succeeded in replacing President Reagan's policy of "constructive engagement" toward South Africa with legislated sanctions. In their wake, many of the leading American firms operating in that country have withdrawn.

Apartheid is the policy that offends the moral sensibilities of many Americans. The South African government, through force of law, endorses policies that discriminate against blacks and those of mixed race in order to preserve the privileged position of white settlers who comprise 17% of the population. The white group, which has dominated the politics of South Africa since the 1948 victory of the Nationalist Party, is composed of the descendents of Dutch settlers who arrived at the Cape in 1652; it is this group, the Afrikaners, rather than the British settlers, that is most zealous in support of apartheid. Blacks are forbidden to own property in areas covering 86% of South Africa's territory, and they can only become land owners if they move to tribal "homelands" designated for their exclusive use, and areas to which they are often forcibly repatriated. Blacks are, also, confined to areas set aside for their occupation outside cities, so they cannot live where they work, and they are often forced to live much of the year separated from their families back in the "homelands" because only males are allowed to occupy the enclaves near their workplaces. Furthermore, they are denied the right to vote, to organize politically, to join unions, to occupy managerial positions; they are paid less than whites for the same jobs and confined by law to nonsupervisory positions. Segregated eating establishments and toilets are legally mandated.

While Americans find such policies morally repugnant, it ought to be recalled that it was only in the 1960s that our own country became sensitized to the brutalizing effects of similar policies against blacks — although certainly not as stringent or pervasive — practiced overtly in our southern states and covertly elsewhere. The South African government claims to be grappling with ways in which to soften the more offensive aspects of apartheid, particularly with a revised constitution, which now allows people of Indian descent and mixed race to each elect a house of the legislature.

Opponents of apartheid both within and outside the country contend that this is a self-serving device to divide nonwhites by a "divide and conquer" strategy. They think the government's motive is to buy the allegiance of the people of mixed race by enfranchising them, while keeping the much larger black population permanently disenfranchised.

Much international attention has been leveled against the South African government, with the General Assembly of the United Nations in 1981 passing an oil embargo against it by 127 to 7 votes. While the Security Council did not go along, and so the measure has nothing but advisory force, all the OPEC countries and other exporting countries have honored the boycott. Despite this profession of adherence, however, the South African government still receives plenty of oil from companies breaching the embargo.[8] American companies are prohibited by law from doing business with the South African military or police apparatus. After the House passed a bill in 1984 to force substantial American disinvestment, Suzanne Garment, reported in the *Wall Street Journal* the reaction to such efforts among South Africans.

When you ask about it here, almost all black and white anti-apartheid activists look at you like you're crazy. They cannot imagine why you would want to threaten the economic growth that has been the chief engine of racial progress and of the current South African political ferment.[9]

Some leading American companies have chosen to pursue actions of various sorts to make their opposition to apartheid known. Polaroid withdrew completely from South Africa in 1977 after it discovered that its independent distributor had violated guidelines that Polaroid established for its operation in 1971 after internal and external pressure for its "Experiment in South Africa." When these opponents of apartheid pointed to the use of Polaroid equipment by the government to maintain its passport ID system (all blacks must carry such internal passports signed by their employers), Polaroid, on the advice of an advisory group of blacks and whites that it had sent to the country, instituted a set of guidelines for their distributor. Business would be continued but with no sales to the government; salaries of blacks would be improved within the distributorship; nonwhites would be trained for managerial positions; and a portion of profits would be set aside for the education of blacks. Black South Africans who had been consulted by the Polaroid advisory group preferred this solution to outright divestiture. But in 1977, Polaroid discovered that its distributor had, in fact, been dealing through intermediaries with the South African government, and they pulled the plug on their operations. This moral stance did not greatly affect Polaroid's bottom line, as sales in South Africa represented only three to four million dollars per year out of total worldwide sales of over one billion.

Some other American companies—and we had about 320 companies doing business in that country—have chosen the same course—Burlington

Industries, Weyerhaeuser, Halliburton, and Interpace among them. Others have chosen to limit their future investments in the country. For most of the largest corporations that operated in South Africa — such as Mobil, Caltex, Ford, General Motors, Chrysler, and IBM — their business in South Africa represents less than 1% of total sales. Yet they have been troubled by the moral implications of that investment, particularly when prodded and subjected to the hostile glare and public exposure of various church groups. In the wake of sanctions, the trend has been for these companies to sell their assets in South Africa to locals.

Another response to public scrutiny was advanced by General Motors in 1977 when one of its directors, himself a black and a minister, promulgated what has come to be known as the Sullivan Principles. Rather than demanding outright divestiture, Sullivan argued that corporations should stay in South Africa, but pursue enlightened social policies to improve the condition of blacks, policies that are mostly illegal according to South African law. The Sullivan Principles called for the following actions: (1) nonsegregation of the races in all eating, comfort, and work facilities; (2) equal and fair employment practices for all employees; (3) equal pay for all employees doing equal or comparable work for the same period of time; (4) initiation of and development of training programs that will prepare, in substantial numbers, blacks and other nonwhites for supervisory, adminis- trative, clerical, and technical jobs; (5) increasing the number of blacks and other nonwhites in management and supervisory positions; (6) improving the quality of employees' lives outside the work environment in such areas as housing, transportation, schooling, recreation, and health facilities.[10] Many other companies doing business in South Africa embraced these principles. Of even greater interest is the fact that the government's Minister of Information approved the Principles, and the government has not thwarted companies that attempted to comply with them despite the illegality of many of the Principles' provisions. In the spring of 1987, Sullivan called upon all American businesses to cease operating in South Africa because that government had failed to end apartheid as he had demanded.

When we examine the arguments of moralists concerning the divestiture question, we are once again confronted with a diversity of viewpoints. John Payton, a spokesman for the National Bar Association, argued that the Sullivan Principles have proven ineffective, and that, given the deaths of 700 blacks in the Soweto rioting of 1976 and the death in prison of black activist Steve Biko in 1977, such palliatives as the Principles are morally offensive. He favored legislation prohibiting companies from directly or indirectly doing business in South Africa, (an embargo), and ending all diplomatic, political, economic, and cultural relations.[11] Robert Moss thinks otherwise. He contends that disinvestment would impoverish blacks, make whites more inflexible, and remove the single most effective catalyst for liberalization—foreign business. The turmoil that might ensue upon divestiture, he thinks, might well lead to a bloody civil war with the potential for a black dictatorial government alligned with the Soviets emerging from the turmoil. Such an outcome would deprive the West of its vital sea lanes around the Cape and of strategic resources contained within the country. Moss also points to the selective moral outrage of critics who bemoan the injustice of the South African system, yet remain almost indifferent to acts of genocide and oppression in other black African states, which make the excesses of the South African government pale by comparison. He points to such outrageous behavior as the expulsion of Asians from Uganda, the expropriation of the property of Asians in Marxist Mozambique, and massacres perpetrated by the security police in Uganda, Zaire, Nigeria, and Equatorial Guinea. "Selective morality is no morality at all," he concludes.[12]

Now, how might a utilitarian moral theorist appraise this divestiture question? On the benefit side—that is, the side favorable to remaining in South Africa—he might include the following considerations: (1) that foreign investment might be a moderating force on apartheid by subjecting such practices to the light of international ethical standards and practices; (2) that divestiture would hurt blacks because as the economy shrunk they would be the first to suffer, while a growing economy, in contrast, would benefit them by increasing the need for skilled labor beyond what could be supplied by the white population; (3) that such a divestiture would have little or no positive effect, as the place of American companies would simply be taken over by European or Japanese companies; (4) that the function of business is not primarily to encourage social change; and (5) that if divestiture destabilized South Africa, its vital resources and sea lanes might be denied to the West; and (6) that even the black African countries that profess their abhorence of apartheid are economically dependent on South Africa as evidenced by the 100,000 migrant workers sent by Marxist Mozambique to the South African gold mines and the acquiescence of the black African countries to a $1.1 billion loan to South Africa from the International Monetary fund. On the cost side—the side of withdrawal— the following factors might be included: (1) even companies that improve the conditions of their own few workers will not undermine the apartheid system by their presence nor will they succeed in improving the condition of the majority of blacks; (2) even those companies professing allegiance to the Sullivan Principles nevertheless aid the South African government by paying taxes to it, thus indirectly supporting apartheid; (3) the government still manages to purchase U.S. technology, which aids their military and police in the suppression of blacks. How a utilitarian resolves this balance, will depend upon the weight he attaches to each of these considerations.

For the Kantian moralist, these pragmatic considerations would not matter, for he would view apartheid as exemplifying a moral principle that if universalized would have unspeakably loathsome consequences. What could the categorical imperative look like? "Act so that one's business investments serve to legitimate racial policies that deprive people of their basic human rights!"

The rights theorist, once again, would consider as relevant to making a moral decision on divestiture the property rights involved. If company A legitimately owns its resources, then it can trade with other willing partners as long as it doesn't deprive other people of their rights. But is it a deprivation of other people's rights when company A operates in South Africa in adherence to laws that deprive blacks of the vote, the right to own property, and mandate lower pay for blacks than whites? If company A is merely adhering to local laws, and is itself not the initiator of such policies, it is difficult to see how the rights violations can be attributed to the company; rather, the source of the rights violations is the South African government itself. Thus, on rights grounds alone, there would be no objection to company A operating in South Africa, and the choice of whether to operate or not could be decided by the company using such utilitarian or pragmatic considerations as it found relevant. This analysis assumes that South Africa falls into that "gray" category that we described earlier—countries who have distasteful regimes, yet fall short of being truly heinous. In recent years, as black street protests have increased and police violence has escalated, many people would argue that South Africa is slipping into the "henious" category.

Robert Moss raised the issue of "selective morality," and, just as an aside, it might be interesting to ponder the question of why there has been so much effort expended to force divesture in the case of South Africa while barely a handful of business publications have even noticed the vital role played by Gulf Oil in propping up the Marxist regime in Angola, a regime that can only maintain its power by the use of Cuban troops, troops whose cost is paid for by Gulf royalties paid to the Angolan government.[13] I do not wish to imply that oppression in Angola somehow neutralizes oppression in South Africa and makes the latter acceptable, but that, rather, our moral decisions should not be guided by personal dislikes born of ideological convictions. In other words, if it is wrong for whites to persecute blacks, then it is equally wrong for blacks to persecute blacks.

Conclusion

How helpful have our three moral systems proven in resolving these two issues—the legitimacy of bribing foreign officials in the pursuit of contracts, and the desirability of American companies divesting their holdings in South Africa? Kantian principles being absolutist have, I think, little usefulness in resolving these issues, since they take too little account of what goes on in the real world. Given the fact that few governments in the world adhere to Western democratic standards even in rough approximation, and no government, our own included, ever behaves in a manner beyond reproach, it is unduly utopian to demand that businessmen adhere to principles so lofty that, if followed, they could never engage in business anywhere in the world.

The solution that I prefer would involve a combination of natural rights moral theory and, in those ever troublesome "gray" cases—where natural rights theory does not direct a clearcut answer—an infusion of utilitarian considerations. My test would go like this.

(1)   Establish whether Company X has legitimate claim to its resources; that is, did it acquire them by noncoercive means, by original acquisition of unowned land or voluntary transfer from individuals who originally had title to land or goods.

(2)   Inquire into the status of the government within whose territory Company A wishes to do business. Is the government a massive violator of the rights of life, liberty, and property of its citizens, is it a "gray" government that violates rights but is not murderous, or is it a rights-observing government? If it falls within the first category, no dealings with it would be morally permissible because such dealings would be analogous to an individual acting as an accessory to murder; if it falls within the third category, no problem arises and business may proceed; if it falls within the second, "gray' category, then apply a further test.

(3)   This further test involves weighing the advantages and disadvantages of doing business with that government or under the laws of that government. Such a balance might include both pragmatic considerations and the personal sensibilities of the businessmen making the decision.

Admittedly, this framework still leaves a lot of room for personal differences in reaching decisions, especially in the application of the third criterion, for utilitarian weighing always involves subjective judgments about how much weight ought to be assigned to each factor. But this may not be as big a liability as it at first may seem because these "gray" cases we have examined are precisely the kind that should be left to individual conscience where people of good will can differ. What these criteria do provide is a way of differentiating these tough cases from ones that invariably ought to be denied American business involvement.

Perhaps, these criteria will be clearer if we examine some instances in which they would prohibit any involvement of American businesses with foreign governments. If we look at the issue of making bank loans to Eastern Bloc countries, an endeavor much favored by our international bankers during the 1970s and the era of détente, our second criteria appears to eliminate such activities as immoral. The reason for this prohibition is that these Communist countries have systematically and as a declared party and governmental policy acted to deprive their citizens of basic human rights, including the right to own productive property; the rights to move freely, to engage in businesses activities of one's choice, to speak one's opinions without fear of persecution, and in many cases, the right to life. The Soviet Union, for example, exterminated an estimated twenty million people during the Great Purges of the 1930s, and the policy of incarcerating political dissidents in slave labor camps and psychiatric institutions continues to this day. To buttress such regimes with Western loans at below market rates, loans that in all likelihood will never be repaid, makes little sense as pragmatic policy, and offends our second criterion because it places our bankers in the positions of subsidizing murderers. As of June 1983, Eastern European countries, excluding the Soviet Union, owed Western bankers and countries almost sixty-two billion dollars. It seems curious, indeed, that our system rallies to legislate against bribe payments to foreign officials, yet our government encourages such loans to Communist regimes.

One more example of a clear-cut case where our criteria can direct businessmen to avoid foreign ventures lies in the area of technology transfer. Recently, there have been some dramatic revelations of Western businessmen serving as intermediaries for the Eastern Bloc in its attempt to circumvent United States export restrictions and acquire advanced computers.[14] Aside from being illegal, such actions are morally culpable, for they endanger American lives by bolstering the Soviet military establishment, to say nothing of their impact on strengthening the organs of internal repression within the Soviet Union.

In conclusion, while the criteria enunciated above can provide moral guidance to businessmen by offering a framework in which to proceed towards making a decision, the "gray" cases can still lead to some companies choosing to continue doing business in South Africa or not, and to offering payoffs to foreign officials or not. But in cases like the banking and spying examples, our moral criteria lead to a decisive conclusion that they are always wrong. Admittedly, the conclusions reached in this chapter diverge rather radically from contemporary legal requirements.

Notes

1. "Big Profits in Big Bribery," *Time,* March 16, 1981, p. 67.

2. "The Antibribery Act Splits Executives," *Business Week,* September 19, 1983, p. 16.

3. *Congressional Record,* July 14, 1982, S8263, testimony by Edward T. Pratt, Jr., chairman, Emergency Committee for American Trade, before the Subcommittee on International Finance and Monetary Policy.

4. *Congressional Record,* August 5, 1982, S9984, testimony of Norman Pacun, vice-president, Ingersoll Rand Company, before Senate Banking Committee.

5. *Congressional Record,* July 22, 1982, S9083, testimony of Mark B. Feldman to the Senate Banking Committee.

6. Mark Pastin and Michael Hooker, "Ethics and the Foreign Corrupt Practices Act," in Tom L. Beauchamp and Norman E. Bowie, eds., *Ethical Theory and Business* (Englewood Cliffs, N.J.: Prentice-Hall, 1983), pp. 280–84.

7. Kenneth D. Alpern, "Moral Dimensions of the Foreign Corrupt Practices Act: Comments on Pastin and Hooker," in W. Michael Hoffman and Jennifer Mills Moore, *Business Ethics: Readings and Cases in Corporate Morality* (New York: McGraw-Hill, 1984), pp. 468–75.

8. "Sanction Busting Again," *New Statesman,* June 18, 1982, pp. 12–13.

9. "South Africa In Policy Ferment . . . Permanently," *Wall Street Journal,* March 1, 1984.

10. "General Motors in South Africa," *General Motors Public Interest Report,* 1976, p. 50.

11. John Payton, "Why United States Corporations Should Get Out of South Africa," in Hoffman and Moore, *Business Ethics.*

12. Robert Moss, "Friends in Need: Five Good Reasons for Standing by South Africa," in Hoffman and Morre, *Business Ethics.*

13. See: "Courting Disaster: Gulf Oil Should End its Relationship with Communist Angola," *Barrons,* July 27, 1981, p. 7; "A Shake-up in Angola Puts Gulf in the Middle," *Business Week,* December 21, 1981, p. 47.

9

AFFIRMATIVE ACTION

NICHOLAS CAPALDI

Introduction

Among the fundamental ideals of American culture is a commitment to judging each *individual* on his or her *personal merit* and the *equal* and open *opportunity* to compete. Free enterprise has long seemed to many to be one of the economic conditions that fosters these values. Nevertheless, some serious questions have to be raised. First, past United States history reveals quite clearly that private individuals, institutions including economic ones such as unions and corporations, and especially the various branches of government have not always lived up to those ideals. Individuals have been discriminated against, that is, they have, because of classification by race or sex, been sometimes prevented from competing at all, or they have not been judged on the basis of their personal merit. The issue of past wrongs must be dealt with in some way. Second, theoretical as well as practical questions have been raised about what constitutes merit, who determines it, and how it is to be measured. Third, there has recently emerged a critical debate about whether equality means equality of opportunity or equality of outcome.

Affirmative action is a public policy designed to deal with the issue of past wrongs (an ethical and legal issue), but any discussion of affirmative action invariably raises theoretical questions about both the determination of merit and the meaning of equality. It also raises questions about the relation of economic institutions to individuals or groups (social philosophy), and the relation between economic institutions and other institutions in our society (political philosophy).

Past Wrongs

Let us begin with a discussion of past wrongs; that is, a discussion of the historical discrepancy between our ideals and the implementation of those

197

ideals. For the sake of simplicity and coherence, we shall focus on blacks, and we shall only mention other groups when important differences have to be noted.

There are some well known facts about the treatment of blacks in America. Not all of these facts are directly relevant to the ethical issues that impinge on affirmative action, but they implicitly influence people's attitudes and perceptions of affirmative action. In order to sort out later what is relevant and what is irrelevant, and in order to make some important distinctions, it is well that we recognize as many of these background factors as possible.

Blacks were brought to America against their will, and their initial status as slaves was sanctified by the United States Constitution. Slavery lasted in the South until 1865. Even after Reconstruction, "white supremacy" prevailed in the South through social custom, the terrorism of clandestine groups such as the KKK, and legal devices such as the poll tax and literacy tests, which discouraged blacks from voting. Such taxes and tests reflected the economic and educational deprivation of former slaves. Toward the end of the nineteenth century, many southern states passed "Jim Crow" laws, which made segregation of facilities a permanent feature of life in the South. Such laws made separate or segregated schools, forms of transportation, public facilities such as lavatories, and even amusements mandatory. These laws were extended in the first two decades of the twentieth century to encompass separate hospitals, churches, and even jails. For a long time, the U.S. Supreme Court upheld the constitutionality of such laws. In the most famous such case, Plessy v. Ferguson (1896), noteworthy for Justice Harlan's dissent, the court upheld the constitutionality of "separate but equal" accommodations.

Organized opposition to "Jim Crow" laws started as early as 1905 with the Niagara Movement headed by W. E. B. Dubois, and in 1910 with the founding of the NAACP. Through the 1930s, opponents of "Jim Crow" laws limited themselves to the contention that separate facilities were not, in fact, equal. The great impetus to overcoming segregation, or legally sanctioned separate facilities, came with the Second World War, largely in response to the newly felt need for national unity. In June of 1941, President Roosevelt created the Fair Employment Practices Committee. The Committee saw to it that anti-discrimination clauses were added to federal contracts. In July of 1948, President Truman formally ended segregation in the armed forces.

On May 17, 1954, the U.S. Supreme Court "reversed itself" and declared that segregation is "inherently unequal." Separate cannot be equal. Further, all blacks proscribed from attending public schools with whites were found to have been denied the equal protection clause of the 14th Amendment. In March 1956, the Court extended this decision, in the case of *Brown v. the Board of Education* (of Topeka, Kansas), to all state-supported institutions of higher learning. In the wake of the historic *Brown* decision, Congress passed the Civil Rights Act of 1957, the first piece of Civil Rights legislation since Reconstruction. Under this Act, the Attorney General is directed to bring suit on behalf of anyone deprived of his voting rights. In addition, the Civil Rights Commission was established. The Civil Rights Act of 1964 struck down "Jim Crow" laws in public accommodations and *prohibited discrimination by employers and unions.* The Civil Rights Bill of 1968 prohibits discrimination in housing.

The History of Affirmative Action

With the Civil Rights Act of 1964, we come to the legal issues of affirmative action as they bear upon business ethics. The most relevant provision of the 1964 Act is Title VII, which prohibits discrimination by employers or unions, whether private or public. It is unlawful for any employer "to fail or refuse to hire or to discharge any individual or otherwise to discriminate . . . because of such individual's race, color, religion, sex, or national origin."

In the most unequivocal fashion, the sponsors of the measure in the Senate made clear that this act was designed to foster equal opportunity, not preference and not racial balance.

Senator Hubert H. Humphrey: "Title VII does not require an employer to achieve any sort of racial balance in his work force by giving preferential treatment to any individual or group." Senator Harrison A. Williams: Title VII "specifically prohibits the Attorney General, or any agency of the government, from requiring employment to be on the basis of racial or religious quotas. Under this provision an employer with only white employees could continue to have only the best qualified persons even if they were all white." In the ensuing debate, the floor manager in the Senate, Senator Joseph Clark, and Senator Clifford Case both stated that: "It must be emphasized that discrimination is prohibited as to any individual . . . The question in each case is whether that individual was discriminated against." Further, in response to the charge that the bill would ultimately require quotas, Senator Clark replied that: "Quotas are themselves discriminatory."

Two provisions were added to spell this out:

703 (h) . . . it shall not be unlawful employment practice . . . for an employer to give and act upon the results of any professionally developed ability test provided that such test, its administration or action upon the results is not designed, intended or used to discriminate because of race, color, religion, sex or national origin.

703 (j) Nothing contained in this title shall be interpreted to require any employer . . . to grant preferential treatment to any individual or to any group because of the

race, color, religion, sex, or national origin of such individual or group on account of an imbalance which may exist with respect to the total number of percentage or persons of any race, color, religion, sex, or national origin employed by any employer.

Congress did not mandate a redress of all past injustices. What it outlawed was discrimination *per se*. If anyone still doubts this, then let him listen to the words of Representative Celler, Chairman of the House Judiciary Committee and the Congressman responsible for introducing the legislation: "It is likewise not true that the Equal Employment Opportunity Commission would have power to rectify existing 'racial or religious imbalance' in employment by requiring the hiring of certain people without regard to their qualifications simply because they are of a given race or religion. Only actual discrimination could be stopped."

The real controversy, legal and ethical, over affirmative action arose with the subsequent interpretation of Title VII by federal bureaucrats. The expression "affirmative action" is not and never was part of the Civil Rights Act of 1964. Its origin is in the executive branch of government. The earliest relevant executive order, so-called, goes back to 1941 and was issued by President Roosevelt ordering an end to discrimination in defense industries. In 1961, President Kennedy issued Executive Order No. 10925 prohibiting job discrimination among contractors doing business with the federal government. In that executive order, he used the expression "affirmative steps" to direct contractors to recruit and actively encourage minority applicants. In the wake of the Civil Rights Act of 1964, President Lyndon Johnson issued Executive Order No. 11246 in 1965, stressing the need for "affirmative action" with regard to minorities. Executive Order No. 11375 of 1967 extended affirmative action to women.

The executive policy of affirmative action was never defined by any president. It was defined by the federal bureaucracy. In May of 1968, the Department of Labor issued Order No. 4.

A necessary prerequisite to the development of a satisfactory affirmative action program is the identification and analysis of problem areas inherent in minority employment and an evaluation of opportunities for utilization of minority group personnel. The contractor's program shall provide in detail for specific steps to guarantee equal employment opportunity keyed to the problems and needs of members of minority groups, including, when there are deficiencies, the development of specific goals and time-tables for the prompt achievement of full and equal employment opportunity. Each contractor shall include in his affirmative action compliance program a table of job classifications . . . The evaluation of utilization of minority group personnel shall include . . . an analysis of minority group representation in all categories.

Further guidelines were issued on February 5, 1970 in which affirmative action was defined as "a set of specific and result-oriented procedures to which a contractor commits himself to apply every good faith." Finally, the guidelines issued on December 4, 1971 spelled out the ultimate logic of affirmative action, namely quotas. It all turned on the term "under-utilization."

"underutilization" is defined as having fewer minorities or women in a particular job classification then would reasonably be expected by their availability.

Anything less than a statistically balanced work force would bring down the wrath of the government.

The lines had now been drawn. The Congressional intent had been to eliminate documentable instances of discrimination against specific individuals. The Bureaucratic assumption was that the law intended to create a statistically balanced work force.

The clash between and the resolution of the controversy between Congressional intent and bureaucratic interpretation emerged in a series of Supreme Court cases throughout the 1970s. The first important case was the product of the so-called "Philadelphia Plan." The construction trades unions in Philadelphia were all white, resulting in large part from father-son practices in the union. The Department of Labor, in 1969, ordered an end to that practice and instituted goals and timetables in minority recruitment. This was the first major application of Order No. 4 of 1968. The Contractors Association of Eastern Pennsylvania took the case to court and appealed Order No. 4 on the grounds that Title VII bans discrimination and that the "goals and timetables" of Order No. 4 are discriminatory quotas. In federal court, the Third Circuit Court of Appeals, the Secretary of Labor was upheld. The contractors then took the case to the U.S. Supreme Court, but the Supreme Court refused to hear it. The reason is quite simple. The Philadelphia Plan was a clear case of existence of previous discrimination.

In the case of *Swann v. Charlotte-Mecklenburg Board of Education* (1971), the U.S. Supreme Court concluded that local communities could voluntarily assign students by race for educational purposes even where no prior *de jure* segregation had existed. But there is a difference between what is permissable voluntarily and what the courts can order in the absence of specific proof of discrimination. As Chief Justice Burger put it,

a prescribed ratio of Negro to white students reflecting the proportion for the district as a whole. To do this as an educational policy is within the broad discretionary powers of school authorities; absent a finding of constitutional violation, however, that would not be within the authority of a federal court.

Courts can impose a numerical remedy only where there is a finding of prior discrimination as in the Philadelphia Plan. Reading this forward to the *Bakke* case, we note that such assignment as the court allows excludes no individual but merely concerns the assignment to a specific school in a noncompetitive situation. The *Bakke* case, as we shall see, involved a competitive exclusionary situation.

More crucial was the 1971 case of *Griggs v. Duke Power Company,* wherein the U.S. Supreme Court interpreted Title VII as forbidding the use of certain aptitude tests and the requirement of the North Carolina power company that employees have a high school diploma. But the court did not literally bar tests or other criteria as long as those tests and criteria are demonstrably and directly related to job performance. Moreover, the court went out of its way to uphold the merit principle. In this case, the merit principle recognizes not just whether people are minimally qualified but who is better qualified.

Congress did not intend . . . to guarantee a job to every person regardless of qualifications . . . (Title VII) does not command that any person be hired simply because he was formerly the subject of discrimination, or because he is a member of a minority group. Discriminatory preference for any group, minority or majority, is precisely and only what Congress has proscribed . . . Congress has not commanded that the less qualified be preferred over the better qualified simply because of minority origins. Far from disparaging job qualifications as such, Congress has made such qualifications the controlling factor, so that race, religion, nationality, and sex become irrelevant.

By 1977 the question of statistical data was becoming increasingly important. In order for a court ordered remedy to be applied it must be established that actual discrimination has taken place. With the passage of time and the working out of the Civil Rights Act of 1964, establishing overt instances of discrimination has become more elusive. Various agencies of the federal bureaucracy such as EEOC (Equal Employment Opportunity Commission) began to argue that discrimination was inferable from statistics alone. In December of 1977, EEOC issued *Interpretation Regulation Guidelines for Remedial and/or Affirmative Action Appropriate under Title VII of the CRA.* Focusing on race and sex, and excluding mention of religion or national origin, Item 4 promised to protect employers from reverses discrimination suits, and Item 5 makes clear that EEOC reserves the right to use its bureaucratic discretion to decide if enough has been done by the employer. The test of discrimination is no longer intent to discriminate but having an *adverse impact* on minorities. This is what is known as institutional discrimination as opposed to intentional discrimination.

We pause to note that if EEOC has had its way, and if as a matter of fact a pure merit system had adverse impact, then the EEOC would have declared a pure merit system to be discriminatory. Moreover, that politically oriented department did here what it did in so many other cases, that is, it distorted the pronouncements of the U.S. Supreme Court. In the 1977 case *International Brotherhood of Teamsters v. the U.S.,* the Supreme Court unequivocally explained when statistics could and could not be used.

The Government bolstered its statistical evidence with the testimony of individuals who recounted over 40 specific instances of discrimination . . . individuals who testified about their personal experiences with the company brought the cold numbers convincingly to life . . . We caution only that statistics . . . like any other kind of evidence . . . may be rebutted. In short, their usefulness depends upon all the surrounding facts and circumstances.

. . . statistical evidence was not offered or used to support an erroneous theory that Title VII requires an employer's work force to be racially balanced . . . 703 (j) makes clear that Title VII imposes no requirement that a work force mirror the general population . . .

. . . figures for the general population might not actually reflect the pool of qualified job applicants . . .

The landmark case in the affirmative action controversy was the *Bakke* case. Alan Bakke sued the Medical School of the University of California at Davis on the grounds that his rejection was an instance of reverse discrimination. Davis had set aside 16 seats out of each class of 100 specifically for minorities. Bakke's attorneys argued that this violated Title VI of the 1964 Civil Rights Act. They did not raise the constitutional issue but merely referred to specific statutes.

In July of 1978, the U.S. Supreme Court ruled 5–4 in Bakke's favor. By the narrowest of margins, the Supreme Court had ruled in no uncertain terms that the Civil Rights Act of 1964 did not condone the interpretation of affirmative action given by EEOC, HEW, and other government bureaucracies.

Although a majority ruled in Bakke's favor, not all members of the majority did so with the same explanation. Four of the justices (Burger, Stewart, Rehnquist and Stevens) ruled on the narrow grounds of Section 601 of the Civil Rights Act of 1964, which prohibits reverse discrimination. The fifth justice who supported Bakke, Lewis Powell, went even further and decided on fundamental Constitutional grounds that the Medical School of the University of California at Davis had violated Bakke's rights under the Fourteenth Amendment and had denied him the equal protection of the laws. Powell reiterated in his decision that the law and previous Supreme Court decisions were directed toward overtly verifiable instances of discrimination and that the discrimination must have been against specific individuals.

We have never approved a classification that aids persons perceived as members of relatively victimized groups at the expense of other innocent individuals in the absence of judicial, legislative, or administrative findings of constitutional or statutory violations.

Most important of all, Powell identifies and rejects the major assumption of quota interpretations of affirmative action. To impose a quota one would have to prove that statistical disparity is the "product" of system-wide discrimination and that in a truly fair system Bakke would never have qualified "because Negro applicants . . . would have made better scores."

As Powell put it so eloquently, "Not one word in the record supports this conclusion."

A subsequent case that is sometimes invoked is the *Weber* decision of 1979. This case involved an agreement between the union and a company to reserve half of the places in a training program for blacks. Weber, an employee with seniority sued on the basis of reverse discrimination, but the Supreme Court upheld the contract agreement. The *Weber* decision does not in any way detract from the Bakke decision. It does not permit EEOC to impose quotas and it does not legitimate the hypothesis that disparate representation is the product of system-wide discrimination. Technically, the case concerns the voluntary self-imposition of a quota formula by mutual contractual agreement between a private business and its representative unions. The *Weber* case did not deal with new jobs, but with a selection from among current employees for a training program; the agreement was temporary and local; there was no commitment to maintaining racial balance; and no decision on defining what is permissable affirmative action.

Another relevant case was *Fullilove v. Klutznick* (1980), in which the Supreme Court accepted a "set aside" statute with regard to federal funds used on local works projects. Under the statute, 10% of the funds had to be spent on services and supplies provided by businesses owned and controlled by minority groups. In his opinion, Chief Justice Burger noted that "Congress had abundant evidence from which it could conclude that minority businesses had been denied effective participation in public contracting opportunities by procurement practices that perpetuate the effects of prior discrimination."

These earlier decisions have been complicated by a number of recent cases. In 1986 (Workers v. EEOC), the Supreme Court approved a 19% minority membership quota to rectify past discrimination even when the persons asking relief are not "identifiable victims of discrimination." In 1987 (Johnson v. Transportation Agency No. 85–1129), the Supreme Court ruled that employers may favor women and minorities *over better qualified men and whites* in hiring and promotion even without a prior history of discrimination. This program is said to be "voluntary" and "temporary" and was justified by appeal to the notion that it is meant to alter social attitudes rather than eliminate actual past discrimination.

What the Law Requires

1. It is against the law to discriminate. That is, it is against the law as passed by Congress and upheld by the Supreme Court to accept or reject people on the grounds of race, sex, national origin, age, or other categories.

2. In addition to the negative prohibition, there is a positive injunction that a reasonable attempt be made to reassure people that employment and promotion is based upon merit. This is normally taken to mean that vacancies will be well-publicized and that talent searchers make reasonable attempts to locate those who may have been previously passed over.

3. Employers who use objective tests or other criteria must be prepared to show that such criteria are related to the actual job or performance.

4. In some cases, it seems permissable for employers to use quotas in hiring and promotion as long as such use is *voluntary* and *temporary*. It remains on open question how these terms are to be defined.

5. Quotas, as remedial compensatory measures, may be imposed only by the courts, not by a federal bureaucrat. Moreover, such numerical remedies require a legally determined history of prior discrimination.

6. The 10% rule in cases involving federal contracts does not apply where the federal government is not involved and only applies because of a finding of past discrimination.

Conceptual Issues

So far we have been using concepts without having attempted to define them clearly. As you will see, how these concepts are defined determines how they are used. The key terms are discrimination, prejudice, adverse impact, compensation, and equal opportunity.

Discrimination is the pivotal term. In its benign general sense, it means simply to make relevant distinctions, relevant to some purpose or goal or standard. In its pejorative legal sense, it means to exclude individuals from access to roles and facilities for any reason other than failure to comply with the traditional, legal, and objective norms of that role or facility. It should go without saying that traditions that are illegal or unobjective are not relevant. It should also be clear that those who wish to suggest changes in the traditional criteria or norms that are legal and objective may do so but not under the rubric of discrimination. Refusing to hire a competent individual because of his black skin color or hiring a less competent individual because he is white is discrimination. Refusing to promote a woman who surpasses her male competitors because she is a female is discrimination. Refusing to allow an individual to perform a role that he or she is incompetent to perform or for which a superior performer is readily available is not discrimination.

Discrimination is an overt, concrete form of behavior whose existence as a policy can be established in an objective way. One clear and incontrovertible example of discrimination is segregation, or the establishment of separate facilities based on race, as in the case of "Jim Crow" laws.

Segregation as a form of discrimination is illegal. The opposite of segregation is said to be integration. But integration is an ambiguous word. If integration is the absence of segregation, then integration is the absence of overt concrete policies which deny access to facilities or roles for reasons which are irrelevant in the traditional, legal, and objective sense. A landlord who refuses to rent an apartment to someone because of race is discriminating and creating segregated housing. A landlord who refuses to rent an apartment to those who cannot afford it is not discriminating and not creating segregated housing. His building is integrated even if everybody who lives in it is white. The same can be said of a work force based upon merit. In popular speech, however, integration is usually taken to mean the presence of individuals formerly excluded through discrimination. Sometimes a distinction is made between *de jur* segregation and *de facto* segregation. The former is the result of law whereas the latter is the result of historical accident or inadvertence.

Part of the obscurity and obfuscation surrounding terms like discrimination, segregation, integration is the result of expectations in the minds of some people about what would happen in an ideal world where no discrimination ever existed. For some, such a projected society would produce a new homogeneous culture or a particular numerical mix. Failure to achieve such homogeneity or such a mix is taken as evidence for the lingering presence of discrimination. But such a projection is not part of the objective meaning of the term and not part of the law. Rather it reflects an idiosyncratic vision or a peculiar kind of social theory we shall discuss below.

The Civil Rights Act of 1964 as well as various state laws outlaws the previous practice of discrimination and provides for remedies or compensation when the previous existence of discrimination has been legally established. The law does not call for or require a specific result.

Discrimination must be sharply distinguished from prejudice. *Prejudice* is a negative personal attitude, not based upon verifiable knowledge, and usually held without any attempt at gaining objective information and sometimes resisting the attempt to do so. Very often, it is assumed that discrimination is the overt effect of which prejudice is the cause. Nothing could be more mistaken. Discriminatory policies may be implemented by individuals who not only are not prejudiced but who even privately disagree with the policies. Moreover, prejudiced individuals may not necessarily discriminate. In fact, some prejudiced individuals may and do show favoritism to the people against whom they are prejudiced for any number of reasons. The existence of prejudice is not at all relevant as evidence of the existence of discrimination. It should also be clear that prejudiced attitudes held about groups may not influence the behavior toward individual members of that group. Finally, a belief about a group that is based upon fact and influences one's attitude toward that group is not prejudice. Those who refuse to hire sufferers of epilepsy for certain jobs are guilty neither of prejudice nor of discrimination.

Discrimination must also be distinguished from *adverse impact*. Any set of criteria for performance will, by its very nature, favor some and not others. Those who are not favored are said to be adversely impacted. For example, the traditional criteria for playing basketball favor, in general, those who are tall. Short people are, in general, victims of adverse impact as far as the traditional norms of basketball are concerned. Now it may very well be that perfectly traditional, legal, and objective criteria will adversely impact on individuals and groups of individuals in totally unpredictable ways. But the point is that this has nothing to do with discrimination, that there is no law against adverse impact, and that what those who are concerned with adverse impact have in mind is a change in the norms. The reader should recall at this point that affirmative action concerns itself with the discrepancy between traditional norms and actual practice, and not with the question of replacing those norms.

It is sometimes said that giving preferential treatment in hiring is a form of compensation for past wrongs. This requires us to raise questions about the meaning of *compensation*. Is compensation applicable to cases of discrimination, and if so in what form? To determine this, let us take some noncontroversial instances of compensation. Let us say that a doctor is paralyzed in an automobile accident in which another identifiable party was at fault. What the doctor is likely to receive is monetary compensation awarded by the court on the basis of projected earnings. Projected or potential earnings are calculated on the basis of what the doctor was already earning. Next, let us imagine that the doctor is killed in the accident. The doctor cannot be restored to life; the members of his family cannot be compensated for the loss of love and companionship. Again, the only meaningful compensation is monetary, based upon actual earnings. It is inconceivable that the courts would guarantee the children of the doctor seats in medical school as a form of compensation.

In order for compensation to be paid to the victims of discrimination we would have to (a) identify the party at fault and (b) show that the discrimination caused impairment of function. As far as (a) is concerned, even our doctor could not collect if there were no party at fault or if the guilty party were not apprehended and in a position to pay (e.g. insurance). Where discrimination is treated as an ascertainable and factual state of affairs, victims can be and have been compensated. For example, applicants for jobs as truck drivers were given the first available jobs after a trucking company was convicted of employment discrimination. When "discrimination" is treated in some vague theoretical sense (e.g. "societal discrimination"), the perpetrators are either unavailable, unidentifiable, or nonexistent. Recall that many who advocate affirmative action talk about discrimination as the concatenation of unintentional social forces. The price they must now pay is to disqualify themselves from using the concept of compensation.

It is this technical requirement of the concept of compensation that critics of affirmative action have in mind when they point out that young white males will be victimized by such a policy in the form of reverse discrimination. A rough analogy would be to require the doctors who acquire the deceased doctor's patients to pay compensation even though they had nothing to do with the accident. The analogy is actually worse because what we would need is the requirement that some doctors pay without our being able to trace who actually got the patients. This, of course, is not compensation, and it can hardly be mandatory.

The issue of harming the innocent has come up again and again. Giving preference necessarily denies positions to presently more qualified nonminority applicants who are not themselves the perpetrators of any of the alleged historical forms of discrimination. One response to this criticism is that the harm is only temporary and the system as a whole will benefit. Not only is this question-begging, and not only does it raise serious questions about social morale, but it is a Pandora's box for illegal and immoral practices that could be based on the same argument. Another response is that although the white male applicant may be better qualified, it is because he is the beneficiary of advantages from a previously unfair system. That is, without the system's malfunctioning, those white applicants would not be better qualified. This response makes assumptions about the distribution of talent among groups that no one has ever been able to prove. The sad fact is that we do not know how talent is distributed short of actual achievement.

With regard to the second requirement in the concept of compensation, calculating the degree of damage, we must repeat that short of actual achievement in individual cases there is no empirically meaningful way to identify what someone might have achieved. Herein lies a second crucial difference. In our previous compensation cases, there was some way of calculating compensation because there had been some performance. In the case of discrimination, there is the absence of performance and hence no way of calculating compensation.

Even the advocates of affirmative action realize the inappropriateness of the concept of compensation to convey what they have in mind. For they assert that to compensate someone is to treat him as if he had his merit intact. What is intended is the restoration of the individual or the group to its rightful position before the damage was done. That is, to give compensation is to give the victim the role that he would have had. How far this is from the ordinary and legal meaning of compensation can be seen with a moment's reflection. The athlete who is paralyzed before he can play in the professional league is not put into the starting line-up. Even if he could play, he would not be permitted to take the place of another and better player. Nor would we routinely change the rules of the game to allow damaged players to participate. What advocates of affirmative action want is a kind of social reform for which there is no clear analogue or precedent. This does not of itself invalidate the recommendation, but it does show that an entirely different argument would be needed. Practically, what is needed is some way of determining what an individual's or group's position would have been.

Let us assume for the sake of argument that talent is distributed in proportion to one's group in the total population. Even here, the argument will not work. Let us grant that a cross-section of the population has a certain talent. How do we know which members of the class in particular have that talent? Let us grant that blacks should be 11% of the members of boards of directors of major corporations. How do we know which from among the group should be selected? Surely it cannot be argued that the ones who went to business schools should be selected since some of those who did not attend might be the relevantly more talented ones but fail to apply because of the continuing effects of earlier discrimination. Surely it cannot be argued that the ones who graduated with the highest grades should be selected since some blacks with lower grades may actually be more talented but past discrimination has taken a greater toll on them. In effect, we face the same problem within any group that we face with society as a whole, and ironically all of the arguments propounded by advocates of affirmative action themselves about why traditional standards should not apply also work against applying some version of those standards within any subgroup. It has not been shown that the right individual in the preferred group is going to get the compensation. Second, the individual who receives preference can know, only at best, that some member of his subgroup deserves the position but not necessarily himself or herself.

This brings us to the last, most important, and most elusive of all concepts, *equal opportunity*. In its oldest, clearest, and original eighteenth-century sense equal opportunity meant that all competitions would be *open*. That is, no one would be denied the opportunity to compete. Against the background of a feudal system wherein all positions were hereditary, this concept of equal opportunity makes sense. As the founding fathers repeatedly made clear, equality before the law meant that all were eligible to compete, but how far they got should depend upon differences of ability or virtue or talent. It was both presumed and explicitly stated that nature creates a disparity of innate capacity.

There are some important qualifications to be kept in mind. Sometimes in order to take part in a specific competition, one must already have been successful in a previous competition. Thus, in order to compete for a scarce place in a medical school one must have been successful in one's previous college work. If an individual was not permitted to go to college but is allowed to take the MSAT exam, it would be a mockery to call this equal opportunity. But what makes it a mockery is the previous closing of the competition at the college level.

A second case occurs when a competition is open only to those who have been previously endowed with certain resources. For example, I cannot compete in some business ventures because I do not possess the relevant amounts of capital, whereas someone born into a very wealthy family can compete because of an accident of birth. However, just as some people are born rich others are born with other resources such as natural talents. Such accidents in no way render the competition unfair. The difference between this case and the previous hypothetical case is that the opportunity to amass a fortune is still present to those not born wealthy, whereas the opportunity to go to college prior to medical school was not available. The whole point of equality of opportunity is that it favors those with special assets of all kinds. It certainly does not mean equality of result or outcome. Therefore, the inequality of results cannot by itself be evidence of a lack of equal opportunity.

Some of the responsibility of developing natural talent is left to the individual, some to the family, and some of that responsibility is accepted by publicly supported agencies such as schools. The only meaningful cases of a lack of equal opportunity that can arise here is where publicly supported agencies fail to provide the stipulated services. Here again, the discrepancy of outcome cannot by itself be evidence of a lack of equal opportunity because prior factors are at work. To the extent that a public agency engages in talent development, it must be unusually scrupulous in not showing favoritism. Moreover, the justification for doing this through public agencies has remained pretty much the same: it is not a natural right but justifiable only if it increases total *productivity* (which in turn increases overall opportunity), and it is the case that private agencies either won't or can't do the job. The issue has never been whether some people come out ahead of others, but whether all advance their positions from where they started.

There are two alternatives to these traditional norms. The first alternative is to have centralized state control of all institutions starting with the family in order to redistribute resources so as to affect the outcome. Here we encroach upon another topic, namely whether free enterprise or a socialized economy and society can do a better job. But this alternative claims to be seeking the same end.

The second alternative actually challenges the traditional norms. It does not necessarily deny that the original norms are more productive, but it does claim that people will be happier in some other presumably more important sense. Here we are also impinging upon a different topic, namely conflicting theories of human nature. It is perfectly consistent for someone who holds this alternative to argue that positions or roles or jobs or promotions be awarded on a basis other than natural talent because there are other social aims or norms that are being advocated. Perhaps the most extreme version was articulated in the eighteenth century during the French Revolution by one Gracchus Babeuf: "Society must be made to operate in such a way that it eradicates once and for all the desire of a man to become richer, or wiser, or more powerful than others." Of course, at this point we have stopped talking about affirmative action as having anything to do with past wrongs.

Conflicting Social Theories

It should be clear from the foregoing discussion that affirmative action can mean different things to different people depending upon what other views they hold. These conflicting ideals and theories have serious repercussions for business in that they involve conflicting notions of the role of economic institutions.

We are now in a position to summarize the three relevant conflicting views presently expressed in public policy debates over affirmative action. These are conflicting views about man, social goals, and the means to achieving them.

1.   According to one view, there is a common core of genetic attributes that define human nature, but some of these (talents) vary widely with each individual. There are or can be significant differences in ability. The goal of social institutions is to foster the development of the individuals who belong to these institutions according to the norms and standards set by those who participate within the institutions. With regard to public policy, it is believed that the state serves both the individuals and the institutions as those entities negotiate on their own behalf with each other. The state provides the minimum necessary conditions for the pursuit of ends, but it does not decide what the ends should be. When the state does intervene, it is to protect the rights of individuals or institutions as those rights have traditionally evolved.

2.   According to the second theory, although talent varies, it is believed to be proportional by group. As stated by one public agency: "Intelligence potential is distributed among Negro infants in the same proportion and pattern as among Icelanders or Chinese, or any other group." Since talent is distributed equally by group proportion, statistical disparities are evidence of a lack of equal opportunity and the persistence of discrimination. The state is now supposed to act not on behalf of individuals and their rights but on behalf of group entitlement.

3.   According to a third theory, although talents may vary widely, such talent differentials are either irrelevant or secondary. They are irrelevant because all human beings are equal in possessing some common core of attributes, and it is these equal attributes that are crucial for public policy.

This theory also involves a different notion of social goals. According to it, social institutions exist in order to foster the common core, and the heart of the common core is the fundamental need to participate in social life in some meaningful way (i.e. to identify oneself with the social whole). The key concepts here are *participation* and *social whole*. This theory is collectivist as opposed to the first two, which claim to be individualist. The means for achieving these goals is state activism on behalf of a new social whole. The state exists to create institutions that foster the common core of participation in a new social whole.

While the first theory permits government intervention into the economy to correct remedial and identifiable past injustices, and while the second theory permits government regulation (monitoring) of economic institutions (unions as well as corporations), the third theory advocates total government control of all institutions. We are now talking about socialism and/or totalitarianism.

There is an interesting transition from the second theory to the third theory. Why do proponents of the second theory take a stand one way or the other to worry over the distribution of talent? Would it not be more consistent to argue that all natural talent is equal and that all differences of individual achievement are environmentally determined? Or, once we admit that individuals differ, why expect these variations to be insignificant in large groups? Why would it matter if some statistically identifiable groups were more successful? After all, in the end it is only individuals who actually possess a talent.

Here the third theory can say to the second theory that what really worries people is the prospect of belonging to a group that is perceived as less valuable (if not inferior). But this is a problem because people do not really see themselves as individuals, it is claimed, but rather as members of a group. This provides the opening wedge. If people perceive themselves as members of a group then the less talented (let us say the bottom 20%) will still feel less valuable (or inferior) even within the framework of the second theory. A female, for example, who is in the bottom 20% of females will not feel better because 51% of the elite is female. Our hypothetical female will still feel left out. Hence a more egalitarian scheme is necessary.

This is not the place to argue which of these theories is correct. Rather, what should be emphasized is that the debate over affirmative action can be construed in one of two ways. Either it can be construed narrowly in terms of our traditional cultural values such as fairness and the way in which those values have been interpreted by Congress and the courts. If so, then the previous section on what the law requires is fairly obvious. Or, it can be constructed as part of a much larger debate in which discrimination and equal opportunity have been redefined to reflect conflicting views about man, the structure of the social world, and the facts of history.

10

THE MORAL FOUNDATIONS OF POLITICAL-ECONOMIC SYSTEMS

TIBOR R. MACHAN

There are probably three or four major political systems that are options in our time. Among these, the most prominent ones are socialism, capitalism, and the welfare state. We will examine briefly the moralities that support each of these systems.

In earlier times, it may not have been a matter of choice as to which system will go and which will stay, but more and more in democratic societies, citizens can influence their political organizations and do so constantly. For this reason, it is important to be aware of the reasons given in support of the several systems. Even within societies with one or the other system in force, people are constantly thinking and writing about whether their political system is sound and might have to be abandoned for an alternative. Such questioning may not be done freely in some cases, but in our time, when international communication is prominent, it can hardly be prevented. And although some writers in political thought express considerable pessimism about our chances for changing our basic political and legal institutions, there is ample evidence that such changes are being precipitated all the time, albeit gradual. For instance, when the teaching of certain values in literature, philosophy, or religion influence the polity, they elect particular political leaders who, in turn, appoint judges or pass legislation to implement those values.

For members of the business community, alternative political-economic systems are very important to think about. In some of these systems, the profession of business is treated with contempt, as an evil—e.g., socialism regards it as morally pernicious for people to trade and sell goods and services. Cooperation, sharing, and not profit, are regarded as morally admirable. In other systems, business is treated as a noble, honorable profession—e.g., capitalism is a system in which trade between people is seen as beneficial, in the main, and those who produce and work for the promotion of trade are to be regarded as decent human beings. If the former stance is correct, those in the business world should rethink their choice of career and help persuade their colleagues to also do so.

Before we consider this issue, it should be noted that one of the foremost ideologies of our time, Marxism, holds that we cannot choose our political-economic systems. For genuine Marxists, a political-economic system is the direct result of the arrangement of the means of production — agricultural, industrial, wage-labor — that dominates a certain phase of society's development toward communism. For Marx, communism was not, as most of us tend to suppose, an ideal to strive for but "the real movement which abolishes the present state of things. The conditions of this movement result from the premises now in existence."[1] Communism for Marx was to be the natural end of humanity's growth process, as the full grown oak tree is the mature state into which the acorn eventually grows. Marx set out to describe a kind of natural history that does not involve "preaching morality" but traces the course of humanity's development.

From this, we see that the Marxist framework is not applicable to us in the context of considering what we ought to do, how we ought to act. This is not because human beings are evil, but because Marxism rejects the view that human beings possess freedom of choice needed to make sense of moral good and evil. If we are part of a natural course of development, then there is no problem of what we should do about our political institutions. These will develop, just as we will develop, as we must, governed by independent laws of nature. Indeed for Marx, we are not quite human anyway, and a mature communist society is not for human beings of today, just as legal responsibility is not applicable to a minor under our system of laws.

Socialism

This is the political-economic theory in which a good human community owns in common or collectively the major means of production, including labor and capital. The whole economy is administered for the use of the entire society. In Marxism, socialism is the penultimate phase of humanity's development, a stage prior to full maturity under communism. But, as noted above, Marxism is not concerned with ethics but views human life from the vantage point of the natural scientist. Non-Marxist socialism resembles this penultimate stage, but there is no doctrine of its necessity in humanity's life.

Non-Marxist socialism may be justified within certain moral frameworks. The central moral ideal underlying socialism is that each person is, in fact, a social being by nature and is obligated to work for the enhancement of society. The determination of what enhances society as a whole (and its members' welfare as social beings) would be best achieved by keeping the interest of the whole of society in mind. This can be done most effectively by subjecting society to efficient government administration, including the distribution of wealth, education of citizens, and control of crime; this may or may not involve extensive citizen participation. Socialism is the system that involves the collective ownership and administration of the values and goals of the society. The promotion of the welfare of society as a whole, then, appears to require socialism.

Socialism and Morality

Two main ethical systems suggest that each of us is obligated to serve society as a whole, utilitarianism and altruism.

Utilitarianism states that everyone ought to act to promote the good that is the greatest happiness or well-being for the greatest number. This view requires promoting the welfare of society as a whole. While some utilitarians believe that a centralized economic direction does not promote the general welfare, others believe that central planning alone ensures the welfare of society. They would choose socialism — or the welfare state — as the best means toward the achievement of their goal.

Altruism, too, supports socialism. If each individual's central moral obligation is to help others, the idea that the government should enforce the fulfillment of this obligation would seem to emerge quite naturally. Since, if everyone has the obligation to support the welfare of the whole society, the society has a right to such help, so the obligation is an enforceable one. A clear example of this are good-Samaritan laws. These laws legally require one to give aid to those who are in need of help (usually, however, only in dire circumstances). Similarly, in a socialist system the well-being of anyone depends on the well-being of the whole of society, which is most vigorously advocated in an altruist morality where each person is responsible for the welfare of other people.

There are a few altruists who believe that a capitalist system creates prosperity for society as a whole, so they do not endorse socialism and its centralized economic planning (just as not all utilitarians do). They believe that by permitting everyone to pursue selfish goals, to fulfill his or her desires, that a society's welfare is most effectively achieved.

So socialism may be given support from several ethical viewpoints, sometimes even contradictory ones, depending on what means are assumed to most effectively promote the socialist goal of society's overall welfare. Even a certain kind of egoist can be a socialist — if the egoist believes that only in a community in which the entire population is ensured of prosperity can the individual flourish best. Nevertheless, most socialist theorists, such as Claude Henri Saint-Simon, Charles Fourier, and more recently, Eric Fromm, embrace and advocate altruist moral ideals.

For most socialists, then, the ethics underlying their political-economic system is usually utilitarianism or, better yet, altruism. Whether there is a *strict* conceptual or philosophical connection between socialism and these ethical systems cannot be established here.

Capitalism

Capitalism is the political-economic system in which the principle of individual rights to life, liberty, and property are protected by law. Without private ownership, free trade and competition is impossible — one may not freely hold or exchange something one does not actually own. The capitalist system, then, presupposes the institution of the right to private property — the more completely capitalist it is, the more pervasive that institution applies in the society.

Capitalism makes it possible for individuals to strive to achieve their own goals, to pursue their own (idea of) happiness. Individuals have the basic right to do so under capitalism.

Capitalism and Morality

Although in its history most defenders of capitalism offered economic arguments in support of the system — namely, that it is the most productive of wealth, whether of individuals or for societies — there are some moral arguments that may be offered for the system. It is, of course, associated with certain religious outlooks, namely, the protestant idea of diligence and the earthly duty to prosper. But more recently, capitalism has been defended on more secular grounds as morally desirable.

Egoism seems to be the ethics that most readily supports capitalism. Why would the right to property or to the pursuit of happiness be important enough in capitalist systems to be classified as "unalienable" unless it is admitted, also, that individuals ought, morally to pursue happiness?

In our time, capitalism is supported either from a narrow type of egoism, in which everyone is supposed to pursue his or her individual conception of well-being or happiness, or from classical egoism, in line with which the well-being of human beings as such, their flourishing as human, thinking, creative animals, requires the institutions of private property and free trade. In both cases, the basic moral idea is that one ought to do what will most likely benefit oneself. But different kinds of egoism define "self" and "benefit" somewhat differently — more or less individualistically and subjectivistically, respectively.

Economists often explain that they believe capitalism is very suitable for human social and economic life because in the last analysis everyone is selfish and pursues his or her own advantage. By this is meant that every human being is naturally, automatically driven, or at least inclined to pursue his or her welfare as he or she understands it.

This is not a normative, moral support of capitalism but it suggests one clearly enough. Although economists would probably not put it this way, if by pursuing our own welfare we act in a way that suits our nature and *if we have a choice,* we *should,* morally, seek our own welfare.[2]

Utilitarianism is also advanced in defense of capitalism as the system that best promotes the public welfare, basing their support on utilitarianism. A few even hold that capitalism rests on *altruism* because when people pursue wealth and happiness in society, they must start out by helping others (e.g., by paying them for their skills).[3]

Welfare State

The welfare state amounts to a kind of balancing act. It embarks upon a balance between two crucial values human beings have cherished throughout history; namely, liberty (or personal autonomy) and happiness (or general well-being).

To put it more precisely, the welfare state is the political system in which human beings are regarded as possessing two basic rights, namely, a right to liberty and a right to happiness. When, in a country such as the United States of America, commercial, artistic, scientific, and educational endeavors, to name just a few, are given legal protection against interference by the authorities and by intruders, it is because those involved are regarded as having the right to embark on these endeavors. The freedom to set out on these sorts of activities is what citizens in such a society have a right to do. Generally, free enterprise means that everyone has the basic right to choose some line of work he or she can find, earn a living from it, and keep the rewards. This is one of those rights a welfare state sets out to protect to a considerable extent.

At the same time, the laws of a welfare state also protect the right to welfare or happiness or a decent standard of living. The welfare state provides people with basic necessities, even some luxuries, in part by redistributing wealth through taxation, regulation, and other political means. This limits the exercise of the right to liberty, just as the protection of a substantial degree of liberty places limits on the government's ability to provide welfare. The welfare state, then, aims at securing both the right to liberty and the right to welfare, as understood above.

What moral viewpoint would support this kind of system? There are essentially two ethical perspectives from which the welfare state gains support — utilitarianism and institutionism.

Utilitarianism gives support to the welfare state because the greatest happiness of the greatest number is the utilitarian ethical goal and many utilitarianists see liberty as a crucial means by which to achieve happiness in most areas of social life. Yet, wherever the welfare state does not yield happiness, the government ought to interfere in support of that goal. This then leads to a balance between the right to liberty and the right to welfare.

Intuitionism, a doctrine also used to support the welfare state, is not some code or system of ethics but a way to arrive at what ethical principles or moral system we should follow and promote. We have some familiarity with the idea of intuition—it is *a way of knowing some things without extensive theorizing and proof.* When people speak of women's intuition, they mean that women sometimes have knowledge that cannot be explained or proven.

Accordingly, it is argued that, intuitively, we have knowledge of what is right or wrong. For example, it is simply wrong for an adult to abuse a child—there is no need for extensive proof of this point. And when one considers that most people "know" what is right or wrong without an ethical system to back up their "knowledge," this position is quite plausible.

There are two values we all seem to be intuitively aware of quite apart from whether we have some ethical theory or not to back up our belief that they are indeed important values. Human freedom (or autonomy)—the liberty from the authority of others who haven't obtained this authority properly—is undoubtedly a value that we all recognize. To become aware of someone's enslavement or subjugation is to become aware of a wrong. To witness freedom of expression, of association, of judgment on the part of another is to witness something that is clearly right. Similarly, to become aware of destitution, of misery, of deprivation, of helplessness, is again to become aware of something wrong. To see prosperity, good health, promise of security, and the like is to see something right.

The intuitionist viewpoint stresses the fact that both values, the right to liberty and the right to well-being, are regarded by us as primary, of the utmost significance. So, a good society must take both of these into account. Capitalism and socialism seem to take note of just one or the other when they promote individual liberty and social welfare, respectively, as their only public goals. The welfare state takes both very seriously and this, it is argued, gives that system its moral support.

Of course, intuitionists realize that a balance needs to be struck between the two values they argue we can all intuitively realize to be crucial, and this is one of the major tasks and distinctions of the welfare state. The rights to liberty and to well-being should not both be protected fully, to the exclusion of each other. So the business of government is to strike a rational balance, which is what the welfare state is designed to do—and indeed appears to be doing. It is for this reason that the welfare state does not fully appeal to either capitalists or socialists. And, indeed, the welfare state leaves most people somewhat dissatisfied as far as their own goals are concerned; yet it seems generally to be a satisfying political arrangement.

There are nonutilitarian, nonintuitionist defenses of the welfare state, of course, so an exhaustive account[4] has not been presented here. Still, the utilitarian and the intuitionist approaches are the most prominent in our time.

Last Reflections on the Moral Economic System

So we have before us a sketch of the three of the main political alternatives we face in our times and some of the moral considerations raised as to why one or the other should be established and promoted. Which of these is the most appropriate, from a moral point of view? That is a crucial question for everyone.

It is not possible to handle that question here but neither would it be honest to simply leave it entirely unattended. My own conclusion is that a capitalist system does human nature and morality greater justice than all the live socio-political-economic options before us. I believe this because capitalism is, as I see the situation, most in tune with human nature and it is the ethical system that is best in accord with human nature and the system of classical egoism.

This view holds that what we are all primarily responsible for in life is to make of ourselves the best we can be. But the best what? The best *human individuals*.

Two important aspects of this view bear on politics and economics. One is that we are all human beings. The other is that each of us is also unique: an individual who can have his or her own individual aspirations and will probably be happy only if these are reasonably fulfilled by himself or herself.

Capitalism is the system most likely to make possible the satisfaction of both of these features of personal development and self-realization. It secures for each a measure of personal (including economic) liberty. And it makes the successful pursuit of individual happiness — by the persons whose responsibility is to pursue them, namely the individuals themselves — more likely because of this freedom.

The kind of freedom involved is called "negative" because it stresses the *absence of intrusion into one's life by other people,* regardless of how well- or ill-endowed this life may be. (Another conception of freedom is called "positive," meaning that one must be free to develop fully, as one should, and society must provide this freedom by having others make it possible. It requires not the absence of others' intrusion but the presence of needed provisions by others.)[5]

With negative freedom, persons are in charge of their own lives, which can be extremely varied. Within their own situations, people are free to do their best, or not. This is what makes the system of capitalism, which secures negative freedom, suitable to the moral nature of human life.

This point is extremely controversial. Critics of capitalism sometimes claim that it is inherently inconsistent and cannot even do what it sets out to do—e.g., produce abundance for most people and secure individual liberty. This "internal" criticism can be supplemented by an "external" type, which holds that there are many values that capitalism fails to secure, values that must, morally speaking, be secured. (Here the ground of criticism is a different moral system and the basic question is whether it is better than the classical egoism on which capitalism rests.)

From the beginning of our political/economic discussions, it has been reasonably clear that capitalism has gained support from egoistic considerations; socialism from altruistic ones; and the welfare state is to be a happy compromise. Defenders of these systems will have their own opinions of them, and before one settles for one or the other—or gives up on them and goes in search of another system—one will do well to examine them all. Have capitalists give their defense of capitalism, socialists and socialism, so that one may find a fair enough treatment from which to draw one's conclusions. The rest is one's own task and the main consideration is to think the matter through before making a choice.

The significance of the controversy cannot be understated. The world today is seeing the continuation of the dispute started several hundred years ago concerning what kind of human community we should live under. And that is ultimately a moral question.

Notes

1. David McLellan, ed., *Karl Marx, Selected Writings* (Oxford University Press, 1977), p. 172.

2. Indeed, one reason Marx regarded capitalism as an immature stage of humanity's development is that it did accord with the nature of egoistic man (at least temporarily, while human beings were egoistic). And the reason Ayn Rand, a twentieth-century novelist and philosopher, defended capitalism is that she held that egoism is indeed the right ethical system for human beings because it is based on a correct understanding of their nature. Choosing to act egoistically is what our own nature requires. Classical supporters of capitalism (or the legal system that makes it possible) John Locke and Adam Smith did adhere to one or another form of ethical or psychological egoism. It is not easy to explain in simple terms how intimately they connected the two. Marx, who criticized them for linking ethical and psychological egoism did connect egoism and capitalism very intimately, and Ayn Rand, who supported the basic economic ideas of those thinkers, did so as well.

3. The contemporary social theorist George Gilder advanced this notion in his best seller, *Wealth and Poverty* (Basic Books, 1980). Nevertheless, what matters in

morality are both motives and intentions, and only egoism advances a moral theory the motives and consequences of which would most clearly require capitalism.

4. See, Alan Gewirth, *Reason and Morality* (Chicago: University of Chicago Press, 1978). For a study of Gewirth's views, see Edward Regis, Jr., ed., *Gerwith's Ethical Rationalism* (Chicago: University of Chicago Press, 1984). See also A. I. Melden, *Rights and Person* (Berkeley: University of California Press, 1977).

5. The case for capitalism and the various controversies surrounding it is discussed in Tibor R. Machan, *Human Rights and Human Liberties* (Chicago: Nelson-Hall Co., 1975), and *Individuals and Their Rights* (LaSalle, Ill.: Open Court Publishing Co., 1988).

Epilogue:

RECENT WORK IN BUSINESS ETHICS
A SURVEY AND CRITIQUE

TIBOR R. MACHAN & DOUGLAS J. DEN UYL

Commerce is satanic, because it is the basest and vilest form of egoism.
— Baudelaire

Money, which represents the prose of life, and which is hardly spoken of in parlors without apology, is, in its effects and laws, as beautiful as roses.
— Emerson

Before we conclude the discussion of various facets of business ethics, it will be useful to give a report of the current thinking of those who have been most active in this field. We will report on and critically assess some of the work others are doing in business ethics and public policy.

The Textbook Boom

Most of the work in business ethics can be found in the proliferation of textbooks or editing. This must be qualified. Some new journals have been introduced, but the impact on the field has been primarily through textbooks. Furthermore, there are very few "trade books" in the field. That is to say, collections of essays and texts in political philosophy, ethics, and metaphysics are common as are also numerous original treatises, such as John Rawls's *A Theory of Justice,* or Robert Nozick's *Anarchy, State, and Utopia.* But nothing of that sort is evident in business ethics *per se.* Few general theories have been advanced, although some special subjects have been dealt with in book length treatments, e.g., Werhane (1985), Stevenson (1980), Goldman (1980), Donaldson (1980), and (one of the earliest special treatments, Garrett, 1966). Some interesting yet far from comprehensive essays have also appeared in the two main journals started in 1980 and 1981: *The Journal of Business Ethics* and *Business and Professional Ethics Journal.*

One of the most widely used and reprinted textbooks is *Ethical Theory and Business.*[1] It contains some traditional ethics, a good deal of modern and contemporary political philosophy (Locke, Adam Smith, Karl Marx, John Rawls, Robert Nozick, et al.), and some normative essays pertaining to business. The selections in another widely used text, *Ethical Issues in Business,* focus primarily on specific public policy topics that affect business.

Most of the "readers" and single author texts are oriented to public policy as well. For example, Manuel G. Velasquez's *Business Ethics,* Richard T. De George's *Business Ethics,* and David Braybrook's *Ethics in the World of Business* all deal extensively with questions bearing on law and public policy. Each, however, devotes space to standard meta-ethical questions, such as relativism versus absolutism, or whether one needs theory to make intelligent ethical judgments.

As already noted in this volume, many people who write about business ethics initially regard business with suspicion. Yet even among those who have an open mind and accept trade as morally proper (or at least unobjectionable), different ethical attitudes are possible. It depends largely on how important the virtue of prudence is within their ethical systems.

Central Normative Topics in Business

We will now explore some of the prominent normative views in the following areas of business: employment (wage-labor, rights, organized labor, discrimination, exploitation, alienation); management (subordination, discipline, codes, organization, authority); advertising (truth-telling, gimmicks, dependence effect, sponsorship, taste, commercialization [of media]); profit (as motive, as goal, as prosperity, as exploited labor, as earnings); corporations (as creatures of state, as entities, as free associations, re social responsibility); and regulation (mercantilist, utilitarian [market failure], democratic [market failure], human rights, judicial inefficiency). These topics do not exhaust what could be discussed within our sphere of concern, and they indicate more the trends in the field than what logically relate to it.

1. Employment

To employ someone is to come to terms with the person about some skill that he or she will perform in the course of the production of some commodity or service. An employer is one who desires this skill and offers payment for its performance. The employee supplies the needed skill and receives an agreed-upon payment for providing it for an agreed-upon period of time.

It is assumed that the employer owns the facilities where the productive endeavor can be undertaken. The employee in turn owns the skill. The ownership may or may not be alienable. An employer may own an idea, e.g., about next fall's design for women's wear, while the employee, e.g., a seamstress, owns the skill to implement the idea. Neither of these items can be easily parted with, thus both are unalienable. Of course, often from the creation of such ideas or the cultivation of skills, individuals may move on to produce various items that are alienable.

More familiar is the case where a group of persons, e.g., a corporation, owns a plant and needs skilled workers to help produce items or render services. The corporation (i.e., its manager) and the workers (sometimes their organization) will arrive at terms, including what the corporation will pay the workers, how many hours the workers will devote to the task per week, how much extra will be paid when overtime is required, and so on.

Although some argue that wage-labor is a necessary component of the capitalist, business economy, this is not so. One can find skilled workers forming corporations or partnerships, and trading their skills for set fees, as attorneys and medical doctors customarily do. This tends to obtain most frequently in highly skilled specialities and may be related to the kind of demand that exists for the skill within the market. Wage labor is more frequently associated with unskilled or semiskilled labor, although this need by no means be a set practice.

Rights. The most feverent ethical issue surrounding labor pertains to workers' rights. There are two dominant perspectives here. One holds that workers have basic individual rights of free choice and no more (Haggard, 1976; Nozick, 1974; Machan, 1987a). In the course of employment, one can freely choose to accept or reject terms; but once terms are set, one is required to honor them. So if workers knowingly agree to work for some company that demands that workers expose themselves to high risks, they must accept the high risks and have no ground for complaint in case of resulting harm. If workers agree not to organize into labor unions while working for some employer, here too, they must honor their agreements or terminate the relationship. Because they are wage-laborers, such employees are also seen to be subject to the "employment at will" condition. Once their employment agreement has been fully honored, they may be laid off or fired by their employer. Such an agreement may, however, specify conditions of prior notice.

Essentially, this view of workers' rights sees workers as party to a freely consented to contract or agreement, the terms of which they are legally obligated to honor. The same applies to employers; so it is fair to say that no special workers' rights are recognized within this viewpoint.

The main opposing viewpoint sees workers as filling a special role within the employment relationship, one that places them at a relative disadvantage, as a class, compared to employers (Nickels, 1978–79; Bowie, 1981;

Werhane, 1985). This is not to be confused with Karl Marx's view of the relationship between labor and capital, which sees the relationship as lamentable and necessarily exploitative. The position we have in mind states that workers, because of their inequality in the bargaining situation, ought to be granted certain special considerations. Employers not only should but *ought* legally be required to provide workers with those work-related benefits that, under equal bargaining terms, workers would demand for themselves. For example, workers should not be exposed to unreasonable risks; they must enjoy safe and healthy working conditions; they must not be hampered by their employers in their effort to form labor organizations; they must not lose their jobs when the corporation that hired them experiences economic setbacks, at least not until other cost-cutting measures have been exhausted. In general, workers have rights to specified forms of treatment unique to their circumstances as a class. Whatever institutional measures are effective in securing the protection of these rights—e.g., a well staffed, powerful enough governmental body (such as the National Labor Relations Board [NLRB])—must be established, just as courts and police departments are established to secure for citizens the protection of their various rights.

The doctrine of workers' rights encompasses numerous areas associated with the employment side of business ethics. One of the positions mentioned above would restrict the scope of rights to treating workers as any others who are party to a contractual agreement. Yet it is arguable that within this scope there could be numerous other ethical dimensions. Besides consideration of rights, one would be required also to pay heed to moral requirements that are not dealt with by reference to rights and corollary obligations. Employees ought to be loyal, diligent, thrifty, prudent, as employers ought to be considerate, just, generous, and honest. The alternative perspective mentioned above would not leave the relationship between employee and employer to freely chosen moral conduct, but would insist that this relationship be supervised by legal authorities, lest the employees be taken advantage of or neglected in the process.

Labor Organization.   In the absence of the legal protection of workers' special rights, it is possible that the one promising moral solution to the vulnerability of workers is the institution of labor organizations, unions. The precise nature of unions is unclear. They are not treated as corporations, nor as partnerships. They are rather a kind of nonprofit social organization, with a hierarchy of leadership, administered in a quasi-democratic fashion.

Unions come into existence by the process of spontaneous worker organization or by franchising whereby an existing union embarks upon the recruitment of members from unorganized employee groups. The process is now highly regulated. This is not the place to consider the history of unionized labor or specific regulations (See Machan, 1981a). In the present legal atmosphere, labor organizations are generally supported by the law; for example, even if only a small percentage of workers express the desire to form a union, elections at plants or factories are mandated by law. The underlying theory is that without such a mandate, the threat of employer retaliation would rarely allow the formation of labor organizations (Haggard, 1976).

The improvement of workers' bargaining power is not always viewed as desirable. Some (Bennett, 1985) argue that unionization simply increases the cost of labor, the cost of production, and finally the price of the commodity or service, which in the end works against the interest of the worker and consumer. Since prices in the market place tend to rise whenever related production costs rise, and since all this reverberates throughout the market, whenever wages rise without some actual scarcity or change of demand, there is only a nominal or temporary improvement for those who receive the wage. Legal protection of unions gives more lasting status to the improvement, but at the expense of other workers (Hutt, 1975).

There are also those who recognize the value of labor organizations but with reservations and qualifications. On the one hand, they argue that nothing would be wrong with labor organizations if they and the firms whose workers they organize stood on equal legal footing. For example, unions are not subject to antitrust laws. So either these laws should be lifted for firms, or imposed on unions. An industry-wide strike, for example, might be permissible only if firms could engage in similar collusion as they consider their hiring practices. On the other hand, there is also the suggestion that labor might go much further than unionization. They could develop themselves into firms, similar to law firms, and pool the skills of the workers who would become partners or associates. Then workers would no longer be wage-laborers but capitalists trading their capital on the market.

Discrimination. One of the most widely discussed aspects of the employment relationship is discrimination. Kinds of discrimination include racial, sexual, religious, ethnic, and others for which no clear concept has been formed, e.g., those based on medical condition, intellectual quotient, weight, or grooming. To avoid misunderstanding, the problem has never been with discrimination as such — this is a judgmental process involved in all thinking and recognition. Rather it is *unjust* discrimination that has been the focus of discussion.

Unjust discrimination can only be identified in terms of some idea of justice. The most prominent approach to conceiving of justice in this context has been that irrelevant factors ought not to be invoked in how one treats other people. The Rawlsian idea, that there must be a large component of fairness in the treatment of human beings, adds to this familiar sense of justice the idea of social conscience. When one hires workers, one ought to consider each application fairly. This, in turn, means that all applicants ought to be given an equal chance. So the issue is whether the hiring, firing, or promotion of an employee is related to performance, or to irrelevant consideration. For example, given that flight attendants have as their central task the safety and comfort of the passengers, hiring only women on the basis of their good looks would probably be unjust discrimination.

Granted that the ethics of business itself may construe unjust discrimination to be a moral wrong, there is considerable dispute as to what measures must be taken to combat this practice. Here again two main schools exist within the literature of business ethics.

One school holds that employees are not properly positioned to fight injustice, and for this reason alone, legal interference with unjust discrimination is necessary (Braybrooke, 1983; Wasserstrom, 1977). A variation on this theme invokes the doctrine of workers' rights, whereby workers have the right to be treated fairly, and government, the protector of the rights of individuals in a free society, is duty bound to restrain such discrimination and punish it where it occurs (Werhane, 1985).

The other view sees unjust discrimination as a violation of business ethics, but not a violation of rights. Those who do the hiring, promotion, and firing ought to follow through on their moral promises and adhere to their legal contracts. They, however, ought not to be forced to do what they morally ought to unless they are violating the terms of a contract. It is arguable that in some cases unjust discrimination is a breach of contract, but more often it is unethical or morally objectionable management. If that is so, then no rights are violated, even though employees, customers, and stockholders are being mistreated. It is further argued that by treating them as such, the realm of personal liberty, wherein one takes responsibility for one's actions without threat of legal sanctions, is diminished (Machan, 1977; Den Uyl, 1984).

Exploitation. Here we face perhaps the most fundamental challenge against the employment relationship. As noted before, Marxism regards exploitation as inherent in capitalism. But this is scarcely an ethical or moral criticism. Rather it is a kind of normative remark on a par with observing that natural processes are destroying a forest or some species of animal life—that is, a value judgment not implying any blame or praise (Fisk, 1980). For Marx, capitalist exploitation may be lamentable but carries no implication that anyone ought, morally, to do anything about it. From Marx's perspective, these matters are viewed as "a process of natural history" (Marx, 1977).

But in some non-Marxist discussions, exploitation is a morally wrong. When a worker is exploited, this means that he or she is being taken unfair advantage of or that a vulnerability is being unfairly used for personal advantage. And such conduct should not be tolerated (Braybrooke, 1983).

Clearly one need not be a Marxist to testify to the existence of exploitation in all kinds of human relationships. For Marx, the exploitation in capitalism was a general, class phenomenon that had many exceptions. For the moral critics of capitalism, exploitation is something that may or may not occur throughout the economic system. Disadvantaged groups, such as women, blacks, or children, are more often the victims of exploitation. Such persons, in need of a livelihood and approaching the marketplace from a position of inequality, have no way of choosing between desirable and undesirable work. Their employers are able to extract from them performance which is ill-paid and demeaning. The typical case would be women working in a typing pool. Many of them are single mothers who cannot live and provide for their children without the work. They cannot protest the treatment they receive.

The non-Marxist exploitation theory usually rests on an egalitarian moral foundation. This view holds that the proper relationship among persons is one of significant equality, meaning that the parties ought to have equal moral standing, without some having to be subservient to others. The egalitarian outlook does not demand absolute equality, but merely significant equality. Workers are moral agents with needs and aspirations, who ought to have equal standing with their employers in matters of work-related preferences, wants, and desires; the employer, in turn, should respect the workers' job-related interests (Braybrook, 1983:204ff).

Alienation. Again, it is the Marxist framework that is the most familiar host to the philosophical discussion of alienation. Within Marxism, alienation means that a person is not living a life in accord with the requirements of his most fully developed human nature. Such a person is not whole, not in place, or is out of alignment, given that the proper conditions for human existence are unavailable to him (Fromm, 1961).*

In Marxist analysis, however, such alienation is inescapable under capitalism. Yet Marx did not originate the term and it clearly has non-Marxist homes as well. So, with an awareness of Marx's insights into the situation of the working class, but without embracing the Marxist baggage of historical relativism, alienation has been understood as a condition of many members in commercial society. The idea is that persons are pressured into conformity with a certain approach to living, namely, competition and specialization, which undermines the full humanity that might be possible outside a capitalist socio-economic context. The desire for private gain is inculcated into the bulk of the members of society, regardless of whether this is really the desire that would serve them best (Fromm, 1961; Schmitt, 1973; Torrance, 1974).

There are those who argue that the condition of being alienated is not at

*A very different account of Marxist alienation is to be found in P.C. Roberts and M.A. Stephenson, *Marx's Theory of Exchange, Alienation and Crises* (New York: Praeger Publ., 1983).

all necessary in capitalist society. It is brought about by two factors, both incidental to capitalism. First, there is the fact that some people fail to invest the will power to demand of life what is suitable to them, settling, instead, for immediate satisfaction. This is not the system's fault but the person's (Branden, 1987). Second, the system is skewed and there are demands imposed on people that are really not the function of capitalism at all but of statism: e.g., taxation makes it necessary for everyone to earn a sufficient income to pay, for example, property taxes. So none are permitted, by the state, to spend a life in contemplation, artistic creativity, or leisure (Nozick, 1976). This pressure to contribute to the public interest, to the redistributionist features of the society, is not part of business but of the state. Its alienating influences, then, cannot be construed as part of the commercial society which, if unencumbered by interventions, would not require all to participate commercially (Machan, 1986).

Clearly there are many other strands to the discussion of employment. For example, there are those who would completely eliminate the employer/employee relationship by establishing worker-owned firms or by fully nationalizing the labor market (Fisk, 1980). There are those who would also leave the entire matter of employer/employee relations to the forces of the market and discount any moral criticism addressed to the results (Friedman, 1962). In between, there are varieties of workers' rights advocates, who demand a regulated market society, and moral defenders of the free market.

2. Management

Businesses require administration or management. Sometimes owners themselves manage their firms, but more often management is itself employed by the owners (e.g., stock holders). Thus, managers typically concern themselves with operations – allocating the workforce, determining the skills required, marketing the product, distributing the firm's revenues between various types of costs, introducing new lines of production.

Managers are hired to make the enterprise function profitably. This is how they benefit the owners, while owners pay managers a competitive salary. Of course, managers are sometimes also (part-)owners, so there is no uniform division of roles involving management and owners. In corporate commerce, however, owners (stockholders) are typically silent partners, with minimal and optional managerial responsibilities. This is obvious in looking at the typical corporate structure especially the limited liability privilege, bestowed by state charter or, less frequently, by explicit contract (Hessen, 1979; Donaldson, 1982).

The first ethically relevant point about management regards the responsibilities of managers to owners of the firm. This is where an explicit normative element is evident: a promise to administer the firm profitably in the nontechnical sense of making the firm prosper economically. Managers hire on with a promise to advance the economic well-being of the company. Unless this promise is made with duress, it would *prima facie* have a binding character. Certainly there are those who have argued (Friedman, 1970) that the primary obligation of corporate managers is to their stockholders, namely, to enrich the latter within the framework of "the rules of the game," i.e., the legal system.

The practical import of this is that management organizes the firm, including the work force, in the most efficient (and lawful) way for the long-term well-being of the company (owners). The authority and responsibility for doing this is delegated to management, with the owners making their evaluation of company performance by buying or selling their shares. In contrast to those who argue that corporations are no longer effectively controlled by their shareholders (Nader, Green & Seligman, 1973), there are those who insist that owners are in sufficient control via the buying and selling of shares (which sends the needed signals to the management) (Manne, 1978). Others deny this and hold that ownership means very little if there is no overseeing responsibility attached to it (Nader, Green, and Seligman, 1976; Chaudhuri, 1971).

For the present, however, our main concern is not with the broad character of corporate commerce. We mention it only because it has some bearing on the moral nature of business management. For example, plant closure is one task that might befall management of a large corporation, leading to the possible layoff of large numbers of workers. The plant closure may be in line with management's responsibility to owners. It may well ensure the solvency or greater profitability of the firm. Yet it also threatens to lead to the unemployment of many workers, some who have invested a lifetime with the firm's plant (division) that is to be closed down (Kavanagh, 1982; McKenzie, 1983).

Less crucial moral topics arise as well, and here we will briefly survey some of them.

Subordination. The central issue here is just how much loyalty is owed to management and what are the limits of ordering employees to comply with management decisions. The most widely aired philosophical views on this topic at present tend to stress a doctrine of worker's rights and responsibilities (Werhane, 1985; Ezorsky, 1987). This doctrine draws its substance not from the promise(s) involved in hiring and accepting payment, but from noncontractual moral features allegedly present in the management-worker relationship. No loyalty, for example, may be demanded from workers that would involve the suppression of information that may serve the public interest (Nader, Green, and Seligman, 1976; Donaldson, 1982; Werhane, 1985).

In general, there is considerable literature that argues against the view that makes subordination part and parcel of management's task in the profitable administration of a firm. The idea that if management's orders are not agreeable to workers the latter may terminate the relationship and thus avoid the sting of the order does not receive much support in recent business ethics discussions. This is a corollary of the criticism that the doctrine of employment at will has received (Blade, 1967), based in part, on certain affinities between the feudal master/servant and the capitalist employer/employee relationships (Werhane, 1985:82).

The manager's own ethical concerns are not frequently discussed, although some exceptions do exist. It might also be argued that the main source of solutions for ethical difficulties to managers is to be found in a neo-Aristotelian self-realization or flourishing ethics, one that stresses the virtue of integrity (Norton, 1976). The point here is that a manager of a firm must treat all his tasks in line with a well-formed set of moral principles. While prudence is one of these principles, it would be self-denying to make this the sole virtue by which to make one's choices. When it comes to treating others, viz., subordinates, the self-actualization ethic requires keeping firmly in mind that others are moral agents whose deception or similar mistreatment would be a blemish on one's own moral character. Placing demands on subordinates is not in itself morally objectionable, provided one does not disguise the nature of the demands and that one treats employees according to their accurate job description. Once managers conduct themselves according to such a moral viewpoint, expecting loyalty from subordinates is not contrary to dictates of respect for their personhood.

Of course here again we occasionally find the kind of argument that is associated with neo-classical economic analysis: whatever practice will be profit-maximizing, within positive law, are morally permissible; those that are unsuitable will, in turn, be met with public rebuke *through the behavior of market agents* (e.g., by the manager's ultimate replacement with one who is more efficient with administering the work force).

While there could be many other phases of managerial ethics, unfortunately, the literature regarding these is scant. Except for the widespread concern shown toward the employee, the problems of managerial ethics are left to be dealt with by instructors of business management and organization

3. Advertising

The first major concern with advertising, judging by the literature in business ethics, is whether advertising is useless, harmful or, is of some social benefit (Leiser, 1979). This again does not so much consider the decisions those in the field need to make, but the moral character of the field itself. The most widely reprinted work on this issue is not by a moral philosopher but by an economist (Galbraith, 1958).

The Dependence Effect. Galbraith's popular work argues that the main thing wrong with advertising is that it creates needs in the population that, without advertising, would never have arisen, thus, ensuring the continued siphoning off of resources that could otherwise go to meet real needs. This may appear at first to be economically advantageous, because the consumption habits thus created sustain a large and productive portion of the market. But under closer inspection, the production created aims at the satisfaction trivial, frivolous, luxurious, or extravagant desires. Advertising is thus seen as a menace to vitally important but neglected possibilities.

In response, it has been noted (Hayek, 1961), that if there is something wrong with creating desires, then much of culture must be condemned. The arts are relentlessly involved in the creation of new desires and tastes. It would seem that the complaint involved in the dependence effect rests on (a) a distrust of human judgment, which then should cut deeply and call into question the complaint itself—to wit, perhaps the critic does not appreciate being left out or having his preferred list of priorities ignored; or (b) a failure to appreciate the creative nature of human life, including human aspirations in areas of lesser and greater significance. In any case, the debate was one of the earliest ones in the field.

Not Enough of the Truth. This criticism of advertising is aimed less broadly. It is alleged that much of advertising commits the wrong of *suppressio veri.* "It is not asking too much of the advertiser to reveal such facts when they are known to him, and he should not be forgiven for 'putting his best foot forward' at his customer's expense" (Leiser, 1973). The problem is that advertising promotes the product of the client (or firm) without making it clear that other products are better or less expensive (and thus an economically more advantageous choice for the consumer). By so misleading the consumer, advertising tends to promote consumer errors and to create misallocation of resources. Although there is no explicit lying involved in this, there is a failure of telling the relevant truth.

Yet it is arguable that there is nothing morally objectionable in not telling the whole truth, since there does not exist some prior obligation to reveal to prospective buyers all they may have use for. The charge seems to rest on the misunderstanding that advertising is primarily a form of product information. Rather it is a form of appeal. This might be illustrated by reference to that very frequently employed instrument, the academic or business resumé. None list the failures of applicants for positions, leaving it to the employer to look into whatever interests him or her about the candidate beyond what the candidate wishes to communicate. It would be odd to demand that applicants inform prospective employers of all that the employer might like to know. Similarly, it seems not to be the task of the seller to inform prospective employers about the possible problems or disadvantages of his or her product. To do so might even call into question the resourcefulness and intelligence of the buyer.

Gimmickry. There are also discussions of advertising gimmickry, which has been charged with being a form of deception (Leiser, 1973). If toothpaste is advertised by depicting happy couples in the background, or cars by showing attractive women approaching men who drive them, the inference may be drawn that the purchase of such products will bring forth results that are quite independent of the use to which they can be put.

One other issue that may deserve separate mention is the relationship of advertising to consumer freedom. Yet in a way, this is a slightly different version of the issue between Galbraith and Hayek. It is argued, for example, that when customers ask for advice from a seller and receive it in a way that benefits the seller, they are not free in a real sense to choose (Benn, 1967). An opposite viewpoint might be that it is not the moral responsibility of sellers to make their customers better off, and customers should be aware of this.

There are, in addition, suspicions about subliminal advertising and complaints about celebrity sponsorship, plain bad taste, stereotyping, and the phenomenon of the commercialization of culture in general. These topics and problems do not dominate the recent discussion, which is focused more on deception, cost, and the broader issue of market freedom in the face of advertising.

4. Profit

To profit from an activity is to gain, not lose from it. The term thus means more than what we understand by it in commerce. In this latter context, profit refers to *economic* gain. "Economic" values are exchangeable and directly or indirectly priced on a market. Thus one may not $profit_1$ from making a $profit_2$ — as when by gaining economically something of greater value, say the love of a spouse, is lost. In connection with the field of business or commerce, only $profit_2$ will concern us here. Business ethics' studies profit mainly because, in pursuing them, one would appear to be often tempted to go morally astray.

Some have argued that the very institution of profit-seeking has built into it a sort of corrupting element, taking our attention from more noble deeds and focusing it on satisfying desires for private gain (Schmitt, 1973). To avoid this, it may be necessary to restructure society rather drastically, so that the very institution of profit-making is abolished. In contrast, others have argued that the profit motive is by no means the central motive of a commercial society. Rather, such a society may embody all kinds of motives — rent motive, wage motive, pleasure motive, artistic enlightenment motive, so that perhaps "no one has any business simply to assume that the desire to make a (private) profit is always and necessarily selfish and discreditable; notwithstanding that the corresponding desires to obtain a wage, or a salary, or a retirement income, are—apparently—not" (Flew, 1976:156).

Some of the confusion in the discussion of profit stems from the economic theory that postulates the existence of a built-in profit motive. This view is often, though probably mistakenly (Billett, 1987) associated with Adam Smith, who said that "It is not from the benevolence of the butcher, the brewer, or the baker, that we expect our dinner, but from their regard to their own interest" (Smith, 1776, 1976). Thus, economists claim that the capitalism Smith argued for is supposed to be resting on the inherently selfish or self-interested motives of human beings. In contrast, it is arguable that such motives are not inherent but institutionally or structurally induced (Schmitt, 1973).

Still, a persistent question about profit-making is whether it is morally justifiable in the first place. Some argue that morality is inherently a matter of looking out for the interests of others, or at least of considering how one might coordinate self-interested conduct so that the general welfare is secured. Thus profit-making is justified not as something one ought to do as such, but rather as it tends to result in the public welfare or embody altruistic results (Gilder, 1979). Some defend profit making on ethical egoistic grounds and argue that it is merely the implementation of the virtue of prudence (Rand, 1967; Machan, 1987b). They hold that while prudence or productivity is not the highest virtue, it is clearly a commendable character trait. There are those for whom seeking profit is justified only after one has properly taken care of the interest of others, including one's competitors and certainly one's customers (Leiser, 1982). For others, however, it is too self-regarding an endeavor to contain morally redeeming features and is almost certainly going to lead to general social malaise (Mead, 1976). Indeed, there are those who favor a restructuring of global economic affairs, so as to remedy the consequences of the pursuit of profit (Nielsen, 1987).

5. Corporations and Morality

The subcategories listed earlier under this main category can all be treated simultaneously. This is because the answer to the question of whether corporations are essentially creatures of the state seems to inform one's view of the concept of corporate social responsibility—the central ethical concern of this category.

As De George points out, there are two main schools of thought on the nature of corporations as creatures of the state (De George, 1982). The first could be called the "legal creator" position. In this theory, corporations are essentially created by law or the state. Corporations owe their existence and nature (not to mention privileges) to the state and its laws (Nader and Green, 1973). Were those laws absent, corporations would not exist except perhaps in such forms as limited partnerships.

In contrast to the legal creator position is the "legal recognition" theory. This position holds that corporations are essentially voluntary associations of private individuals (Hessen, 1982; Pilon, 1982). The state's role is simply to formally recognize the association by offering it legal protection—the same type of protection being offered many other voluntary associations not initially created by the state (e.g., marriages). We cannot assess the merits of these conflicting theories here. Suffice it to say, that the weakest element of the legal recognition theory concerns explaining limited liability. The weakest element of the legal creator theory concerns explaining the prelegal origins and development of corporations.

These two views have, nevertheless, influenced the debate over "corporate social responsibility." If corporations are creatures of the state, they are likely to be viewed as "trustees" of society's resources. The state has entrusted them to manage society's resources. As trustees of the state, corporations will have responsibilities to the public at large, because the state itself is charged with securing the public welfare and should therefore insure that those sanctioned by it do so as well. Consequently those who adopt the legal creator theory are also likely to adopt a strong sense of corporate social responsibility.

On the other hand, if corporations are voluntary associations of individuals recognized, but not created, by the state, it becomes difficult to imagine why corporations have any special obligations to society beyond those that individuals may have. Furthermore, if individuals are not "trustees" of society in the resources they employ, it is not clear why combinations of individuals should become so, whatever the utilitarian effects on society of large scale associations. Clearly, then, theorists sympathetic to the legal recognition theory are likely to hold to a weak or nonexistent conception of corporate social responsibility.

Although a number of schools of thought have been proposed on the question of corporate social responsibility (Sohn, 1982), it has been argued that there are really two main perspectives with variations under each (Den Uyl, 1984). These two perspectives are closely linked to the two theories on the nature of corporations just discussed. Aligned with the legal creator theory are those who see corporations as operating by permission of society and/or the state. This is the predominant position in the field with variations ranging from social contract arguments (Bowie, 1982), to legal approaches (De George, 1982), to combinations (Donaldson, 1982), to the essentially amoral (Davis/Frederick/Blomstrom, 1980). Those linked to the legal recognition theory are less commonly represented in the field of business ethics and tend to have fewer variations on the main theme. The arguments tend to be either quasi-moral with an economic emphasis (Friedman, 1962; Johnson, 1978) or based upon a theory of individual rights (Hessen, 1982; Den Uyl, 1984).

We could continue by discussing the responsibilities corporations do or do not have in specific areas such as the environment, product safety, discrimination, working conditions, and the like. But to do this would carry us too far afield and would not affect our basic point that the types of recommendations made in specific areas are generally a function of the answers given to the basic questions discussed here and elsewhere. And since the main body of this volume contains an essay discussing government regulation, a topic closely related to corporate commerce, we will leave off this topic presently.

Conclusion

We have now provided a brief survey of ideas that are prominent in contemporary discussions of business ethics. In total fairness, however, we would have had to go into far greater detail in order to cover the field thoroughly. The reader and student should supplement his reading with other works. In that way, a balanced picture will emerge and an informed choice can be made as to how best to approach either business ethics in general or some particular topic in it.

On the critical side, we should make the general observation that within the normative philosophical literature bearing on business, there seems to be no clear distinction being maintained between several branches of normative philosophy — e.g., ethics or morality, social ethics, public policy, law, and political theory. Both from a philosophical and a pedagogical viewpoint, such distinctions are vital. Ignoring them has had a number of negative consequences. For example, the excessive orientation towards public policy has turned the field into little more than an arena for ideological expression, almost all of which is decidedly hostile to business and to capitalism, in particular. Unlike medical, legal, or education ethics, all of which seem able to generate ethical issues that are not directly related to public policy questions, business ethics is still in search of an identity distinct from political ideology. Perhaps this is inevitable, but then it should be clearly understood.

Pedagogically, the failure to maintain clear distinctions has had, in many cases, the effect of misrepresenting courses in business ethics to students who expect and desire from them what doctors and nurses get from courses in medical ethics — an idea of how they ought to conduct themselves in their chosen profession, not simply what laws ought to be passed or repealed. Yet even if we regard business ethics as exclusively concerned with public policy questions, professionals in the field have generally not done a good job in keeping informed about recent theoretical work in related fields such as economics and law. There is, for example, an appalling lack of understanding among most writers in business ethics of how markets even work. This has the effect of alienating those who might otherwise be interested in, and benefit from, a course in business ethics – the business person himself.

But the field is still in its infancy. Perhaps in time, these problems will work themselves out. It may also be possible, however, that philosophers will conclude that there is little to this subject beyond the classical debates in political philosophy and political economy. We hold to the belief that there is the potential for a distinct subject of business ethics, but the direction of the field at present seems to have lost sight of what that distinct subject might be.*

*A longer version of this essay appeared in the April 1987 issue of *The American Philosophical Quarterly*. Permission to use the portions above is gratefully acknowledged.

Bibliography

Acton, H. B. 1971. *The Morals of Markets.* London: Longman Group.

Aranson, P. H. 1982. "Pollution Control: The Case for Competition," in Poole, pp. 339–93.

Arrington, R. L. 1982. "Advertising and Behavior Control." *Journal of Business Ethics* 1: 1–12.

Arrow, K. J. 1981. "Two Cheers for Government Regulation." *Harpers* (March): 17–21.

Ashmore, R. B. 1981. "The Public Interest and Business Decisions." *Proceedings of the Catholic Philosophical Association* 55: 278–87.

Baden, J. A., and R. L. Stroup. 1983. *Natural Resources.* San Francisco: Pacific Institute.

Baram, M. S. 1968. "Trade Secrets: What Price Loyalty?" In Beauchamp and Bowie, pp. 179–89.

Bayles, Michael. 1981. *Professional Ethics.* Belmont, Calif.: Wadsworth Publ.

Beauchamp, T. L., and Bowie, N. E. 1979. *Ethical Theory and Business.* Englewood Cliffs, N.J.: Prentice-Hall.

Benn, S. I. 1967. "Freedom and Persuasion." *The Australasian Journal of Philosophy* 45:259–75. In Beauchamp and Bowie, pp. 367–76.

Bennett, J. T. 1985. *Does a Higher Wage Really Mean You Are Better Off?* Springfield, Va.: National Institute for Labor Relations Research.

Benson, G. C. S. 1982. *Business Ethics in America.* Lexington, Mass.: D. C. Heath & Co.

Billett, Leonard. 1987. "Adam Smith and Justice." In Machan, pp. 292–310.

Blades, L. E. 1967. "Employment at Will versus Individual Freedom: On Limiting the Abusive Exercise of Employer Power." *Columbia Law Review* 67: 1404–35.

Bowie, N. E. 1982. *Business Ethics.* Englewood Cliffs, N.J.: Prentice-Hall.

Branden, Nathaniel. 1987. "Alienation." (in Machan, pp. 62–82).

Braybrooke, David. 1983. *Ethics in the World of Business.* Totowa, N.J.: Rowman and Allanheld.

_____. 1984. "Justice and Injustice in Business." In Regan, pp. 167–201.

Brenkert, G. G. 1981. "Privacy, Polygraphs and Work." *Business and Professional Ethics Journal* 1: 19–35.

Buchanan, J. M., and Gordon Tullock. 1962. *The Calculus of Consent.* Ann Arbor, Mich.: University of Michigan Press.

Camenisch, P. F. 1981. "Business Ethics: On Getting to the Heart of the Matter." *Business and Professional Ethics Journal* 1: 59–69.

Chaudhuri, Joyotpaul. 1971. "Toward a Democratic Theory of Property and the Modern Corporation." *Ethics* 81: 271–86.

Childs, M. W., and D. Cater. 1954. *Ethics in a Business Society.* New York: Harper and Brothers.

Cohen, David. 1982. "How Business Can Influence Government Credibil. *Journal of Business Ethics* 1: 109–118.

Davis, K., W. C. Frederick, and R. L. Blomstrom. *Business and Society: Concepts and Policy Issues.* New York: 1980.

DeGeorge, R. T. *Business Ethics.* New York: 1982.

DeGeorge, R. T., and J. A. Pichler, eds. 1978. *Ethics, Free Enterprise and Public Policy.* N.Y.: Oxford University Press.

Den Uyl, D. J. 1984. *The New Crusaders.* Bowling Green, Ohio: Social Philosophy and Policy Center.

Donaldson, Thomas. 1982. *Corporations and Morality.* Englewood-Cliffs, N.J.: Prentice-Hall.

Donaldson, T., and P. Werhane, eds. 1979. *Ethical Issues in Business.* Englewood-Cliffs, N.J.: Prentice Hall.

Ewing, David. 1982. *Do it My Way or You're Fired.* New York: John Wiley & Sons, Inc.

Ezorsky, Gertrude, ed. 1987. *Workers' Rights.* Albany, N.Y.: SUNY Press.

Fisk, Milton. 1980. *Ethics and Society.* New York: New York University Press.

_____. 1987. "Property Rights. In Machan, pp. 250–71.

Flew, Antony. 1976. "The Profit Motive." *Ethics* 86:312–22. In Donaldson and Werhane, pp. 155–64.

Friedman, Milton. 1962. *Capitalism and Freedom.* Chicago: University of Chicago Press.

_____. 1970. "The Social Responsibility of Business is to Increase Profits." *The New York Times Magazine,* September 13, pp. 122–26.

Fromm, Erich. 1961. *Marx's Concept of Man.* New York: Ungar.

Galbraith, J. K. 1976, 1982. "The Dependence Effect." In *The Affluent Society, 3rd ed.* N.Y.: Houghton Mifflin.

Garrett, T. M. 1966. *Business Ethics.* New York: Appleton-Century-Crofts.

Gilder, G. F. 1981. *Wealth and Poverty.* N.Y.: Basic Books.

Goldman, A. H. 1980. *The Moral Foundations of Professional Ethics.* Totowa, N.J.: Rowman and Littlefield.

Haggard, T. R. 1976. "The Right to Work—A Constitutional and Natural Law Perspective." *Journal of Social and Political Affairs* 1: 215–43.

_____. 1983. "Government Regulation of the Employment Relationship." In Johnson and Machan, pp. 13–41.

Hayek, F. A. 1961. "The *Non Sequitur* of the 'Dependence Effect.' " *Southern Economic Journal* 3 (in Beauchamp and Bowie): 363–66.

Hermann, D. H. J. 1983. "Property Rights in One's Job: The Case for Limiting Employment-at-Will." *Arizona Law Review* 24: 901–57.

Hessen, Robert. 1979. *In Defense of the Corporation.* Stanford, Calif.: Hoover Institution Press.

Horton, J., and A. P. Baroutsis. 1973. "An Economic Strategy for Environmental Quality." In *The Environment: Critical Factors and Strategy Development,* R. A. Gabriel and Sylvan Cohen, eds. New York: MSS Information Corp, pp. 61–93.

Hutt, William. 1975. *The Strike Threat System: the Economic Consequences of*

Collective Bargaining. Indianapolis: Liberty Press.

Jacoby, Neil. 1973. *Corporate Power and Social Responsibility.* New York: Macmillan.

Johnson, M. B., and T. R. Machan, eds. 1983. *Rights and Regulation: Ethical, Political, and Economic Issues.* Cambridge, Mass.: Ballinger Publishing, Co.

Johnson, M. B., ed. 1978. *The Attack on Corporate America.* New York: McGraw-Hill.

Jones, D. G. 1982. *Business, Religion, and Ethics.* Cambridge, Mass.: Oelgeschlager, Gunn & Hain, Publ. Inc.

Jung, L. S. 1983. "Commercialization of the Professions." *Business and Professional Ethics Journal* 2: 57–81.

Kavanagh, J. P. 1982. "Ethical Issues in Plant Relocation." *Business and Professional Ethics Journal* 1: 21–33.

———. 1982. "The Sinking of Sun Ship: A Case Study of Managerial Ethics." *Business and Professional Ethics Journal* 1: 1–13.

Kipnis, Kenneth. 1981. "Engineers Who Kill: Professional Ethics and the Paramountcy of Public Safety." *Business and Professional Ethics Journal* 1: pp. 77–91.

Kipnis, Kenneth, and D. T. Meyers, eds. 1985. *Economic Justice: Private Rights and Public Responsibilities.* Totowa, N.J.: Rowman & Allenheld.

Lee, D. R. 1982. "Environmental Versus Political Pollution." *International Institute for Economic Research.* Original Paper #39, Sept.

Lee, J. R. 1983. "Choice and Harms." In Johnson and Machan, pp. 157–73.

———. 1987. "Morality and Markets." In Machan, pp. 84–110 (this work is an extended version of Lee's essay in the present volume).

Leiser, Burton. 1973. *Liberty, Justice and Morality.* New York: Macmillan Publishing Co., Inc.

———. 1979. "Beyond Fraud and Deception: The Moral Uses of Advertising." In Donaldson and Werhane, pp. 59–66.

———. 1982. "The Rabbinic Tradition and Corporate Morality." In Williams and Houck, pp. 141–58.

Levine, P. J. 1973. "Towards a Property Right in Employment." *Buffalo Law Review* 22: 1081–1110.

Machan, T. R. 1975. *Human Rights and Human Liberties.* Chicago: Nelson-Hall Co.

———. 1981a. "Some Philosophical Aspects of National Labor Policy. *Harvard Journal of Law and Public Policy* 4: 67–160.

———. 1981b. "Wronging Rights." *Policy Review* 17: 37–58.

———. 1983. "Should Business be Regulated?" In Regan, 1983, pp. 202–34.

———. 1984. "Pollution and Political Theory." In Regan, 1984, pp. 74–106.

———. 1986. "The Virtue of Freedom in Capitalism." *The Journal of Applied Philosophy* 3: pp. 49–58.

———. 1987. "Human Rights, Workers' Rights and 'Right' to Occupational Safety." In Ezorsky, pp. 45–50.

———. 1987b. *The Main Debate: Communism versus Captialism.* N.Y.: Random House.

Mack, Eric. 1980. "Bad Samaritanism and the Causation of Harm." *Philosophy and Public Affairs* 9: pp. 230–59.

Manne, H. G. 1978. "Should Corporations Assume More Social Responsibility?" In Johnson, 1983, pp. 3–12.

Martin, D. L. 1980. "Is an Employee Bill of Rights Needed?" In Westin and

Salisbury, pp. 15–20.

Marx, Karl. 1977. *Selected Writings* ed., D. McLelland. Oxford: Oxford University Press.

McKenzie, R. B. 1979. *Restrictions on Business Mobility.* Washington, D. C.: American Enterprise Institute.

_____. 1983. "Hostage Factories." *Reason* (April): 35–39.

McMahon, Christopher. 1981. "Morality and the Invisible Hand." *Philosophy and Public Affairs* 10: pp. 247–77.

Michalos, A. C. 1981. "Loyalty Does not Require Illegality, Immorality, or Stupidity." *National Forum* 61: 51–54.

Melden, A. I. 1980. *Persons and Rights.* Berkeley, Calif.: University of California Press.

Missner, Marshall, ed. 1980. *Ethics of the Business System.* Sherman Oaks, Calif.: Alfred Publ. Co.

Nader, R., M. Green, and J. Seligman. 1976a. *Taming the Giant Corporation.* N.Y.: W. W. Norton.

_____. 1976b. *Constitutionalizing the Corporation: The Case for Federal Chartering of Giant Corporations.* Washington, D.C.: Corporate Accountability Research Group.

_____. 1973. *Corporate Power in America.* N.Y.: Grossman Publ.

Newton, L. H. 1981. "Lawgiving for Professional Life: Reflections on the Place of the Professional Code." *Business and Professional Ethics Journal* 1: 41–53.

Nickel, J. W. 1978–79. "Is there a Human Right to Employment?" *The Philosophical Forum* 10: 149–70.

Nielsen, Kai. 1987. "Global Justice, Capitalism, and the Third World." In Machan pp. 440–53.

Norton, D. L. 1976. *Personal Destinies: A Philosophy of Ethical Individualism.* Princeton, N.J.: Princeton University Press.

Nozick, Robert. 1974. *Anarchy, State, and Utopia.* N.Y.: Basic Books.

Novak, Michael. 1981. *Toward A Theology of Corporations.* Washington, D.C.: American Enterprise Institute.

Pastin, Mark. 1986. *The Hard Problems of Management: Gaining the Ethics Edge.* San Francisco: Jossey-Bass Publ.

Philips, Michael. 1982. "Do Banks Loan Money?" *Journal of Business Ethics* 1: 249–50.

Pilon, Roger. 1982. "Corporations and Rights: On Treating Corporate People Justly."*Georgia Law Review* 10: 1245–1370.Poole, Robert, Jr., ed. 1982. *Instead of Regulation.* Lexington, Mass: Lexington Books.

Rand, Ayn. 1967. *Capitalism: The Unknown Ideal.* New York: New American Library.

Rasmussen, D. B. 1982. "Ethics and the Free Market." *Listening* 16: 77–88.

Rawls, John. 1971. *A Theory of Justice.* Cambridge, Mass.: Harvard.

Regan, Tom, ed. 1984a. *Just Business: New Introductory Essays in Business Ethics.* New York: Random House.

_____. 1984b. *Earthbound: New Essays in Environmental Ethics.* New York: Random House.

Sayer, K. M. 1980. *Regulation, Values and the Public Interest.* Notre Dame, Indiana: University of Notre Dame Press.

Schmitt, Richard. 1973. "The Desire for Private Gain." *Inquiry* 16: 149–67. In Machan 1987b, pp. 162–77.

Schwartz, Adina. 1982. "Meaningful Work." *Ethics* 92: 634–64.

———. 1983. "Autonomy in the Workplace." In Regan, pp. 129–66.

Shue, Henry. 1980. *Basic Rights.* Princeton, N.J.: Princeton University Press.

Smith, Adam. 1776, 1976. *The Wealth of Nations.* Indianapolis, IN: Liberty Classics.

Stewart, Robert. 1984. "Morality and the Market in Blood." *The Journal of Applied Philosophy* 1: 227–38.

Thomson, J. Jarvis. 1983. "Some Questions About Government Regulation." In Johnson and Machan, pp. 137–56.

Titmuss, R. M. 1970. *The Gift Relationship.* London: Allen & Unwin.

Torrance, T. S. 1974. "Capitalism and the Desire for Private Gain." *Inquiry* 17: 241–48.

Velasquez, M. G. 1983. "Why Corporations Are Not Morally Responsible for Anything They Do." *Business and Professional Ethics Journal* 2: 1–18.

Walton, C. C. 1980. "Business Ethics: the Present and the Future." *Hastings Center Report* 10: 16–20.

Wasserstrom, R. A. 1977. "Racism, Sexism, and Preferential Treatment: An Approach to the Topics." *UCLA Law Review* 24: 581–622.

Werhane, P. H. 1985. *Persons, Rights, and Corporations.* Englewood Cliffs: Prentice-Hall.

Westin, A. F. and S. Salisbury, eds. 1980. *Individual Rights in the Corporation.* New York: Random House.

Williams, O. and J. Houck, eds. 1982. *The Judeo-Christian Vision & the Modern Corporation.* Notre Dame, Ind.: University of Notre Dame Press.

Wurf, Jerry. 1982. "Labor's View of Quality of Working Life Programs." *Journal of Business Ethics* 1: 131–37.

Contributors

TIBOR R. MACHAN is professor of philosophy at Auburn University. After being smuggled out of Hungary in 1953, Dr. Machan emigrated to the United States and served in the United States Air Force. He later earned his Ph.D. in philosophy from the University of California at Santa Barbara.

He is the author/editor of numerous publications: *The Pseudo-Science of B. F. Skinner* (1974), *Human Rights and Human Liberties* (1975), *The Libertarian Alternative* (1974), and *The Libertarian Reader* (1975), *Rights and Regulation* (1983), and *Recent Work in Philosophy* (1983). His most recent book is *The Main Debate: Communism versus Capitalism* (1987). In addition to contributing to numerous scholarly journals, including *The American Philosophical Quarterly, The Review of Metaphysics, The Southern Economic Review, The Journal of Applied Philosophy, and The American Journal of Jurisprudence,* Dr. Machan is cofounder and senior editor of *Reason* magazine and is editor of *Reason Papers*. His forthcoming work, *Individuals and Their Rights,* will focus on natural rights theory.

JOHN AHRENS is assistant director of the Social Philosophy and Policy Center and a member of the graduate faculty at Bowling Green State University. He received his Ph.D. in philosophy from the University of Iowa in 1978. Since then, he has developed and taught courses in business ethics and a variety of other topics in political philosophy and public policy. The author of *Preparing for the Future: An Essay on the Rights of Future Generations* (1983), his current research focuses primarily on issues in environmental ethics and policy.

NICHOLAS CAPALDI is professor of philosophy at Queens College, City University of New York. He is a noted authority on the philosophy of

David Hume and the author of a well known text on informal logic, *The Art of Deception* (1979). His other publications include *An Invitation to Philosophy* (et al., 1981) and *Out of Order* (1985), a study of affirmative action. He is coeditor of *Journeys Through Philosophy* (1982) and has published widely in the *Journal of Philosophy, Reason Papers, Policy Review,* and the *Review of Metaphysics.*

JAMES E. CHESHER earned his M.A. in philosophy from the University of California, Santa Barbara. He teaches philosophy at Santa Barbara City College. He has taught at Ventura City College, as well as at Pioneer High School, San Jose, California. His publications have appeared in *Poet Lore, Reason Papers,* and *Reason.* As vice-president and co-owner of the Pacific Painting Company in Santa Barbara, he has had extensive experience in employee relations.

DOUGLAS J. DEN UYL is associate professor of philosophy at Bellarmine College, Louisville, Kentucky. He is the author of *The New Crusaders* (1984) and *Power, State, and Freedom* (1983). Other publications of his have appeared in the *American Philosophical Quarterly, The Journal of the History of Philosophy,* and *Man and the World.*

JOHN HOSPERS is professor of philosophy at the University of Southern California. He is the author of the widely discussed work *Libertarianism* (1971), which has become the premier statement of the political philosophy of that name. Other publications are *Meaning and Truth in the Arts* (1967), *Human Conduct* (1961), and *Understanding the Arts* (1982).

J. ROGER LEE teaches philosophy at California State University, Los Angeles and at other colleges in the Los Angeles area. He has published in the fields of political philosophy, criminal punishment, government regulation, and the philosophy of economics. His work has appeared in *Philosophical Studies* and other journals, as well as in numerous anthologies (e.g., M. B. Johnson, et al., *Rights and Regulations* [1983]).

FRED D. MILLER, JR. is professor of philosophy at Bowling Green State University and executive director of the Social Philosophy and Policy Center. His wide ranging interests include both ancient Greek philosophy and modern political theory. His article "The Natural Right to Private Property" appeared in *The Libertarian Reader* and his monograph, *Out of the Mouths of Babes* (1983), was a study of the infant formula controversy. He was instrumental in introducing business ethics curricula at Bowling Green State University and continues to do research in this area. He is presently writing a book on the modern relevance of Aristotle's theory of rights.

ELLEN FRANKEL PAUL is deputy director of the Social Philosophy and Policy Center and professor of political science at Bowling Green State University. She received her doctorate from the government department of Harvard University in 1976. She has held faculty positions at Miami University and the University of Colorado and, in 1980–81, was a fellow at the Hoover Institute of Stanford University. Her published works include *Moral Revolution and Economic Science; Studies of the Third Wave: Property Rights and Eminent Domain;* and the forthcoming *Equity and Gender: The Comparable Worth Debate.*

DOUGLAS B. RASMUSSEN is associate professor of philosophy at St. John's University, Jamaica, New York. He is co-editor of *The Philosophic Thought of Ayn Rand* and has published in *The New Scholasticism, The Thomist,* and in *Reason Papers.* He is co-author of *The Catholic Bishops and the Economy* and is the author of the forthcoming *The Philosophy of Freedom.*

Index

Business manager, 23, 34, 156
  obligations of, 23, 34 passim
  role of, 229
Business regulations, 170, 174–75, 177

Calculation problem, 96–97
Capitalism, viii, 7, 94, 113n, 141–42, 148,
  151, 213, 216–20, 228–29
  critics of, 220, 228
Capitalists, 105, 113n
Case, Sen. Clifford, 199
Categorical imperative, 182
Caterpillar Tractor Co., 156–57
Christian ethics, 13
Civil disobedience. See Law
Civil Rights Commission, 199
Civil War, 136
Clark, Sen Joseph, 199
Coercion, 174
Commerce, vii, viii, 1, 3, 6–7, 11, 18, 163,
  180
  regulation of, 161–62, 171
Communication, nonpersonal, 51
Communism, ix, 7, 102, 214
Communist regimes, 195
Competition, 48
  wasteful, 45–47
Comte, Auguste, 12
Concepts, 27
Conduct
  in business, viii
  human. See also Ethics
  standards of, 1
Consciousness, 2, 27
Constitution (United States), 17, 133, 198
Constitutional Democracy Act of 1980,
  147–48
Consumer greed, 60
Contractors Association of Eastern Pennsylvania, 201
Cooperation, 100
Corporate charters, 164
Corporations, 140–42, 145, 186, 234
  as "creatures of the state," 163–64, 170–71
  as private, 159
  as public, 143–48
  as quasi-public, 141–42
  contractual origins of, 145
  legal creator theory of, 234
  legal status of, 140–41
  modern, 142–59
  nature of, 234–35
  legal recognition theory of, 235

social responsibility of. See Social responsibility
responsibility of, 140, 145–47, 149, 152–53,
  157–58, 235
Cost, total, 48
Council of Better Business Bureaus, 61
Criminal Law. See Law

"Daimon," 36–37
Declaration of Independence, 87
Democracy, 165
Democracy Act (1980), 147–48
Demsetz, Harold, 48
Den Uyl, Douglas, 157–58
Deontology, 58. See also Ethics
Dependence effect, 232
Department of Labor (DOL), 200–201
  Order No. 4, 200–201
Discrimination, 197, 199–200, 202, 205,
  211–12, 226–27
  adverse impact of, 207
  compensation of, 206–8
  degree of damage, 208
  in employment, 226
  illegal, 204
  institutional, 202
  intentional, 202
  unjust, 226–27
  reverse, 203–4
Divestiture, 189–92
Dubois, W. E. B., 198
Due caution, 52–53

Economic democracy, 140, 158–59
Economic efficiency, 165
Economic well-being, 7
Economics, 3, 5, 12, 219
  cost-benefit analysis, 169, 175
  labor theory of value, 105
  science of, 2, 4–5
  stable preferences, 3
  utility maximization, 3
  as value free, 4
Economist's view
  of human nature, 3
  of science, 3
Egoism, 9–11, 16, 216, 219–20
Egotism, 9
  objective, 10–11, 16
  subjective, 10–11
Emergency Committee for American Trade,
  184
Employment, 223–24

A